Economics for Normal People:

An Economist's Memoir

Jon R. Miller

Table of Contents

Introduction

When I was a first-year student at Pacific Lutheran University in 1966, we had mandatory chapel, and I mean mandatory. Members of Spurs, a women's service organization, roamed the aisles of Eastvold Chapel in their tight, white, knit sweaters and took attendance every day. If you missed a few days, you could count on a visit with the Dean of Students. The adult Lutherans in power were no dummies; the seating was boy-girl-boy-girl down each row. Some married their chapel partners, which, of course, was the goal: to propagate more Lutherans. My chapel partners didn't interest me romantically, but I did meet my future wife, Solveig, during my sophomore year in "The Bible," Religion 201. This biblical union has lasted over five decades. I thought I'd introduce her to you at the outset, as she appears often in these pages.

The next year, when some of our high school classmates were fighting in Vietnam, we ran a successful protest, not against the war, but to end mandatory chapel. It felt good at the time, but today, I regret it because, on rare occasions, we heard amazing chapel talks by visitors and members of the faculty and administration. Most chapel talks were horrible, some so horrible they were funny. One week, though, the chapel speaker was the legendary Walter C. Schnackenberg, chair of the history department and author of *The Lamp and the Cross: Sagas of Pacific Lutheran University From 1890 to 1965*. I can remember each day "Schnack" came to the podium and delivered one of his "Vignettes on Faith." He started each with the words, "Our purpose today is to sing a hymn, but in a slightly different setting." I can't remember the specifics, but I do remember the power of using story to make a point. I never forgot it and have told economics stories for over forty years in college classrooms. In the last twenty of those years, I used a collection I called Economics Vignettes as a course supplement. Many of those comprise the bulk of this book. The collection has expanded and evolved over the years, but it all started in those rare days in chapel in the mid-sixties. So, when you read this book, please remember that our purpose is to use economics vignettes to learn economics concepts in many different settings. Hymn singing is optional.

Economics has always been an easy subject to teach and a difficult one to learn, mainly because economists are different from normal people. I address some economist peculiarities in Part One, but I want to address a major characteristic of economists and standard economics here in the Introduction to differentiate *Economics for Normal People* from other approaches. Introductory economics, even the most basic, is usually delivered with a lot of technique. I often ask those who went to college whether they took an economics course while there. If they answered yes, I asked if they remembered anything about it. Some say they remember nothing. Some say supply and demand; others say it was hard. The most common answer, however, is that it had a lot of graphs. Graphs are just simplified representations of mathematical relationships. Economists confront reality by stepping away from it, using mathematical models to represent it, and manipulating those models to understand it. This is what I call abstract thinking.

On the flyleaf of his *Foundations of Economic Analysis*, the book that launched a career that won him the Nobel Prize in Economics, Paul Samuelson wrote "Mathematics is a Language." Because of this statement, I was allowed to take Linear Algebra to fulfill my graduate school language requirement in the 1970s at Washington University in St. Louis. Economic thinking is abstract thinking. Normal people are not abstract thinkers. No graphs appear in this book.

I'm certainly not alone in recognizing the weirdness of standard economics. An entire field of economics, behavioral economics, is about how the human beings of standard economic theories are not human at all but rather rational, calculating, optimizing machines. Economics Nobel laureate Richard Thaler, one of the founders of behavioral economics, divides people into two groups, Humans and Econs, the former close to what I call normal people in this book. Behavioral economists study how people make decisions using shortcuts, rules of thumb, and biases.

This is not a behavioral economics book. While I address the field of behavioral economics in Part One, in the remainder of the book, I try to teach Thaler's Humans (or my normal people) the economic thinking of Econs. Even Thaler himself says it's not wrong to think like an Econ. He shows that in many (most?) instances, they don't act that way. In this book, I'm acting like Thaler's "clinical economist." Please lay down on my couch and let me attempt to improve your life by showing you the standard economic way of thinking. When we are finished, feel free to get up from the couch and resume normality. There is nothing wrong with being human.

While this book differs from standard economics books in its lack of technical analysis, it resembles it in topical coverage and organization. In sixty-one short vignettes on economics, we cover many of the most basic economics principles, such as the basic economic problem, marginal analysis, supply and demand, market structure, collective goods and the role of government, and topics in macroeconomics. The book ends with topics in personal finance, including how to get rich slowly with seven rules for riches. These economic vignettes are mostly self-contained. They can be read in any order. I'd suggest you read Part Seven before Part Eight, but other than that, if something interests you, give it a go. I begin each part with an introduction summarizing each vignette to help you decide how to proceed.

As we've already seen, this book contains a lot of memoir and history, too. When you're as old as I am, you can't avoid it. For example, in Part Four, a beer-influenced sabbatical in Germany shows that even a professed Econ like me can make bad decisions if he ignores potential movements in foreign exchange rates. A trip to the NCAA Final Four in Seattle with my economist buddies shows the forces of supply and demand in action in an unofficial ticket market.

That's it, in a nutshell. See what you think. If you read this book, I'm sure you'll agree that economists are a little weird, but you might appreciate that there is some value in their strange way of thinking. You might improve some of your decisions and take comfort in knowing that you are not alone in your bad ones. You might even realize that economists are less cynical, rude, uncaring, or even less amoral than you thought previously. They think a little differently than you and other normal people do. And who knows, you might take pity on or even befriend an economist someday and invite him or her to a party. As one of the lonely and the weird, if that's the only good that comes from this book, it's enough. Thanks.

Part One

Economists and
Normal People

Introduction

Economists are weird. We are not normal. We think differently than normal people and often talk funny. Sometimes, we say the darndest things. Economists have talked to each other for so long that we think we are normal and normal people are strange. When we try to teach economics to normal people, frustration reigns.

The first vignette, "Economists Say the Darndest Things: Reflections on Economists and Normal People," begins with a conversation between a mother and her daughter, who has just come home from Lutheran College. The girl has a new boyfriend. Let's say Mom has something in common with the Willie Nelson lyric, "Mamas, don't let your sons grow up to be cowboys."

The second piece in this part, "Maps, Model Airplanes, Barbie, and Ken: Using Models to Understand Reality," shows that recognizing the everyday use of models and abstraction can help a normal person deal with economists' use of models to analyze social phenomena.

"Science, Advocacy, and the 'Miller Wave:' Positive and Normative Economics" shows a striking difference between economists and normal people, how they address issues of right or wrong and good or bad. Normal people are more likely to proceed directly to judgment about the appropriateness of someone's action, while the aphorism "different strokes for different folks" could be a professional economist's mantra.

"An Economist's Christmas" uses gift exchange to illustrate that no one knows a person's tastes and preferences, likes and dislikes, better than that person. To an economist, electronic funds transfer would be a good substitute for the traditional gift exchange on holidays. Because of this and other weird ideas, we aren't invited to many Christmas parties. We sit home in December brooding about why everyone is so much more irrational yet has so much more fun. It's not easy being an economist.

The final piece in Part One compares the approach in this book with the new and rapidly growing field of behavioral economics. Behavioral economists point out human departures from rational choice, a fundamental assumption of standard economics. Such behavior is demonstrated frequently in this book through boneheaded actions taken by the author. That said, much of this book follows the advice of many good parents and me: "Do as I say, not as I do."

I hope that after reading Part One, you don't dismiss economics due to the strangeness of its practitioners. I want to note that differences in thinking rarely lead to understanding and learning unless these differences are understood. Furthermore, there is nothing wrong with being normal. This is not an evangelical book. I hope for learning, not conversion.

Economists Say the Darndest Things:

Reflections on Economists and Normal People

A young woman comes home from Lutheran College in her junior year. "Mom, I've met a nice boy," she says.

"Oh?" Mom says.

"He's really cute, and smart, too, and he treats me so nice."

"That's good. What's his name?"

"Izzy Friedman," she says.

"Sounds Jewish," Mom says.

"He is," she says. "Is that a problem for you?"

"Of course not. Where's he from?"

"He's from the Chicago area, a place called Elgin."

"Oh, yes. They make watches there. Know anything about his parents?"

"Not much. I think his dad's an engineer or something. He hasn't said much about his mom. I think she's from Senegal, in Africa."

"Oh, that's interesting," Mom says.

"His parents are divorced."

"That's too bad, but many people are these days," Mom says. "It's a funny thing that this Izzy would go to Lutheran College."

"Not really," she says. "He learned about Lutheran when he was in the area for drug and alcohol rehab."

"I see," says Mom. "Sounds like he got straightened out okay, though. What's he want to do after he graduates?"

"He's going to graduate school in economics. He wants to be an economist."

"Oh dear!" Mom says.

Mom's point is well taken. Economists often say the darndest things, and the way they say them frequently confuses or irritates a normal person. Normal people conclude that the world needs economists but hope their children don't marry one. Normal people also don't invite economists to their parties. Do you have any friends who are economists? Of course not.

Economists say strange things because they have a way of thinking that's different from the way normal people think. We will have a chance to see many of these peculiar economic ideas in this book, and delve into them more deeply, but for now, let's briefly look at just a few to get started.

Economists have a strong commitment to the market economy as a way of addressing the basic economic problem. To the economist, markets exist where trade happens, and trade is mutually beneficial. Normal people distrust markets, and often think that trade is a way for the powerful to take advantage of the weak.

Economists worry about how to make the national economic pizza bigger. Normal people are more concerned with the relative size of each piece.

Economists are abstract thinkers. They form theories and use models to simplify reality and understand it better. Normal people dislike formal abstraction, like reality, and learn by example.

Economists assume people are rational. Normal people know they are not.

Economists emphasize the future, where all choices lie. Normal people can't shake the memory of bad choices in the past and make worse ones today, attempting to compensate for regret.

Economists withhold judgment about the appropriateness of a person's values, preferences, and choices. We reserve statements with the word "should" for the arcane sub-discipline of social choice theory. Normal people could care less about social choice theory. They are much more normative and judgmental about the preferences and actions of others.

Economists emphasize that for every benefit, there is a cost. Normal people don't like to think about the "downside" of actions, and we economists are quick to remind them about opportunity cost, the value of opportunities foregone by choice. Normal people interpret this as negativity and don't invite economists to parties.

Over two centuries ago, a Scotsman named Adam Smith developed one powerful idea espoused by economists. It's called the invisible hand principle. By pursuing one's own self-interest, one is guided by an invisible hand to benefit others in society as well. Most normal people believe that self-interest leads to a "zero-sum society," where a self-interested gain is balanced by someone else's loss. Normal people are more romantic than economists, believing that good in society comes from a noble perfection of the individual, not through the vulgarity of self-interest.

Economists think that eliminating badness in the world is almost always unjustified. Economists know we can have too little of a bad thing and too much of a good thing. Take crime, for example. To rid the world of crime would require the use of resources that have a higher value if used elsewhere, not to mention the value of lost intangibles such as personal freedom and privacy. Economists think in terms of an optimal level of crime, where the value of another unit of crime reduction is equal to its cost.

Because they are comfortable abstracting from reality, economists would not feel the least bit uncomfortable with an economic theory of marriage. Thinking about marriage, economists would emphasize rational economic choice rather than the whims of romance and passion. "Let's see," says the suitor. "I've made my list of attributes of a potential mate and have weighted them appropriately. I've ranked potential mates according to how they measure up to my criteria. Now, I need to make proposals of marriage in declining rank order. Where are the phone numbers?" Mom's right. This is a funny idea, indeed!

Because they assume people act rationally in their own interest, economists often point out self-interest in lofty human behavior. Need-based financial aid at colleges is price discrimination. The NCAA is a successful buyers cartel, exploiting college athletes for the good of the institution. Bureaucrats are not passive conduits through which legislative decisions get channeled into our lives but, rather, act in their own interest. Churches can best be understood as profit-maximizing institutions. Normal people see this as cynicism, but an economist believes that if you are going to use your head to explain the way the world works, you need to professionally remove your heart from your sleeve and confine it out of sight in your chest.

I could give you many other examples of economists' strange ideas, but if I did, you might quit reading now. I don't want to overload you with economic weirdness too soon. For normal people, the weirdness of what economists say makes economics hard to learn.

Maps, Model Airplanes, Barbie and Ken:

Using Models to Understand Reality

The snapshot reveals so much. I'd seen it many times before, but most recently, my Auntie Edythe sent me a copy of it as a birthday card. I'd guess it's the summer of 1950. I'm sitting on the front right fender of a large mass of American steel, probably a '41 Dodge or Chevy. The large firtrees in the background suggest Portland, perhaps my grandparents' driveway. Auntie Edythe, in her striped sun dress, stretches over the headlight, her finger extended toward my inviting, chubby little left arm, one that cries out for a tickle. I had a lineman's body in the summer of my third year. Two years earlier, when Mom had taken me into Dr. Gordon for a checkup, he inquired, with more surprise than alarm, "What are you feeding that boy?"

Yes, the photo says much about my family and physical nature, but I clutch the most revealing aspect of the photo in my right arm, a large doll. Now, this is not a stuffed animal, a cowboy doll, or some other 1950s gender-appropriate toy. It's an honest-to-goodness likeness of a baby I nurtured that summer day, albeit with a mild stranglehold. To my father's chagrin, in my earliest years, I played with dolls. Maybe this foretold a later life of teaching, certainly a nurturing profession. But at the least, it indicated a preference for abstraction that would serve me well in economics. Dolls are models, abstractions from reality that help us understand reality.

Most reasonable parents would not encourage a toddler football lineman to learn nurturing through playing with a three-month-old baby. But a model of a baby allows the benefit of learning something about the reality of babies, without the cost of experiencing reality itself. Later, when my modeling turned from dolls to model airplanes, my dad was happy. These models were more appropriate for the ten-year-old boy and represented the only way a kid in East Wenatchee, Washington, could learn about WWII instruments of war. You can't buy a bomber or a fighter jet, and it's difficult in a small Inland Northwest town even to see a real one in person. But as I drifted off to sleep at night, a model B29 Superfortress, suspended with fishing line from the ceiling of my bedroom, reminded me of American might and how we won the war. Models have power.

Economists can't study economic reality by experiencing it either. Reality is too complicated. Everything is moving. Nothing stands still long enough. You can't even have a physical model of an economy to cuddle or fly around your bedroom. We economists create economic theories about the way the real world works and represent these theories of cause and effect with mathematical equations and graphs that help us visualize these equations. This formal theorizing and the representation of economic theory with models infuses the teaching of economics.

I did an experiment with former economics students, not those who were majors in economics, but those who had me for a course in economics principles sometime in the past. I asked them if they remembered anything from the course. Often, with just a little reflection, they say, "Graphs, there were lots of graphs." And there were lots of graphs. Modern economics is very formal in its method and those who gravitate toward economics as a profession like formal abstraction. When economists teach economics, they emphasize this formal, abstract modeling. After all, we're good at it. But normal people are less formal in their approach to abstraction than economists, and because of this, learning economics is hard.

It's not the use of models, per se, that is hard for normal people. Everyone does it. Few would attempt a drive from Seattle to Miami without a map. A map is a model of a real landscape. Driving from Seattle to Miami requires not just any model, but an appropriate one. A map of France won't help much. One with contour lines contains too much detail. In fact, for this trip, many would be willing to assume away all but interstate and U.S. highways, with some state boundaries, towns and cities, and the mileage between them. The nature of modeling is one of assuming away, of doing violence to reality. When a normal person drives, it's OK to use a map, but to negotiate the landscape of an economics course, the common model, the graph, is more foreign and more difficult.

The idea of an appropriate model is an important one in economics, as it is in choosing the right map or the right doll. We want just the right amount of abstraction. We want to pare reality down to only the essential elements important to the task at hand. We also try to worry about assuming away too much, especially important stuff that might alter the conclusions of our modeling effort. And always, we want to be careful when we apply conclusions from a high level of abstraction to reality itself. We don't want to commit, as Alfred North Whitehead called it, the fallacy of misplaced concreteness. When we as economists tiptoe back to reality, armed with conclusions from our modeling, we want to be humble, careful, and cautious that reality might not conform to our stylized version of it.

Economists have no monopoly, however, on the problem of inappropriate models. Go to the toy store. You can now buy dolls that cry and wet their pants. I'd assume this part of reality away immediately. And the Cabbage Patch doll, with its face like a dry rotten potato, seems a little much. But of course, American males might think that the makers of the ever-popular Barbie have assumed away all but the most essential aspects of American womanhood: beautiful long blonde hair, long legs, a thin waist, and enormous breasts. The Ken model, on the other hand, abstracts away from one important part of male reality that is certainly inappropriate. Considering these examples, even a normal person might conclude that economic models, even formal ones, are not so bad.

Science, Advocacy, and the Miller Wave:

Positive and Normative Economics

Radical Cambridge economist Joan Robinson once accused her mainstream brethren of running to hide in thickets of algebra while abandoning the important questions to journalists and politicians. She acknowledged that everyone must recognize the difference between the words "ought" and "is," but suggested that this difference should not define the economics profession.

Mrs. Robinson had a point. Rather than use economics to prescribe what individuals or governments ought to do, economists prefer to develop theories, often expressed in mathematics, about the actions of those individuals and governments. Then, they like to test these theories with the facts to see if the theory explains how the social world works, especially the relationship between cause and effect. Economists prefer science to advocacy. They want to practice positive economics rather than normative economics.

Economists' reluctance to advocate for a particular government action is captured in the old joke about President Truman and his economic adviser. Mr. Truman was the first president to appoint a Council of Economic Advisers. He even enjoyed listening to them, up to a point. Once, he asked an adviser about some matter of economic policy, and the economist responded that, on the one hand, the action would have one effect. On the other hand, it would have another effect. Confronted with the economist's preference for explanation over advocacy, Mr. Truman yearned for a one-armed economist.

Today, much of this type of thinking still pervades economics. We do have a Nobel Prize in Economic Science; one we don't wish to jeopardize with excessive professional opinionating and advocacy. Economists are still more likely to study the causes of poverty and inequality, rather than advocate a particular government program to address the issue. We would be more comfortable explaining the causes of inflation and unemployment rather than advocating a particular target level for these macroeconomic indicators. We would rather explain why the price of oil has risen, rather than opine on whether this is good or bad.

Normal people are much more normative than economists, especially those working for the government. As Mrs. Robinson correctly observed, normative questions are important. Economists have responded over the years to the demand for normative economic analysis. At the beginning of the 20th Century, economist Vilfredo Pareto came up with a normative economic flag that economists were able to salute. As economics is about maximizing human well-being, could we support an action that makes someone better off while hurting no one? Economists would rarely question what came to be called the "Pareto Criterion."

Unfortunately, in the practical world of government policy, someone suffers from most government actions. From a practical standpoint, normal people think that a one-armed economist with the Pareto Criterion can't do the heavy lifting of normative economics. A less stringent social choice criterion would help. The Net Benefits or Benefit-Cost Criterion is an example.

With the Benefit-Cost Criterion, we consider a collective action to be justified if the sum of the gains exceeds the sum of the losses from an action. Note that losses are now allowed, where they were not under the Pareto Criterion. Here we slide further down the slippery slope of comparing someone's gains against someone else's losses. The Benefit-Cost Criterion requires the stronger value judgement that losses are OK, if gains are greater.

Economists can continue to maintain at least some degree of scientific objectivity in the calculation of gains and losses under the Benefit-Cost Criterion. They can merely compute the relevant magnitudes, and still allow the politicians to use this "evidence" to inform their normative decisions. Unfortunately, economists don't have it quite that easy. Hiding in the technical tidepools of benefit-cost analysis lurk small stinging creatures called assumptions. For example, to add up all the individual benefits and costs, economists must assume that all benefits are to be treated equally, or that the politicians (and journalists?) have at least provided a socially valid interpersonal weighting scheme. Can we value my $100 benefit the same as your $100 cost? Is the rich woman's $50 loss the same as the poor woman's $50 loss? These questions require answers that are unavoidably normative in nature.

The Flood Control Act of 1936 codified the Benefit-Cost Criterion in government policy. The act stated that the government should undertake a flood control project if the benefits exceeded the cost. This piece of legislation was a full-employment act for economists. Today, in water resources policy, environmental regulation, and many other areas, benefit-cost analysis plays a key role.

Even though modern-day economists have proved Mrs. Robinson's statement incorrect by involving themselves in important normative questions, one type of normative analysis remains strictly outside the bounds of standard economics. As a matter of doctrine, mainstream economists never question the validity of an individual's tastes or preferences. If you want to own a large, gas-guzzling sport utility vehicle, eat cocoa crispies for breakfast, and rent only movies sold behind a curtain at the video store, that's OK. If a proposed government policy creates benefits or costs to you in the areas of driving, eating, or video viewing, we would willingly measure these effects and add them up across all those affected. But we won't question your preferences.

Finally, any normal person can use scientific economic analysis for advocacy purposes. Normal people are not bound by doctrinal requirements that guide the professional economist. If used correctly, economic analysis in a public hearing, say, can further your cause and make you look smart in the process. At various stages in life, the latter is important. Over the years, I've related this to my students in the form of the Miller Wave.

The Miller Wave is a polite gesture used to get the opportunity to ask an economic question. You execute the Miller Wave usually from the back of the room. You raise your hand as high as it will go and wiggle it rapidly while, at the same time, saying excuse me, excuse me, excuse me, over and over politely until called upon. My friend Bob says it's like the hand gesture he made in a 1950s Catholic school when he knew the answer to a question. "Sister, Sister," he had said, with shoulder nearing dislocation.

Suppose you are a landlord attending a city council meeting where council members are about to impose an upper limit on rents in the city. If you rise and state that you are against rent control because it will lower your income, all in attendance will solidify their beliefs that landlords deserve their traditional occupational stature ranking near used car salespeople and payday loan shop owners. But suppose you use the Miller Wave, and when called upon, say, "In every economics textbook I've seen, rent control reduces the number of apartments offered for rent. Is it the intent of the Council to reduce housing availability for the poor?" As you slowly take your seat, members of the Council are at first silent. Then they look at the table or their shoes. Then, they make panic-stricken glances at staff members sitting in the corner of the room. The glances are futile, as staff members have already run for cover. Members of the Council table the proposition, realize the lateness of the meeting, and adjourn. You've politely advanced your position on an important issue and looked smart in the process. It doesn't get much better than that!

An Economist's Christmas

Charlie Leven, my major professor in graduate school, used to say, "Nothing cures poverty like money." Yet many poverty programs don't give money to the poor. Rather, they give a good itself, like food or housing. Economists often point out the inefficiency of these gifts of goods, these in-kind transfers. Only if someone bought the same amount of a gift with the money spent on it, does the in-kind transfer maximize the increase in the receiver's well-being. And economics is about maximizing well-being.

Similarly, economists are troubled by Christmas, not the religious aspects, which remain well outside the standard discipline, but the economic aspects, the gift exchange. We see the world's largest gift exchange as an exercise in inefficiency. In our basic model of consumer choice, we assume that no one knows the tastes and preferences of a person better than that person herself. The best way to increase the well-being of a person is to let them spend additional money on the goods and services they want. This is one of the reasons we like market economies so much. If you want to increase someone's well-being, give him or her more to spend.

Have you ever heard of someone choosing a gift because it is something the receiver would not buy for himself? This might be a good gift if the receiver didn't buy the good because he lacked sufficient income. Perhaps he would have bought the exact gift himself if he had received cash instead. But often receiving a gift that one would not buy is the result of ignorance on the part of the giver, or worse yet, an act imposing the preferences of the giver on the receiver. The mother of a friend of mine once gave her six-year-old grandson a certificate indicating that he was a sponsor of a whale in the Pacific Ocean. When he visited his grandmother on Orcas Island, WA, he asked, "Where's my whale?"

So, at Christmas or on other gifting occasions, an economist is likely to give cash as the perfect gift. An economist would not be troubled by a Christmas of electronic funds transfers. People would buy what they want, and with less shopping and exchanging, the transaction costs of Christmas would be much lower. It even makes it easier to answer the seasonal question, "What did you get for Christmas?" The answer is, "Oh, about $125, net."

My mother once gave everyone in Solveig's family a lottery ticket for Christmas. All seemed pleased. They at least had a positive probability of cash. But usually, Christmas gifts, just like food stamps, are rarely valued by the receiver at their purchase price. The day after Christmas is one of the largest shopping days, partly due to exchanges and refunds. Black markets in food stamps arise because some recipients want to consume alcohol and tobacco, not food.

Most normal people think the economist's Christmas is unimaginative and impersonal. This is because normal people behave according to a more complex economic model, one where the well-being of the giver is considered, and well-being is also derived from the whole Christmas allocation mechanism itself. Because normal people don't want the poor to spend the money they give them on alcohol and tobacco, they invent a food stamp program. Normal people avoid the economist's Christmas because an important part of the game is trying to buy someone something he or she will like. Perhaps they didn't know a particular item even existed. They then receive information along with the gift, and the giver enjoys the giving even more.

But actual Christmas behavior is too complex for economics. We simplify the model and concentrate on the receiving of gifts. And sometimes we forget that our model, while a good one, is an abstraction from reality. We start believing that our model is reality and suggest to normal people that Christmas should involve only monetary gifts. Then we don't get invited to Christmas parties.

Humans, Econs, and Normal People

Watching TV after a rare dinner without a dessert course, I needed something sweet. Solveig brought a small dish of M&Ms for us to share. After I had moved the dish closer to my recliner and powered through a few handfuls, I pushed the dish to her side of the small table between us and said, "Get these away from me, before I eat any more." I had no willpower to stop eating, a telling statement for an economist who spent a career teaching about rational choice, a block in the foundation of standard economics.

Richard Thaler, one of the founders of behavioral economics and winner of the Nobel Prize for doing so, tells a similar story about cashews in two wonderful books, *Misbehaving: The Making of Behavioral Economics*, and *Nudge: Improving Decisions About Health, Wealth, and Happiness* (with Cass R. Sunstein). Thaler devoted his professional life to drawing a distinction between the decisionmaker in standard economic models, whom he calls Homo Economicus, an Econ for short, and one more familiar to normal people, a member of the species Homo Sapiens, a Human.

In the following, I'll summarize and give examples of some of the many challenges that Thaler and his behavioral economics colleagues create for standard economics. Let's start with my favorite. Thaler once asked Harry Markowitz, one of the founders of modern portfolio theory, how he diversified his investments and how he allocated his wealth among various asset categories to deal with differences in risk. After stating how he should have used his very technical financial economic analysis to make the decision, he admitted to using a common rule of thumb. He split his investments 50-50 between stocks and bonds. Behavioral economists love to show that Humans often use heuristics, rules of thumb, in decision making, rather than more complicated analysis consistent with rational choice.

I, too, used this naive diversification rule of thumb, when I allocated my retirement investments equally between TIAA (bonds) and CREF (stocks) in the University of Utah's retirement plan in the 1970s and 80s. Little did I know at the time that I also succumbed to "status quo bias" by sticking with this naive plan. I ignored economic evidence that over the long run, which I had in my favor then, monetary returns in CREF greatly exceeded those in TIAA, with little increase in long-term risk.

Behavioral economists, as well as their compatriots in psychology, show that Humans are subject to predictable and persistent biases in their decision-making, which lead to blunders that rational Econs don't make. Two of the most famous psychologists in behavioral economics, Nobel economics laureates Daniel Kahneman and Amos Tversky, who died before they could share the Nobel Prize, noted that standard economists and behavioral economists differ by the types of theories they use. Standard economists use what Kahneman and Tversky call normative theory to model how decisions should be made to optimize something, e.g., maximize profit, minimize cost, or maximize an individual's utility or well-being. Standard economists also use this type of theory to predict how Humans behave. Behavioral economists separate the two types of theory, using what they call descriptive theory to explain human decision-making. Behavioral economists don't deny that applying the decision-making principles of standard economics would result in a better outcome for the decision-maker. They just don't think Humans act that way.

One of the most important findings in behavioral economics is loss aversion, sometimes called the endowment effect. Humans are much more unwilling to sell something they already have than they are willing to buy the same thing. This complicates the applied standard economic technique of benefit-cost analysis. The assignment of rights, a value judgment, can affect the outcome of the analysis. Here's an example.

Suppose we are considering whether to build a dam that will eliminate recreation on a river. What is the cost of this action to those currently recreating on the river? Two conceptual possibilities exist to guide this analysis. We could measure what river recreators are willing to pay to prevent this action. Alternatively, we could ask how much they are willing to accept in compensation. Standard economic theory suggests that the difference in these magnitudes will be small. In fact, behavioral economics experiments in laboratories with human subjects and benefit-cost studies in the real world show the difference to be large.

Other important behavioral economic descriptive theories come under the general heading of "mental accounting," how Humans think about money and cost. One aspect of this is the Human tendency not to ignore sunk cost. To an Econ, all costs are opportunities foregone by a choice. Sunk cost is the result of a past choice that we cannot reverse by a current one. In standard economics, we should ignore sunk costs. To a Human, sunk costs loom as something that can be "made up for" by a current choice.

Here's a sunk-cost example, one dear to my heart, about skiing. Suppose there are two identical skiers, both Humans. One has a season pass to the local ski area, and one has purchased a non-refundable $75 ticket to ski that day. Suppose a blizzard arrives, accompanied by cold temperatures and high winds. The access road to the ski area is treacherous, as well. The season pass holder loses no money by staying home and makes a sensible decision to do so. The second skier, using mental accounting and attempting not to realize a loss of $75, might brave the bad, risky weather and go skiing. Because the ticket is non-refundable, an Econ realizes that both skiers face the same choice. The $75 is the sunk cost. Both skiers lose no money by staying home. To an Econ, the only cost of going skiing is the opportunity foregone by doing so.

Escalating commitment can be another result of ignoring sunk costs. I recently spent $1,200 to replace the timing belt and water pump in my 1997 Subaru Legacy. Even at 225,000 miles, I expect (hope?) to grind some more use out of the vehicle. This might turn out to be a bad decision, but I think it was a rational one. But suppose that the transmission now fails. How do I think about the decision? The Econ's choice, and mine, I hope, will be based on whether the cost of the transmission will provide the best use of the money going forward. As a Human, I would be more likely to think about fixing the transmission to justify the past expenditure on the timing belt and water pump. This is like sending more troops to Vietnam so that previous troops would not have died in vain.

Humans also make decisions different from those of Econs because of framing. One form of framing is saying the same thing in different ways. I have a bad back. I've never had surgery on my back, but someday I might consider it. Suppose in a consultation with a back surgeon she tells me that "Eighty-five out of one hundred people who have this surgery have a completely successful outcome." As an alternative, suppose she says, "Out of one hundred people who have this surgery, fifteen are no better than they were before." An Econ would see these statements as equivalent and make the same decision with either form of information. A Human would be more likely to decline the procedure after receiving the second message.

Humans tend to make decisions based on information that is more readily available. When I walk on a sidewalk in a city, I always avoid walking across grates and metal covers for basement access. I do many riskier activities, but the proximity and immediacy of the hazard overcome my reason. Many are concerned about death by homicide, well-publicized in the press, while suicide is much more common. Humans have anxiety about air travel, but think little about death from asthma or stroke, which is much more likely. Recent events influence us more than distant ones. When my brother-in-law's garage burned at his lake cabin, I bought a fire pump that sucks water from the lake, even though the probability of a fire at my cabin was no higher than it was before his fire. Flood and earthquake insurance sales rise after well-reported floods and earthquakes.

These are just a few examples of the differences between Humans and Econs shown in behavioral economics. As I noted in the Introduction, I will not try to explain the reasons for human (normal) behavior. Rather, I will try to show how normal human decisions might be improved by rational economic thinking. But, as in the previous vignette, "An Economist's Christmas," I must warn you that this thinking often has social consequences; you may get invited to fewer parties.

Part Two

The Basic
Economic Problem

Introduction

Late 19th-century economist Alfred Marshall once said that economics is the study of mankind in the ordinary business of life. Marshall, one of the all-time greats, was right, but with this broad, bland view, he'd define biology as the study of plants and animals. One of my professors in graduate school, Hyman P. Minsky, had a succinct, more pithy definition. Minsky once said, "The purpose of an economy is to feed its people and provide tomorrow." The providing tomorrow part is about saving, investing, and financial markets, which we will address in Part Nine of this book. The feeding the people part provides a good metaphor for the overall purpose of economics, addressing what we call the basic economic problem.

In modern economies, we have gone beyond the mere provision of necessities, Minsky's food, but we still "feed" our people goods like houses, cars, clothing, computers, and caviar, and services such as haircuts, hotel stays, and banking. But the question remains. Which of these goods and services should we provide in an economy? Because our resources are limited, we can't produce and consume all we want of everything. Economics is about what to produce, how we produce it, and who gets to consume these goods and services. These questions appear everywhere, in entire economies and in the choices facing three aging baby boomers as they backpack in the canyons of Southern Utah.

"Backpacking with the 948 Boys" illustrates the basic economic problem on a small scale. When planning a backpacking trip, ends (mostly potential locations) are limitless, and the means to achieve them are limited. This familiar conflict gives rise to the basic economic problem of scarcity. Scarcity forces choice, and when you choose one destination, you forego another. If you put apples in your backpack, you might have to leave a bird book behind. Backpacking teaches you about scarcity, choice, and cost, the essence of economics.

The second story in this part, "From Spokane to St. Louis on the Bus," addresses the third part of the basic economic problem, cost. Cost is not defined in terms of money. Solveig and I learned this in the otherwise wonderful summer of 1972. Cheap transportation can be very costly, indeed.

In these modern times, when offices of diversity, equity, and inclusion occupy floor space in most university administration buildings, it might come as a surprise that economists are uncomfortable with normative issues of equity and fairness, leaving these determinations to others. "How Big is the Pizza?" shows that economists are, again, different from normal people. When normal people divide a pizza among many hungry pizza eaters, they worry about the relative number and size of pieces going to each eater. By contrast, economists strive to make the pizza as big as possible so that, despite the relative size of your piece of pizza, it's as big as it can be.

The fourth economic vignette in this part, "Dealing with Drought," explores alternative economic systems and how these systems address the basic economic problem. Water allocation, especially in the arid West, provides the context. There are "many ways to skin an economic cat," in western water policy. We contrast the prevalent command socialist approach with a market capitalist approach. We also define a Green economic system and suggest how Green Economics would deal with drought in the arid West.

The final piece in Part Two shows why economists are so enamored with the use of markets to address the basic economic problem. If we have markets where people are free to buy and sell goods and resources, each person can specialize in what he or she does best. This sounds easy enough until we encounter the economist's definition of best, something called comparative advantage. "Associate Deans, Babe Ruth, and Hawaiian Pineapples" shows how markets, through the signals of prices and wages, lead people to their comparative advantage and how a public university system contains perverse incentives created by a political, uneconomic salary hierarchy.

I hope that after Part Two, you will understand the universal nature of economics. It's about more than money, more than business, and more than the stock market. With economics we can examine money, business, and the stock market, but we can explore any kind of human activity, as well. Alfred Marshall was right, because his "ordinary business of life" is just scarcity and the basic economic problem. If resources cannot satisfy wants, we face the basic economic problem, personally, and in families, businesses, clubs, governments, and economies. Scarcity is everywhere, and because economics is about dealing with scarcity, economics is everywhere.

Backpacking With the 948 Boys:
The Basic Economic Problem

We stood by the bed in a motel room in Kanab, Utah, on which we'd piled a small mountain of "common gear" and food, which we would separate into three piles, one for each of our backpacks. In the morning, we'd start a five-day trip into Paria Canyon on the Utah-Arizona border. For Bruce, David, and me, it was one of the 20 times we'd stared together at this forbidding pile of life-sustaining stuff and faced the basic economic problem of scarcity, choice, and cost.

Bruce and David had known each other from their days of low-income advocacy in Salt Lake City in the early 1970s. I arrived in Utah in 1977 and became friends with both even later. While the cultural trailheads of our lives differ, paths leading from these beginnings were destined to merge sometime. On one of our early trips together, on a luxuriously lazy morning, gazing from our alcove at a red world of Wingate sandstone, pink clouds in a sky of Utah blue, pinion pine on the canyon rim, and the green grotto of a Southern Utah canyon bottom, we discovered an eerie commonality of experience. Not surprising, as the three of us were born in September 1948. We've called ourselves the 948 Boys ever since.

The annual 948 backpacking trip shows the basic economic problem as well as any activity. Economics is about satisfying human wants (ends) with limited resources (means). As all wants cannot be satisfied with limited resources, we must choose which wants to satisfy, and which resources to use in satisfying them. Economists call this the problem of scarcity.

On the annual 948 trip, we sought a quality experience in the desert of Southern Utah. But where should we go in this vast area of natural splendor? Which trip had the highest value? We could hike from the mountains south of Moab down Dark

Canyon to the Colorado River. We could visit famous Ancestral Pueblo ruins in Grand Gulch, or less famous, but no less-spectacular ones in Slickhorn and Road Canyons on Cedar Mesa. And always, the canyons of the Escalante River called to us, and now also to millions of others. Death Hollow, Twenty-five Mile Wash, Coyote Gulch, Fools Canyon, and Sleepy Hollow, all 948 destinations, offered sublime backpacking experiences. We wanted to do them all, but time was limited, as was the ability of our aging bodies to schlep our life on our backs. Every economy must choose what it will produce and consume. The 948 Boys had to choose where to go. And when we went somewhere, we couldn't go somewhere else. By choosing one trip, we incurred the opportunity cost of another trip foregone.

Limited means helped to constrain our choice of other backpacking ends. Our packs were only so big, and our aging Boomer bodies could carry less and less for shorter and shorter distances. One year, due to my ailing back, I spent a good portion of a trip in a small alcove in the Upper Gulch, about a quarter mile from the trailhead on the Burr Trail. In his hiking book, Rudi Lambreschtse refers to it as occurring too early to be of any overnight use. Obviously, Rudi's resources were less constrained than mine. On the Paria trip, David's gout-inflamed foot was so sore that we avoided a helicopter rescue only by an inadvertent placebo effect. I thought I was giving him hydrocodone from my emergency drug stash, when, in fact, it was an antacid of similar size and shape. He was strong on the way out, in any case. Yes, it's fortunate the mix-up didn't go the other way, resulting in a zonked-out treatment for heartburn.

Filling the space in a pack of limited size involves choices about resources. Just as people in an economy must choose how to produce their goods and services, backpackers must choose the resources they carry in their packs. When I was younger, thinner, and stronger, I carried a naturalist's library on every trip: bird book, flower book, trail guide, and an appropriate book to read, like Ed Abbey's *Desert Solitaire*, or *The Monkey Wrench Gang*, or anything by Wallace Stegner, or Muir's *Wilderness Essays*, or something new by Terry Tempest

Williams. In Paria Canyon, facing the prospect of collapsing in the first mile, a high cost indeed, I took no books of any kind.

And what about food? Nothing tastes better than an orange, an apple, a cucumber, or a slice of Bermuda onion about the third or fourth day of becoming one with the desert dirt, but on that bed in the Kanab motel room, each looked like a lead ingot. We took some of Bruce's dried fruit instead. As science had failed us in developing dehydrated beer, what about whiskey? Some things are essential. We took two plastic traveler fifths. Even the teetotaler guests on a trip drink in the desert. And, of course, if we didn't take the fresh fruit, we could take the tins of smoked oysters. Even vegetarian Bruce downed one of these slimy delicacies on many occasions. To make room for these treats, we'd bring only one-pot, dehydrated dinners. Some lentil chili and black beans for burritos from the Moscow Co-op, a meal of polenta, pasta, or couscous.

As in all economies, we'd try to augment our capital and improve our technology to conserve and extend the productivity of our labor. We bought new internal frame packs that didn't catch as easily on the willows, tamarisk, and slots in the slickrock. The top of my pack also doubled as a fanny pack for day hiking, so I didn't need to take a daypack. Lightweight stoves, sleeping bags, and water filters helped lighten the load. Fleece, nylon, and Gore-Tex were substituted for wool, cotton, and denim. We left the metal cup behind and took a plastic measuring cup instead, from which we could eat, drink, and measure. Cut an inch off your toothbrush. Carry pills in baggies, not in plastic bottles. Everyone doesn't need to take a compass, camera, and binoculars. These were just some of the ways we substituted capital for labor.

Finally, any economic problem requires an economic system to help allocate limited resources. Backpacking is no different. The 948 boys had a traditional economic system. By the time we reached Point of the Mountain heading south in the Salt Lake Valley, tradition said we should have decided our destination, but, of course, schmoozing with the ranger always provided information that altered our routes and even destinations.

"Sounds like it's going to be too crowded for me," said Bruce. "I've heard that one hundred parties have been checking in daily to the Escalante Visitor Center. Let's go somewhere else."

"Like your idea of hiking Steep Creek from Boulder Mountain to the Escalante," I said. "Sounds like a Death March to me."

"I kind of like the base camp mode," said David, massaging his foot.

Most economies are either capitalist or socialist, or a mix of both, with centralized or decentralized decision making. Traditional economies, like the 948, are different. The 948 Boys addressed the basic economic problem like it always had been. In our case, the tradition was consensus decision making, with implicit and explicit rules, supported by trust and respect for the individual and his role. Small group size helped. Of course, a set of common values acquired from a common history, since September of 1948, greased the skids of our traditional economy, and helped allocate limited resources among competing ends to produce great trips enjoyed by all.

From Spokane to St. Louis on the Bus:

The Economics of Opportunity Cost

In the spring of 1972, I had just finished my second full year of graduate study in economics at Washington University in St. Louis. Having passed theory qualifying exams the previous fall and two field exams in May, I had entered the vast, daunting space called Ph.D. candidacy, sometimes referred to as "all but dissertation" (ABD). For many graduate students, this space turns into an inescapable academic black hole. I feared it might be for me as well.

Like many before and after me, once I had sailed past a mark on the academic voyage, through what seemed at the time very stormy weather and rough seas, the past stretch began to look calm and easy, and the future sail very strenuous indeed. From the vantage point of graduate school, the challenge of an undergraduate program pales in comparison. When reflecting on the friendly bay cruise of graduate exams, authoring a dissertation seems like a transoceanic voyage. Once land is cited in the new world, the voyage doesn't seem so bad, but getting a job, publishing, and getting tenure resembles a trip through the Bermuda Triangle.

In the spring of 1972, I had no idea about a dissertation topic. My wife Solveig's job was okay, but not great. I had a monthly stipend coming from my National Defense Education Act fellowship. One day with Steppenwolf wailing from our small stereo, "Get your motor running, head out on the highway," we made a great, uncharacteristically irresponsible decision. Flee, procrastinate, avoid, and deny are just a few words that describe our thinking. We decided that even the St. Louis Cardinals couldn't entice us to spend another hot humid summer in St Louis. It was time for a break, a time to defend the nation in the Pacific Northwest.

Our 1961 Volkswagen had shelf paper flowers applied to its dents. It had made it to St. Louis, but we didn't think it could get us home again. We had friends who had had good luck with Drive-Away cars. That's when someone wants a car transported, and you drive it away for them. We were lucky. Someone wanted a 1971 Ford LTD transported to Seattle. We paid a fee of $50 and the gas. When we picked up the car, the Drive-Away person said we would have to get a permit to cross Iowa. I said we weren't going through Iowa. She said we had to go through Iowa to get to Washington, as it was just to the east, and all the major roads went through it. I convinced her she was thinking of Idaho.

"Iowa, Idaho, you still have to get a permit," she said.

We loaded the LTD with five summers of gear. In addition to clothing and books, we took our bicycles, a guitar, and a sewing machine. We had people to stay with along the way. We just had to pay for gas in the LTD, the nicest car we'd ever driven. We drove north and visited Solveig's grandparents in Black River Falls, Wisconsin, and then headed west. I remember we left at 8:00 in the evening. We had planned to drive through the night and part of the next day to somewhere in Montana. A 1971 Ford LTD was a fast car. We crossed the Montana line early the next morning and drove into Billings around noon.

It's hard to stop at noon when you're heading home for the summer. We kept incrementing ourselves across Montana until we saw the sign in Missoula that said Spokane, 198 miles. After going over 1300 miles in the last few hours, and with lots of daylight left, this seemed like a Sunday drive. Black River Falls to Spokane in 25 hours. I think we wanted to get home!

We had a wonderful summer in the Northwest, hitchhiking around and visiting friends and relatives. We capped the summer with two glorious weeks camping at Priest Lake. But then, in late August, it was time to return to St. Louis. Guess what? More people were going from St. Louis to Seattle in 1972 than were going from Seattle to St. Louis. I'm embarrassed to reveal that one of the field exams I passed in the spring was in regional economics. I had failed to predict an important implication of this difference in net migration: no Drive-Away cars from the Northwest to the Midwest.

As the out-of-pocket cost of airline tickets back to St. Louis seemed way beyond our means at the time, and our parents didn't appear overly willing to help us out after we had spent a summer essentially goofing off, we decided we'd take the bus. And here is the economic moral of this travelogue. Cost in economics is not simply money spent on something, what we economists call explicit cost. Cost in economics is much more fundamental. We use the term opportunity cost in economics. The cost of one action is the value of an alternative forgone. Cost can also be implicit, like time spent or pain and suffering incurred.

Taking a 55-hour bus ride from Spokane to St. Louis was one of the costliest things we have ever done. Even with young bones and muscles, in the middle of the second night, we wanted to mortgage our entire future for a helicopter ride. Please, I don't care about the monetary cost, send the helicopter to Fargo, North Dakota. I can't be on this bus for another minute. After 48 hours, we had a two-hour layover and a change of buses in Chicago at midnight. If you didn't manage to make it to the Chicago bus depot in 1972, take my word for it. Frightening. I almost wet my pants waiting to get on the restroom-equipped bus. At least in the Chicago bus depot, at midnight in late August 1972, I had come to my economic senses and correctly assessed the implicit cost of using the restroom in the bus station.

We made it back. My dad managed to get a friend to put our bikes on the back of a load of apple trees he hauled to Louisiana, Missouri. We drove up there a month or so later and picked them up. We paid to have the sewing machine shipped. I don't think either of us has taken a bus trip since. To this day, if I ride one of those airporter buses from the airport to a hotel or ride a charter on a wine tour, I remember my embarrassing lesson in the economics of opportunity cost. I'm better at ferreting out "false economy" traps today than I was in the summer of 1972.

How Big is the Pizza?

Picture yourself as a member of a small group. Each of you is very hungry. Maybe you are teammates after a softball game, a few friends returning from a hike, college roommates returning from a night of studying, or ten-year-old boys at a birthday party. You order a pizza. It arrives at the door, and ooooh, it smells so good.

Your group has a limited amount of money to spend on pizza. You expect that the pizza you ordered is not large enough for all members of the group to have their fill, to become satiated, to say, "No more, please, I can't eat another bite." You and your friends confront the issue of dividing up the pizza, an example of a basic economic problem.

A Norwegian-American Grandma might say, "Just give me half a piece."

A presidential candidate from the Green party might say, "I don't want to be manipulated by the corporate power of the pizza industry. Don't give me any."

Comrade Jones, a communist, might say, "Who needs this pizza the most?" Comrade Jones would set up a committee to decide on the relative levels of need. And, of course, the committee must be fed, so there wouldn't be much pizza left for ordinary members of the group.

Most normal people, however, would worry about the number and size of their own pieces of pizza, and this would be related to the number and size of others' pieces.

"Touch that other piece, and I'll play T-ball off your head!" says a softball player.

"How'd you like to have lug sole marks on your face, pizza pig?" asks the hiker.

"Jenny, like, how many pieces have you had already? I can hear you, like, oinking," says the college student.

"Mommy, Mommy, Jimmy got a bigger piece than me," shouts the ten-year-old.

To economists, who gets what size piece is not the main consideration. Where normal people are concerned primarily with fairness and equity, economists worry about the size of the entire pizza. Once, my students assured me that the day of the super-giant 24-inch pizza had arrived, evidence to them that we live in a great country. With a moderate-size group, you can have a small piece of a super-giant, 24-inch pizza and still get enough to eat. On the other hand, a large piece of a 15-inch pizza, roughly four-tenths the size (if you are geometry-savvy, you can do the math), is not much to eat.

If asked to divide a pizza, economists would have some weird ideas about how to do it. Given their interest in maximizing the value of the pizza consumed and faith that market allocation can accomplish this, economists would have everyone submit sealed bids stating the number of pieces they want and the price they are willing to pay per piece. We would then award pieces to the highest bidders—those who value pizza the most.

Economists care about equity. We just don't have any special expertise in the area. Normal people are as good as we are at deciding what's fair. Religion, sociology, and the law are fields populated by many well-educated, normal people who care deeply about fairness and have careers devoted to it. But, because few normal people care about the size of the national pizza, we economists devote a great deal of time and energy to it. And when it comes to setting up systems to give people big and bigger national pizzas, no one knows more than weird economists do.

Dealing with Drought:

Command, Market, and Green Economic Systems

If you want to grow things in the summer in the Inland Northwest, it's best to irrigate. This is not Seattle, where blackberry bushes are weeds and regular rains water the lawn and garden. The folks in Dusty, Washington, receive less than eight inches of precipitation a year, with little of that falling in the summer. Dusty is, well, dusty, especially when the wind blows across the fallow wheat fields. You can grow dry-land wheat and some grass for cattle even in Dusty, but for anything else, you'd better irrigate.

A few miles farther west in Othello, Washington, it doesn't rain much more than in Dusty, but farmers grow apples and potatoes, and almost everyone grows another important crop, grass in the front yard. In the Columbia Basin, in central Washington, and elsewhere in the Inland Northwest, we've made the desert bloom by building dams. Like water squirrels, we catch the runoff from the mountain snowmelt and store it for later. Unlike our acorn cousins whom you see working by themselves getting ready for winter, we usually work collectively in water storage. We finance dams with appropriations from the U.S. Congress to agencies like the U.S. Bureau of Reclamation and the U.S. Army Corps of Engineers, and expenditures of state and municipal governments. Because we have both government ownership and management of dams in the Inland Northwest, economists would say we use a command socialist economic system to make our desert bloom.

Economists define economic systems according to how resources are owned and allocated. Two rare economic systems are pure market capitalism and pure command socialism. In market capitalism, we have private ownership of resources and private allocation of them through markets. In general, we have much market capitalism in the U.S. In command socialism, we have collective (government) ownership and political or administrative non-market methods of resource allocation. We see a lot of command socialism in Cuba and North Korea. And, as noted above, we see it in western U.S. water management.

In the Northwest Museum of Arts and Culture in Spokane and at other museums around the region, you can learn about Indian cultures that inhabited our region for centuries. These cultures depended on salmon for their existence at places like Celilo Falls on the lower Columbia River and Spokane Falls on the Spokane River. Rather than changing the landscape to produce goods like apples and potatoes to export from the region, members of traditional Indian economies adapted to the landscape for the purposes of self-sufficiency.

Members of the modern Green movement think we should be more like the Indians. We should adjust our wants rather than manipulate Mother Nature. To a Green, Mother Nature is a good mother, and she doesn't like high stream flows and lake levels in the summer. She likes high stream flows and lake levels in April and May when the snow melts so baby salmon can catch a ride to the sea. Later in the summer and fall, the low flows also concentrate the returning spawning salmon population so that you can catch them with a dip net or a wash tub.

I doubt that adherents to a Green economic system would have dammed the Columbia and Snake Rivers at the scale generated by command socialism. The West would look much different today if Greens had controlled Congress and Western state legislatures in the 20th century.

A market capitalist approach to water development would have led to a different West as well. Many water resource development projects could not have passed market tests. Revenues from water and electricity sales could not justify the large expenditure on facilities. Much marginal agriculture that depends on heavily subsidized water for its existence would not be here today. We would sell more electricity from hydropower outside the region at higher prices rather than sell it to locals at low prices.

The economic fabric of the Inland Northwest, and the arid West in general, would look much different today had different economic systems prevailed in the 20th century. We can only speculate about the exact texture of this fabric. By contrast, we can examine the water allocation in our present economic system with a little more certainty because we see it happening all the time. Resource allocation systems are easier to examine and classify when we see them under stress. In the case of water resources, drought provides an informative stress.

In a drought, we have less water to distribute to water users. We must reduce our water use because our water resources are now more limited. Even within a command socialist water system, we could use an allocation system analogous to a market mechanism. Water managers could raise the price of water. At a higher price for water, people would use less.

Even this little bit of market system is rarely used in drought management. Politically imposed shared reduction usually beats out pricing in a drought. Command economies give greater emphasis to the equity aspects of reduced water use. For example, water departments often share water reduction by imposing alternate-day watering schemes. If your house number is odd, you water your lawn on odd-numbered days. If your house number is even, you water on the even days. If odd-even watering doesn't reduce water use enough, water departments might ban certain activities, like washing cars, squirting dirt off the sidewalk, or even lawn and garden watering itself. In Moscow, Idaho, where I lived for 28 years, a malfunctioning pump drastically reduced the water supply. Watering your lawn any day before 8:00 p.m. earned you a ticket from the water police. A capitalist owner of a water system or a socialist water manager who believed in markets would simply raise the price of water. However, the market allocation of water is politically dangerous.

A Green approaching drought would worry less about ownership and allocation issues than would market capitalists and command socialists. A Green would want to use a policy that improved environmental quality, improved the equity and social responsibility of the water system, followed grassroots, participatory politics, and did little violence to humans or nature.

A Green water policy would start with a town meeting with an open microphone, where anyone could express his or her views. Greens at the microphone would have a variety of suggestions for reducing water use, but most of the suggestions would work best if everyone adopted Green values. We should do desert landscaping instead of planting Kentucky bluegrass far from Kentucky. We should install low-flow toilets and showerheads that use less water. We should install drip irrigation systems in our vegetable gardens. A Green would argue that if we changed our values and practiced water conservation, we might even be able to remove dams and give salmon a better chance at survival.

In the Inland Northwest, a combination of Green and command socialist policies triumph over market capitalism in dealing with drought and dealing with water in general. It's one of the reasons our economic system is a mixed one, at neither the market capitalist nor command socialist extreme. Our water system contains elements of both private and government ownership, and elements of both market and political control. Private individuals own shares of stock in McDonald's and Walmart, but all Americans own Grand Coulee Dam. If orange blossoms freeze in Florida, the market price of orange juice rises, and we drink less of it. If the winter snows stay away, next summer, we will have the same price of water, odd and even day watering, and pleas for water conservation. Different economic systems are everywhere, even in our economy. You can see them if you know what to look for.

Associate Deans, Babe Ruth, and Hawaiian Pineapples:

Stories of Comparative Advantage

Comparative advantage, when combined with specialization and trade, allows individuals and societies to get the most value from their limited resources. I encountered the Law of Comparative Advantage in a very real-world context. The College of Business and Economics at the University of Idaho, where I used to work, decided that we needed an associate dean. The dean had decided that he needed an associate dean to handle administrative matters of the college, as he continually traveled out of town begging for money. An associate dean is like the vice principal of a high school. In addition to some interesting tasks related to program and curriculum development, he handles all the dirty jobs, such as dealing with disgruntled faculty and attending painfully boring meetings on things like outcomes assessment and responsibility center management. People who take these jobs usually hope to climb the ladder of academic administration, to someday become a dean, and hit the road to beg for money.

After a short time, two candidates emerged as finalists, both of whom possessed the requisite qualifications. At the time, I thought each would do the job well. I thought one candidate, call him Bill, would be the best associate dean. In my letter to the dean, I suggested that we offer the job to another competent, yet second-place, candidate. Let's call this candidate Jim. How could I recommend my second-place candidate, Jim, for the job? Only an economist knows the answer. In addition to better abilities for "associate deaning," Bill was also a better teacher and researcher than Jim. Many would argue that Bill was among the best teachers and researchers in the college and maybe in the entire university. Jim was solid in these areas but not as good as

Bill. Bill was better at both academic tasks: "associate deaning," and teaching and research. We economists say he had an absolute advantage over Jim in both areas. His advantage over Jim, however, was much greater in teaching and research. For that reason, making Bill the associate dean incurred a much higher opportunity cost in terms of foregone teaching and research than giving Jim the job. Bill had a comparative advantage in teaching and research. Jim, lacking an absolute advantage in either job, was less disadvantaged in administering. He had a comparative advantage in "associate deaning," even though Bill was better at it. If Bill and Jim specialized in the jobs in which they had a comparative advantage, the value of their combined efforts would be higher than it would be under some other allocation of their resources.

In my 43 years as a university professor, I saw countless quality teachers and researchers promoted to positions of pushing paper in the corner office, all based on their outstanding qualifications in teaching and research. It was a waste of talent. Why not make administrators out of tenured bad teachers and researchers, a move that involves a low opportunity cost, and keep the good academics in the classroom and laboratory?

The marketplace is much better at getting people to pursue their comparative advantage than government institutions like state universities and public schools. Here are just a few examples. Babe Ruth, the legendary "Sultan of Swat," came into the major leagues with the Boston Red Sox as a pitcher. He was the best left-handed pitcher in the American League from 1916 to 1920. Babe Ruth pitched 29 2/3 scoreless innings in World Series play against the Brooklyn Dodgers in 1916 and the Chicago Cubs in 1918. He had an absolute advantage in pitching. Once traded to the New York Yankees, he never pitched another game. The opportunity cost was too high. His comparative advantage was in hitting, not pitching.

Billy Rose, a theatrical performer, lyricist, and producer in the 1940s and 50s, was considered by many to be the world's fastest stenographer. The pay for stenography was low compared to that of an American impresario, so Billy Rose chose the latter occupation, in which he had a comparative advantage.

A brain surgeon has many of the skills necessary to be a good auto mechanic. Both involve diagnosing and fixing problems with specialized tools. In fact, a brain surgeon might have an absolute advantage over many auto mechanics in the auto repair business. Do brain surgeons repair their own cars? Of course not. Relative wage differences between brain surgery and auto repair lead brain surgeons to the operating room, their comparative advantage, and their cars to someone else's garage for repair. Specialization and trade increase the value of resources devoted to brain surgery and auto repair. Specialization by the brain surgeon also creates opportunities in auto repair for those having an absolute advantage in neither occupation but a comparative advantage in auto repair. A favorite textbook example of this idea involves the TV comedy Gilligan's Island, where even hapless Gilligan has something to do, the activity he is least worst at.

The principle of comparative advantage works for resources other than labor, as well. Something interesting has happened in Hawaii, on the island of Lanai. Lanai is one of the best places in the world for growing pineapples. Lanai has an absolute advantage in pineapples, but every year on the "Pineapple Island," owners of land remove acres and acres from pineapple production. The reason is tourism. Because Lanai has an even greater advantage in tourism than it does in growing pineapples, the opportunity cost of pineapple plantations is huge. Landowners on Lanai are beginning to pursue their comparative advantage in tourism, by building hotels and condominiums where pineapples used to grow.

Comparative advantage, specialization, and trade make up an economic trinity causing economists to wax rhapsodic about markets. Markets involve trade, by definition, but also send signals to actors in the marketplace. Wages and prices established in markets provide incentives to market participants to pursue their comparative advantage in the form of the highest-valued opportunity. By choosing the highest valued opportunity in the marketplace, the individual avoids the high opportunity cost of not choosing this activity and follows his or her comparative advantage. Markets work well when they do this.

Wages and prices established in socialist institutions such as state universities provide incentives, as well, but often perverse incentives that turn good teachers and researchers into administrators at great cost. If the New York Yankees were managed like a state university, Derek Jeter would have had to replace manager Joe Girardi to raise his salary, and we would have missed the opportunity to watch one of the best shortstops in baseball, a high opportunity cost, indeed.

Part Three

In the Beginning was the Word,
and the Word was Marginal

Introduction

As the title of Part Three suggests, the word marginal attains nearly religious importance in economics. In the index of any encyclopedic economics text, it appears more than any other term. Some would claim that modern economics grew out of a marginalist revolution in the late 19ᵗʰ century. Many normal people find the whole economics discipline revolting and think the entire subject is marginal, but that's a different usage and a different story.

Two synonyms aptly define the economics terms marginal: "incremental" and "change in." Both terms suggest action. Choice is an action. For example, if we choose one alternative, we forego another. The value of the foregone alternative is the cost of the choice, its marginal cost. But cost is only one word we can insert after the word marginal. The stories in Part Three bring a few of these to life.

In "Oh Dad, It's Just Another Osprey," diminishing marginal utility reduces the excitement from additional encounters with one of nature's wonders, just one of many diminishing returns concepts in economics. As we do more of something, the additional, incremental value of it declines. The concept applies to Oreo eating and beer drinking, too, but we use the Osprey example here to protect you, gentle reader, from the sophomoric standard classroom application, the economics of throwing up.

In "Snowbird Ski Tickets and Latah County Garbage," seven hundred miles of rugged western landscape cannot separate the unifying importance of marginal cost. To make good decisions, we must understand marginal cost and avoid the temptation of average cost, whether choosing the number of days to ski the dry powder of the Wasatch Range or the number of cans of smelly garbage to place at the end of a rural Idaho driveway.

We know from the old adage that nothing is certain but death and taxes. But if you eat well, don't smoke, drink moderately, and exercise regularly, you can push back the former. And if you understand tax deductions and marginal tax rates, you can reduce the latter. "Marginal Tax Rates and the Three-Martini Lunch" shows the incentive effects of tax rates on behavior as varied as the fabled lunch, home improvement, family work choices, the housing buy-or-rent decision, and the choice of where to buy things in a border community.

My buddy Larry's marriage history provides the context for our next foray into marginal analysis. Larry's experience shows that all costs and benefits lie in the future, all true costs are marginal costs, and that costs incurred in the past, which economists call sunk costs, must be ignored. In economics, as in marriage, we must look forward, not backward, and be sure we are "Giving up Hope of a Brighter Past."

The final vignette in Part Three brings marginal analysis into the normative sphere of social choice, with examples of lawnmower safety, crime prevention, and water quality. Only to an economist can lawnmowers be too safe, water too clean, and crime rates too low. When economists think about the optimal level of anything, we think of *Goldilocks and the Three Bears*. Porridge should not be too hot nor too cold but just right, where the marginal benefit equals the marginal cost.

Oh, Dad, It's Just Another Osprey

Summer doesn't start until July 5th in North Idaho. At least we have one. Solveig and I lived for a few years way upstate in Potsdam, New York, where I took my first job after graduate school. Early on, I asked my Clarkson College economics colleague, Dascomb B. Forbusch, what the summers were like. "Actually," he said, "We have a highly protracted spring." We never spent a summer there.

On a lovely summer day in the mid-1980s, Solveig and I and our daughter Amanda were part of a family canoe trip on the Priest River, which flows south out of Priest Lake, the most precious jewel in Idaho's triple-jeweled-crown of northern lakes. One section of the river, from Dickensheet Campground to McAbee Falls, provides a leisurely meander punctuated by occasional Class 1 rapids. With only Class 1 rapids to negotiate, ripples to all but the novice canoeist, we were able to watch the world unfold anew around every bend and to marvel at the lush forest, clear, sparkling water, and amazing wildlife, not the least of which was the osprey.

The osprey is a fish-eating hawk inhabiting coastal and inland waters of all continents. My students, even non-birders, would say, "For a bird, it's pretty cool!" And if you've been around ospreys, you know they make large, reusable nests atop a variety of objects: a tall snag in the Northwest, a large, coastal desert cactus, a stationary mark in an estuary, a bridge piling, or a power pole. They're beautiful, large, soaring birds with loud, distinctive calls. But this all pales in comparison to the way they fish!

Unlike the bald eagle, which swoops and glides toward its meal of live animals or carrion, the osprey circles 50 to 100 feet above a living fish. It hovers for an instant, then free-falls to the water's surface, like a cat shot from a tree. But wait, at the last second, the cat's not shot; it lands feet-first, talons ready, and grabs the fish. The osprey then begins its takeoff, like an old WW II bomber, overloaded with fire retardant, struggling for altitude. When it finally picks up speed, the osprey turns the still-living fish lengthwise for lower wind resistance. As you would expect, ospreys drop a few fish.

We witnessed this amazing avian behavior that day on the Priest River, not at a distance through powerful binoculars but 50 feet from our canoe. At mid-day, we usually had some warning, as the watery shadow of a circling osprey repeatedly woke us from our sleepy drift. In mid-afternoon, as this shadow appeared again, eight-year-old Amanda looked up with a start and said disappointingly, "Oh, Dad, it's just another osprey."

At age eight, Amanda exhibited the fundamental economic principle of diminishing returns, in this case, the law of eventually diminishing marginal utility (value). While another osprey sighting, and the possibility of seeing it fish, had value, each ADDITIONAL sighting gave us less ADDITIONAL value than the last sighting. If this were not true, robin sightings would elicit a gasp, and we would make all bouquets out of dandelions. The more we do, the more we have, the lower the value of an ADDITIONAL amount of something. If you understand this simple concept, understanding economics becomes a lot easier.

Snowbird Ski Tickets and Latah County Garbage:

The Importance of Marginal Cost

I'd probably been an economist my entire life without knowing it, but like a born-again Christian, I can pinpoint the time of my actual conversion to the discipline of economics. In the spring of 1967, in Professor Pierson's macroeconomics class at Pacific Lutheran University, I felt a call. By the end of the term, I had changed my major to economics. If one of my students asked me about choosing a major in economics, I usually asked her if she'd seen a burning bush lately.

I used my economics training many times in subsequent years, not just to pass exams and publish papers but to improve a decision here and there, to gain a small advantage in the quest for quality living. Of all the practical applications of economic principles I made over the years, I'm most proud of using marginal analysis in deciding how many ski tickets to buy at Snowbird Ski Resort in Utah.

I'd moved to Utah in 1977 and skied every winter until the economics department Marxists threw me out in 1989. I wouldn't live in New York City without going to great restaurants and the theater, and I couldn't live in Utah without skiing. It's just too good. I learned to ski at the spectacular Alta Ski Area and skied there mostly with economist colleagues. We had to ski together because normal people don't want to ski with economists.

We eventually recognized that because Alta lift ticket prices were low, long lift lines emerged (at least long by early 1980s Utah standards) at the Germania lift, which provides access to Alta's best "steep and deep." In addition to low pricing, Alta managers contributed to long lines by resisting the installation of improved ski lifts that would have shortened the lines. They wanted to preserve the "Alta Experience" on the mountain by limiting the number of skiers on a run at any time. Of course, as economist skiers, we focused on the long lines. Economists hate lines.

In the early 1980s, we fled Alta to neighboring Snowbird. At that time, Snowbird did not have an unlimited ski pass, where, for a fixed price, you could ski for an unlimited number of days. Instead, Snowbird sold skiers as many days as they wanted at discount prices. They gave quantity discounts. The more days you bought, the lower the cost per day. For example, in the 1988/89 ski season, Snowbird sold tickets in blocks of five, with a minimum purchase of fifteen tickets. If you bought before Labor Day, you could buy fifteen tickets for $285, an average cost of $19 per ticket, quite a bit lower than the regular lift ticket price of $32. Twenty tickets cost $340, or $17 per ticket. The average ticket cost remained $17 until you bought fifty or more tickets. The average price then fell to $15 a ticket.

There we were in the depths of summer, temperatures 90 to 100 degrees, deciding how many tickets to buy. Even though we were avid skiers, we did have teaching jobs at the university that we couldn't avoid entirely, even in Utah in the winter. We weren't going to ski 50 days at Snowbird. We did, however, have the luxury of a flexible schedule. The University of Utah was on a quarter system then, and our teaching obligation was six courses over three quarters. We often managed to snare an internal or external research grant to buy our way out of a course in the winter quarter. We then taught one night class and watched the local evening news to see if weather forecaster Mark Eubank was wearing his snow coat. If he wore that ugly off-white sports jacket, we knew we would be on the slopes in the morning. While we couldn't ski 50 days at Snowbird, we certainly could ski 15 or 20 select powder days. The big question for us was whether to buy 15 or 20 tickets. If we purchased 20, the average cost would be two dollars less per ticket. Um, what to do?

Luckily, we knew something about marginal cost. Marginal cost, like marginal anything, involves increments or changes. The marginal cost of Snowbird ski tickets is the **change** in the total cost of tickets divided by the **change** in the quantity of tickets purchased. Buying 20 instead of 15 tickets increased the total ticket cost from $285 to $340, an increase of $55. Dividing $55 by the number of **additional** tickets, five in this case, yielded a marginal cost of $11 per ticket. At $11 apiece, the additional tickets were not just $2 cheaper, the difference in their average cost ($19 minus $17), but $8 cheaper, the difference between the per ticket cost of the first 15 tickets ($19) and the per ticket cost of the additional five tickets ($11), the marginal cost. Was this enough savings to justify buying 20 instead of 15 tickets? Maybe, maybe not, but one thing is certain. To think about the decision correctly, you must consider marginal rather than average cost. To the economist skier, the only thing better than tunneling down the Peruvian Cirque at Snowbird in three feet of light powder was knowing that you used marginal analysis in the decision to do it. Well, maybe not better.

A normal person wouldn't think Snowbird Ski Tickets and garbage collection in Latah County, Idaho, have much in common. But to the economist, they have a lot in common. In the 1990s, Latah County began rural residential garbage collection. Before this, we had dumpsters in several locations around the county where we took our garbage. Unfortunately, the dumpsters became dumpsites for people in the towns and cities, and people would dump things like televisions, mattresses, and couches. It was a real mess, and I was happy to have the garbage trucks stop at the end of my driveway once a week.

The Latah County Solid Waste Department charged me $174.12 a year, about $3.35 weekly, to pick up one standard garbage can. I could put out two cans for $194.16 a year ($3.73 per week, $1.87 per can), three cans for $207.36 ($3.99 a week, $1.33 per can), four cans for $215.76 ($4.15 per week, $1.04 per can), and five cans for $222.48 ($4.28 per week, $.87 per can). I can't imagine five cans of garbage, but if we had wanted to increase our material throughput, it would not have cost much to do so. Here, again, marginal cost is important. Once I decide to have at least one can of garbage picked up each week at the end of my driveway, the marginal cost of additional cans is extremely low. Remember that marginal cost is the change in total cost divided by the change in quantity. Because we are considering increments of one can here, the quantity change is one can. Anything divided by one is whatever it is. So, to figure out the marginal cost of garbage cans, we look at the difference in total weekly cost. The first **additional** can of garbage, the second can in this case, has a marginal cost of thirty-eight cents a week ($3.73 minus 3.35). Putting out a third can has a marginal cost of twenty-six cents ($3.99 minus 3.73). If I'm already putting out four cans, I can put out the fifth can at a marginal cost of just thirteen cents per week ($4.28 minus 4.15). In Latah County, Idaho, once you decide to have one garbage can a week, there is little incentive not to be a garbage hog. Note also that the marginal cost is much lower than the average cost, as in the case of Snowbird Ski Tickets.

The proper information about the cost of being a garbage hog might not have been as important as knowing the marginal cost of Snowbird ski tickets, but it was important nonetheless. For one thing, I felt smug when I made my quarterly pilgrimage to commune at the Shrine of Our Lady of Sustainable Development, the local recycling center. As I filled up the back of the '86 Isuzu Trooper with box upon box of wine and beer bottles and bag upon bag of *Wall Street Journals* and *Spokesman Reviews*, I gave myself an environmentally religious pat on the stiffening back. I was saving less than 40 cents a can per week by recycling. I could have put out an additional can, but I didn't. I recycled instead. Even economists are normal sometimes.

Giving Up Hope of a Brighter Past

After congratulating Solveig and me on one of our twenty-something wedding anniversaries, our bachelor friend Larry noted that he had been married as long as we had, only to three different women. Wife number one, the mother of his children, had lasted the longest, nearly fifteen years. With wife number two, whom he affectionately called the Black Widow, things were rocky after about six months.

"Marriage is like golf," he said, "Everybody deserves a mulligan."

Wife number three was the costliest, as their six-year marriage matched a period of substantial growth in his engineering business, half of which he lost in the divorce.

"It's funny," he said, "Even though I just bought my fourth weed sprayer, it doesn't bother me. I've given up all hope of a brighter past." I realized right then that Larry, a professional engineer, was an economist in his heart of hearts. He understood the meaning of cost.

Economics is about choice, and we have no choice about the past. All past actions and all past opportunities foregone are sunk costs. We can't do anything about them, so we ought to learn what we can from our mistakes, then forget about them and move on. All benefits and costs lie in the future.

Normal people have difficulty ignoring sunk costs. Here's an example to prove the point. Imagine you are the owner of a small business in North Idaho, a shop that sells machines used by homeowners, such as lawn and garden equipment and snowblowers. In October, a snowblower manufacturer runs a promotion. For every snowblower you buy from the manufacturer, you get a free night's lodging at a nice hotel on the beach in Maui. If you buy ten, the manufacturer will throw in airfare as well. You know how long North Idaho winters can be, and the thought of palm trees, beach time, and drinks with little umbrellas in them race through your head. You buy ten at $1,000 each.

Right after Halloween, you run snowblower ads in the newspaper and on the radio that cost you $1,000. You pay the local mall another $1,000 to leave one of the machines on display, where people will walk by it during holiday shopping. You price the machines at $1,799 (They're great machines.), sit back, and dream of Maui. You'll sell the snowblowers for nearly $18,000, and after subtracting your advertising cost, you will have a nice $6,000 profit. That will pay for a lot of golf, meals, and fancy drinks with little umbrellas on your trip.

Unfortunately, North Idaho experiences one of the driest, warmest early winters on record. No snow falls. No one buys snowblowers. It's January, and all ten are still on the showroom floor. You want to go to Hawaii, but you can't stop thinking that you haven't sold a single snowblower.

One day, a snowblower wholesaler from Minnesota contacts you. They are having one of the worst winters in years. She offers to buy your ten snowblowers for $600 each. You reject the offer, telling the wholesaler that the machines are worth at least $1,000, which is what you paid for them, and you have also incurred advertising expenses of $2,000. Selling at $600 means you would lose $6,000 on the deal ($6,000 revenue minus $12,000 in cost). Did you make a good decision?

Only if you are a budding economist will you have the right answer. Economists would say it depends on what you expect to happen in the future, noting that the $10,000 outlay for the machines and the $2,000 advertising cost are sunk. Actions have costs, but things don't. Whether you sell the machines at $600 each should depend on what you expect to sell them for in the future and the additional costs you expect to incur in the interim. A worst-case scenario is that you won't be able to sell them at all, which means you just made your loss $6,000 higher by not selling each one at $600. The cost of selling at $600 is the opportunity (a choice, an action) foregone by doing so. If you expect to sell them for more than $600 in the future, and the amount above $600 is greater than your expected other future costs, then rejecting the offer is sound business and economic reasoning. But if you think the offer is bad because you are regretting your past decision and hoping that things will work out, so you don't have remorse on your trip to Hawaii, you are not being a good economist or business owner. It's time to minimize your loss by giving up hope of a brighter past.

Marginal Tax Rates
and the Three-Martini Lunch

Senate Democrats Max Baucus (MT) and Harry Reid (NV) once called for the restoration of full tax deductibility of business meals and entertainment. I guess if ardent anticommunist Richard Nixon could embrace The People's Republic of China, two Western Democrats could openly support the ultimate antithesis of Progressive politics: business tax breaks. They were not totally exposed on the issue, however. Former Speaker of the House Jim Wright (D. TX) had said, "If the Lord hadn't intended to have a three-martini lunch, then why do you suppose He put all those olive trees in the Holy Land?"

For years, the symbolic three-martini lunch had rallied the moderate American Left. President Jimmy Carter failed to eliminate the deduction, but not for lack of effort. In a populist appeal, he noted that a businessman could deduct a $50 martini lunch, but a truck driver got no tax break on his $1.50 sandwich.

Perhaps opposition to a deductible three-martini lunch was good politics then. President Gerald Ford lost the election to Carter. In a rare foray into economic theory, President Ford had opined that the three-martin lunch was the epitome of American efficiency. "Where else could you get an earful, a bellyful, and a snootful at the same time?" he asked.

We won't address the merits (or lack thereof) of this little bit of U.S. tax policy here. Rather, in the following, we explore how tax deductions work, how they depend crucially on marginal tax rates, and how they have incentives that affect behavior. And when looking at the behavioral effects of tax deductions and marginal tax rates, we'll use a couple of examples that have a much greater impact on the economy than business meals and entertainment, work, and housing decisions.

Normal people sometimes think people get things free when they have tax "write-offs." In fact, the tax code doesn't provide quite that good a deal, but it does provide a deal, and the amount of the deal depends on the marginal tax rate.

When you see or hear the word marginal associated with anything economic, you know something important is happening. And happening is the operative word here. The word marginal or the phrase "at the margin" means that we are talking about a change, an action. When we have action, we have a choice, and choice changes well-being. Economics is about well-being.

A marginal tax rate is the change in the tax you pay as a percentage of the change in the tax base to which the rate applies. From your point of view, any tax payment or tax revenue from the government's viewpoint is the product of a tax rate times a tax base. In the City of Spokane, Washington, where I live, we have an 8.9% sales tax. Here, the tax base is the value of taxable purchases, like beer, automobiles, and nights in a hotel. In Washington State, the tax does not apply to food purchases (No, beer is not food.). The marginal rate in this case is 8.9%. If you spend an additional $100 at the hardware store in Washington, your sales tax is $8.90. The change in the tax base is $100; the change is the tax paid is $8.90. The marginal tax rate is $8.90/$100, which, when converted to a percentage, is 8.9%.

Other tax payments involve tax rates multiplied by tax bases, as well. The base of the property tax is the assessed value of the property. The marginal property tax rate is the sum of rates applied by all the separate taxing districts and authorities in the state, the school district, the county, and the city. For example, where we live, the marginal property tax rate is 1.17%. If our property's value increases by $1,000, we pay $11.70 more unless the taxing authorities change the rate.

The most important marginal tax rate for people with low or moderate income is the payroll tax, which funds social security payments and health benefits for the U.S. elderly. Employees face a marginal tax rate of 7.65 % for the payroll tax. If you get a raise of $100 a week, Grandma takes 7.65% off the top.

The most important marginal tax rate for middle and upper-income people is their federal income tax rate. Unlike sales taxes, property taxes, and payroll taxes, federal marginal income tax rates differ for different levels of the tax base, taxable income in this case. In general, the higher your taxable income, the higher your marginal tax rate. For the 2023 U.S. tax year, we had seven different federal marginal income tax rates: 10%, 12%, 22%, 24%, 32%, 35%, and 37%. The range of taxable incomes to which each tax rate applies is called a tax bracket. For example, the Miller family was in the 22% bracket in 2023, along with other tax-paying American couples with taxable incomes between $83,550 and $178,150.

Marginal tax rates are often at the heart of political and economic tax policy discussions. Economists are fascinated by marginal tax rates because they provide incentives, and incentives affect behavior. Moscow, Idaho, is eight miles from Pullman, Washington. Washington doesn't have a sales tax on food. This might give some an incentive to buy groceries across the border. Payroll taxes affect the net after-tax income from working and are a consideration in whether to work for pay or not. Property tax rates might have incentives with respect to property maintenance or improvement or whether to get a building permit for a property improvement and alert the county assessor to an increase in the value of your property.

The largest tax-induced effect on behavior is from federal and state marginal income tax rates. Let's first look at the decision to work. Nonmarket leisure or non-market (unpaid) work are not taxed. Time allocated to market (paid) activity is taxed, and the proper measure of the tax disincentive is the marginal tax rate. Imagine an upper-middle-income married couple with two young children. Suppose Dad works outside the home, and Mom works in nonmarket "home production," taking care of the kids, shopping, cooking, cleaning, and gardening. You might find one of these families on a cable channel somewhere, e.g., Ward and June Cleaver of the series "Leave it to Beaver." Feel free to substitute Murphy Brown married to Mr. Mom, if you like, or any other TV couple.

Let's imagine that the present-day Cleavers are having a family meeting, and the main topic of conversation is whether June should get a job, perhaps to generate some savings for the boys' college education. Suppose Ward and June are in the 24% federal income tax bracket. Let's also assume they live in a state that has an 8% marginal state income tax rate. June must also pay a payroll tax of 7.65%. This combined marginal tax rate is about 40%, meaning June would be working for sixty cents on the dollar. Maybe the job is worth it. Maybe not. However, economists would certainly recognize that marginal tax rates are an important consideration. If Ward and June were in a higher tax bracket, the tax bite out of additional family income would be larger. When economists consider tax policy, they always suggest considering the incentive effects of marginal tax rates and recognize that changing the rate can also affect the base.

Another important incentive effect of marginal tax rates is the pursuit of tax deductions, arranging spending to receive economic advantages through lower taxes. A tax deduction is an amount the government allows you to subtract from your gross income to arrive at your taxable income. Most U.S. taxpayers take the standard deduction, but for higher-income households, it pays to itemize deductions. The largest itemized deduction in the U.S. tax code is that for interest payments on home mortgages (loans). For cultural reasons, we may want a nice house with a white picket fence, but economists focus more on the tax advantages of borrowing to buy a home.

If a family is in, say, a 40% marginal tax bracket (federal and state combined), Uncle Sam or Uncle Governor pays 40% of its housing costs. A numerical example helps here. Let's make a few assumptions. First, assume that 100% of a house payment is either interest on a home mortgage or property taxes (also deductible). In the early years of a 30-year mortgage, this is close to the actual truth. And for the purposes of illustration here, let's ignore other housing expenses, such as insurance and maintenance. Suppose house payments are $2000 a month, $24,000 a year. Does the family pay $24,000 a year for housing? Not at all! When filing their federal and state tax returns at the end of the year, this family will be able to deduct $24,000 from their taxable income. The amount they save in taxes depends on their marginal tax rate. If it's 40%, their taxes are $9,600 lower (40% times $24,000). So, their housing cost is not $24,000 but $14,400 after taxes. The homeownership incentive is even greater if their marginal tax rate is higher. Not many rich people rent houses. Understanding marginal income tax rates is crucial to the rent-or-buy housing decision.

Three quite different decisions, whether to have a three-martini lunch, to work for pay, or to rent or buy a home, are all very much related. And it's not that if you have the former, you are in no position to do either of the latter. Each decision is affected by federal and state tax policy, and a key ingredient in each decision is one's marginal tax rate. Again, in the beginning was the word, and the word was marginal.

The Optimal Level of Lawnmower Safety:

Social Marginal Benefit and Social Marginal Cost

When I was a kid, we didn't use rotary lawnmowers at our house. My dad preferred the reel-type mowers you could walk behind, the motorized version of the standard push mower. He thought rotary mowers were too dangerous. They had a propensity to fling nasty projectiles out the side of the mower at unsuspecting kids and little old ladies in the neighborhood. Better to have a reel mower and fling projectiles back at yourself, I guess.

I remember spending a night in the hospital after some minor surgery in the early 1960s. I forget the name of the kid in the bed across the room. He was older, a Wenatchee kid (I lived in East Wenatchee.). He lay on his back with his leg elevated, blood still seeping through the gauze bandage on his big toe.

"What happened to you?" I asked.

"Lawnmower accident," he said. "I mowed around some trees and pulled the mower back over my foot. Pretty stupid, huh?" He demonstrated the mowing motion in the air with his arms.

"Rotary mower?" I asked.

He nodded yes.

"My dad won't have one of those," I said, deciding not to comment on the stupidity issue directly.

Despite the danger, almost all lawnmowers are rotary mowers these days. They have more safety features now. Many shut down automatically when you stop to empty the grass-catching bag. This would never have worked in the old days because getting the mower started in 1962 took enormous skill and a solid vocabulary of words boys were astonished to hear their fathers use. Once you got the mower running, you didn't shut it off until you finished mowing. Some modern mowers, like my John Deere, have a blade clutch that allows the blade to stop even when the motor is running. Safety features like these add some cost but protect people from what must be an overwhelming human urge to put hands or feet into a whirling maw of death. At the insistence of their lawyers, I suppose, lawnmower manufacturers even print a warning on the side of the mower. My warning says, "DANGER. ROTATING BLADE! Don't place hands or feet under or into mower when engine is running." Gee, thanks for the warning.

Lawnmower accidents are painful and sometimes even deadly. But we economists would be the first in line to argue that we shouldn't attempt to eliminate all lawnmower accidents, to have 100% safe mowing. At some accident level greater than zero, the additional cost of improving mower safety becomes greater than the additional benefit of doing so. Of course, we don't want everyone who pulls a starter cord to become instantly maimed, either. This means there is an optimal level of lawnmower safety somewhere between zero and 100%. This also means there is an optimal level of lost fingers and sliced toes.

Economists describe the optimal level of lawnmower safety as the level where social marginal benefit equals social marginal cost. Again, the word marginal means "change in," or "additional," or "incremental." If mowers are very unsafe, the additional benefit of safety (fewer accidents) is likely much greater than the additional cost of safety. Designing a mower with a cover over the blade is one example. It costs something not to have an exposed blade, but the additional benefit of reduced suffering and death is greater than the additional cost of a blade housing. If we add more benefits than costs, each additional level of safety moves us in the right direction. However, as we increase safety, the benefit of additional safety will eventually be less than the cost. When this is the case, we need to stop making lawnmowers safer.

An ugly side of the economic approach to lawnmower safety becomes more transparent when we consider lawnmowers that are too safe. Put this way, many normal people would think that a mower could never be too safe. But to an economist, it's simply a comparison of the social marginal benefit and social marginal cost. By reducing the level of lawnmower safety, we will reduce the benefits of that safety. But if we reduce the cost of lawnmower safety more than the benefit lost, we need to have less safety. We need more lawnmower accidents. See, this is another reason none of your friends are economists.

Of course, the principle of comparing social marginal benefit and social marginal cost is not limited to issues of lawnmower safety alone. Just substitute the words crime prevention, water quality, air quality, or any other good thing for lawnmower safety in the discussion above. If the change in the benefit (marginal benefit) of water quality is greater than the change in the cost (marginal cost), cleaner water is justified to an economist. Here, the economist and the Green or environmentalist would be on the same side regarding the water quality issue. However, only economists would consider water to be too clean. If the reduced benefit from lower water quality is less than the reduction in the cost from lower water quality, we need to allow the water to become dirtier. These arguments, so sensible to economists, are like a shrill, piercing, screeching noise to many normal people.

Again, by thinking with their heads and not with their hearts, economists exclude themselves from even more parties. No one wants to have cocktails with someone who tries to figure out just the right amount of maiming from lawnmower accidents or who thinks water can be too clean. I guess that's okay, though. If we aren't invited to parties, we will have lots of time to mow the lawn.

Part Four:

Markets and Prices

Introduction

To understand how economies work, especially ones with a large dose of market capitalism, we must understand how markets address the basic economic problem. To do this, we start with prices and their important role in transmitting information to buyers and sellers.

The first vignette, "Auctions and the Clearance Sale," takes us to rural Washington, Missouri, in 1970, when Solveig and I attended our first auction. We've loved auctions ever since. As a normal person, Solveig likes the bargains or treasures she finds there. As an economist, I love seeing the forces of supply and demand in action. And if we avoid formal models, as we do in this book, nothing illustrates supply and demand better than an auction. The auction's price-lowering counterpart, the clearance sale, also paints a good market picture.

In my teaching career, I used newspaper articles as "experiments" in what I called the supply and demand laboratory of the real world. One such experiment, "Racehorse Venereal Disease, Freshwater Rough Fish, and Convention Prostitutes," shows how the same analytical tools can explain disparate events, such as breeder reaction to an outbreak of venereal disease in Kentucky thoroughbreds, an increase in demand for rough fish in Chicago fish markets, and the higher price of prostitute services in New York City when the Democratic National Convention comes to town.

In "Tug and Stretch, the Elasticity of Demand," common household items enable an experiment that explains the responsiveness of quantity demanded to a change in price. This piece also shows how knowledge of the elasticity of demand can win arguments, make you look smart, and avoid boneheaded decisions.

The next two pieces in Part Four explore attempts to maintain a price below or above the market-clearing price, where the quantity supplied equals the quantity demanded. In "But Only Rich People Will Get Tickets," price ceilings motivated by concerns about equity or fairness create a shortage. We examine price ceilings on hotdogs at student picnics, tickets to events, rent-controlled apartments, river running, university parking, water in a drought, and electricity policy in California, among other examples.

In "Willie Nelson and the Mom-and-Pop Grocery Store Concert," a hypothetical corollary to Willie's "Farm Aid" events, a price floor creates the opposite of a shortage, a surplus, where the quantity supplied by sellers persistently exceeds the quantity demanded by buyers. Willie's support of farmers and none for small grocery stores, similar family enterprises, stems from a romantic attachment to agriculture. Agricultural price floors have predictable economic results, crop surpluses and financial transfers from consumers to farmers.

The next vignette shows that prices in the international economy depend not only on the supply and demand for goods and services but also on the supply and demand of national currencies. In "A Sabbatical in Germany, a Depreciating Dollar, and the Price of Beer," even an economics professor can make poor decisions about adverse movements in foreign exchange rates and their effect on the prices of important goods purchased by his family while abroad.

Finally, we end with a longer story of markets in action, where I go with two economist friends to the 1995 NCAA basketball Final Four in Seattle without tickets in hand. Our attempt to buy tickets on the street illustrates several economic principles. Unlike normal people, we obtained as much satisfaction from participating in the ticket market as we did from the basketball we watched.

Auctions and the Clearance Sale:

An Introduction to
Supply and Demand Analysis

Thomas Carlyle once said that you could teach a parrot economics. Just teach it to say, "Supply and Demand." No other economic theory explains so much of what happens in an economy. Few real-world events better illustrate the principles of supply and demand than the auction.

Solveig and I first started going to auctions while in graduate school in St. Louis, in the early 1970s. We had been married for a couple of months and had little income and an apartment to furnish. One beautiful fall morning, we went with friends to an estate sale on a farm near Washington, Missouri. We bought just a few small items but learned so very much. We learned that once one left the St. Louis metropolitan area, Missouri became *Missoura*, and little boys asked, "Mommy, can I have a sodie?" (As in sodie-pop, we presumed). We also learned how auctions worked. Solveig found a way to get good deals on household items. As an economist, I found extreme beauty, a market in action.

You may have seen something like this before. The auctioneer watched his assistants bring something like an oak chest of drawers to the stage.

"What do we have here?" he asked. "Looks like a nice one. Look at that quarter-sawn oak on the top and sides, brass pulls, nice carvings, and good action on the drawers. Hold it up, boys, so the folks get a good look at it."

Members of the audience would stifle their oohs and aahs, attempting to camouflage their true feelings about the piece. No need to telegraph one's assessment of its value to other potential bidders.

"I've seen pieces like this in antique shops in St. Louis for $200," said the auctioneer. He was working on a commission basis, and $200 was rent for two months in 1970. "Who'll give me a hundred dollars to start things off?"

Silence reigned. Probably one-third of those in attendance would have been willing to pay that price, but all hoped to get it for less. He tried a few lower prices, commented on the "reverse auction" going on, and finally, in mock disgust, said, "Okay, then, what <u>will</u> you bid?"

"Twenty-five dollars," shouted a woman from the back of the room.

"I've got twenty-five; who'll give me thirty?"

About twenty hands shot into the air. And we were then on our way in a glorious, controlled, frenzy, a Missouri version of the English auction. The auctioneer, in his rhythmic chanting of the existing price and one just higher, climbed the ladder of prices until only two bidders remained. One bidder was a dealer from the city, a kind of animal feared and scorned by regular folks. Dealers bid the prices up too high. Of course, we later learned that even bidding against dealers could obtain a good price, as antique stores often had a 100% or more markup.

"One forty-five, going once, going twice," said the auctioneer. He looked at the other bidder, the one not with the current bid, and said,

"Don't leave me now. Are y'all through? One forty-five, going once, going twice, SOLD, to number thirty-six. What do we have now, boys?" he said.

We had just witnessed supply and demand in action. In this case, the supply was a single item, an oak chest of drawers, with the seller willing to sell at any price. At low prices, like the $25 starting price, we had what economists call excess demand, where the number of items wanted at that price outnumbered the number for sale. As the price rose in the marketplace, the auction, in this case, previously willing buyers fell by the wayside. Excess demand drives prices up, at the auction in the fall of 1970 near Washington, Missouri, and every day, anywhere around the world. It's the way we decide in a market economy who gets the goods; whoever is willing to pay the market-clearing price.

Excess demand changes prices in a market, but sometimes a market price is too high for sellers to sell all they want to at that price, just the reverse of the initial $25 price for the oak chest of drawers. This excess supply changes prices, too.

Another kind of auction, a Dutch auction, illustrates this process. In a Dutch auction, the price starts high and falls, eliminating the excess supply when someone is willing to buy. Dutch auctions reach a market-clearing price faster than English auctions, good for selling cheese and tulips on hot days in Holland.

A more familiar example of a market dealing with excess supply is the clearance sale at the local department store. Suppose the weather cools, the economy slows, and store managers overestimate the demand for summer shorts, shirts, and blouses. It's not easy to correctly forecast future demand for anything. As fall approaches, the department store finds stacks and stacks of summer items still on the display racks and tables, the very same racks and tables that the store uses to display fall clothing. The store must move the merchandise, and to do this it has a sale. The store lowers the price, and as the price falls, people buy more than they did at higher prices.

Market economies are good at eliminating excess demand and excess supply. If prices are free to adjust, we won't see piles of unsold clothing in department stores, nor frustrated buyers at auctions with their bidding hands permanently in the air. In market economies, we take this process for granted. When was the last time you went to the grocery store and saw piles of unsold peanut butter jars in the middle of the aisle? Before that happened, the grocer would lower the price, sell more, and order less from his supplier the next week. Likewise, we don't often see long lines to purchase gasoline. Gas station owners seeing long lines at their pumps will take this as a signal to raise prices, and at higher prices the lines predictably disappear. If prices don't rise, because of, say, government price controls, long lines will persist, but this is another story we will deal with later in Part Four.

Racehorse Venereal Disease, Freshwater Rough Fish, and Convention Prostitutes

Compared to the natural sciences and the social science of psychology, laboratory experiments in economics are less common. We can't bring a family into the laboratory, take away some of their income under controlled conditions, and see if they buy less. But in 2002, economist Vernon Smith won the Nobel Prize in Economics for his pioneering work in experimental economics, and economists now use experimental methods more and more in many economics sub-disciplines.

Even without lab experiments, if we read the newspaper carefully and are willing to make a few assumptions about other things held constant, controlled by assumption, we can observe empirical tests of economic theories in the laboratory of the real world. In the following, we look at three of my favorite "lab reports."

On a slow news day in the spring of 1978, the University of Utah student newspaper, the *Daily Utah Chronicle,* ran an article from the Associated Press. They knew it would appeal to a sophomoric sense of humor. Little did they know that it would become one of my (and my students) most cherished experiments from the Supply and Demand Laboratory of the Real World. The article described an outbreak of equine venereal disease among Kentucky thoroughbreds.

In the classroom, I usually shared a few jokes about Black Beauty, Trigger, and horsey safe sex before we delved into the outbreak of the contagious disease *equine metritis* that had forced the Kentucky Agricultural Commissioner to require artificial insemination at any farm with infected horses. Breeders traditionally frown on unrestricted artificial insemination, as it might drown the thoroughbred market in a flood of new Secretariats and Seattle Slews. Kentucky breeders had even asked the Jockey Club in New York, which registers thoroughbreds, to ban the practice and control the potential for "abuse through overbreeding."

The abuse feared by this thoroughbred semen cartel is nothing more than an increase in the supply of thoroughbreds. Like the department store forced into a late summer clearance sale because of an excess supply of summer clothing, an excess supply of thoroughbreds would cause their prices to fall. At lower prices, the sport of kings becomes a more popular pastime, and buyers purchase more racehorses. The market eventually clears at a lower price. To an economist, no "abuse through overbreeding" occurs, just a fall in the price and an increase in the quantity of racehorses bought and sold in the marketplace.

The bluegrass fields of Kentucky differ greatly from the murky waters of Wisconsin's Lake Winnebago, but supply and demand analysis applies to both. A wonderful lab report appeared in September 1976 in the *Wall Street Journal*. A rise in the price of regular, tablefood fish had increased demand for rough fish. Sheepshead, carp, suckers, alewife, buffalo fish, and other even less-appealing species were finding more acceptance on dinner tables in the Chicago area. And the reason? In its typical, valiant attempt to bring human interest to the pages of a business and economics newspaper, the author quoted Oshkosh, Wisconsin, fish dealer John M. Follett. "The price of other fish has gone to the sky," he said. So, with the price of rockfish and salmon rising, the demand for rough fish increased, causing an increase in its price, and an increase in the amount bought and sold, as well.

Unlike normal people, economists know that substitutes exist for everything. Sometimes, the substitutes are obvious. Coke substitutes for Pepsi, and TOP-FLITE golf balls for Titleist balls. A Big Mac at McDonald's substitutes for a Whopper at Burger King. To most young women in America, a nice guy in the apartment down the hall might substitute for Brad Pitt or George Clooney. Subtle substitutes exist as well. I can wear a sweater and use less electricity to run my furnace or substitute consolidated trips for gasoline in my car.

Demand for a good increases if the price of a substitute for it rises. Think of the above examples: If the price of Pepsi rises, some Pepsi drinkers will switch to Coke. If the price of kilowatt-hours rises, I reach for my sweater. And if the price of regular fish rises, the demand for a substitute, rough fish, goes up.

Our final lab report from the Supply and Demand Laboratory of the Real World comes from the streets of New York City. In May1980, a couple of months before the Democratic National Convention, the *Daily Utah Chronicle* again picked up an Associated Press article that speculated on the convention's effect on the New York prostitute market. The first paragraph reads as follows:

"Four years ago, Manhattan rolled out the red carpet for delegates to the Democratic National Convention. This year, even the city's prostitutes say they'll work overtime—but at new higher prices." Real world economics experiments don't get much better than this one.

Let's do the easy part first. With thousands of randy Democrats descending upon New York City, demand for prostitutes increases. One of the fundamental determinants of demand is the number of demanders. More demanders cause more demand. Simple. This alone would lead to a price increase. Excess demand, analogous to that in our earlier auction example, puts upward pressure on the price. But this is only half the story. The supply of prostitutes will decrease, as well.

We can think of supply in two ways. One, the most common way, counts the amount supplied at a schedule of different prices. If less would be supplied at each price, we say supply decreases. But in this case, it helps to think of supply the other way around and ask what prices sellers would require for various quantities of the good or service. If a supplier requires a higher price to sell a quantity they previously sold at a lower price, we also say supply has decreased. Sellers are more reluctant to sell.

Cost of production influences the price at which suppliers are willing to sell, and during the convention, the cost of producing prostitute services was going to rise. The article noted that a spokesperson from the mayor's office said that police would be stepping up enforcement of prostitution laws. The article quoted Iris Dela Cruz, head of the professional organization Prostitutes of New York. She said fines against prostitutes are a reason for the higher prices. "Somebody's got to pay for them," she said. Fines are costs. Sellers will attempt to pass them on to consumers in the form of higher prices. Supply decreases.

Final evidence from the experiment shows the unambiguous effect on price when demand increases and supply decreases at the same time and testifies to the desirability of staying in school and doing your math homework. The article quotes Margo St. James, head of the organization COYOTE (Call Off Your Old Tired Ethics):

"…hookers will be charging up to twice the usual rate. If it's $50, it'll be $100. If it's usually $100, it'll be $150."

When supply decreases and demand increases, we know that price will rise, but the effect on quantity bought and sold in the marketplace depends on a tug-o-war between supply and demand. If the increase in demand is stronger than the decrease in supply, quantity will increase. If the supply decrease is stronger, the market quantity will decrease. The lab report is uncharacteristically detailed, even in this bit of evidence. In an interview, the spokeswoman for the New York Prostitutes Collective indicated that the number of prostitutes working Manhattan during the convention would likely increase by one-half. The demand-increasing effect of visiting Democrats would exceed the supply-decreasing effect of increased police efforts.

Tug and Stretch:

The Elasticity of Demand

Several years ago, I was watching the original *Firing Line* on PBS. *Firing Line* was William F. Buckley Jr.'s vehicle for advancing the cause of political conservatism in America, and to prove to the world that he was smarter than anyone who appeared on the program, or if not smarter, at least a better debater with a bigger vocabulary. On this episode, Mr. Buckley was debating with Robert Strauss, the Washington attorney and long-time Democratic power broker. I forget the topic of the debate, but I remember that uncharacteristically it wasn't going well for Mr. Buckley. Robert Strauss was ahead on points, backing Mr. Buckley into the ropes, preparing for a knockout punch. On PBS, Mr. Buckley couldn't even break for a commercial and collect his considerable wits. Then, when he was about to hit the canvass, Mr. Buckley summoned his own knockout punch. Some might call it a sucker punch, but not an economist. I remember clearly, Mr. Buckley asked Mr. Strauss, "Wouldn't that depend on the elasticity of demand?" The look on Mr. Strauss's face said it all. He didn't know about the elasticity of demand. With a couple of combination punches, Mr. Buckley had Mr. Strauss down for the count. Winner, Mr. Buckley, by a knockout.

Knowing something about the elasticity of demand can make you look smart at crucial times and help you and your organization avoid incredible economic blunders. We'll get to one of these blunders below, but first, we need to understand this important concept.

Let's perform a small experiment or demonstration. You need two stretchy things, like a thin rubber band and a fat rubber band. Bungee cords of different thickness will also work. You also need one un-stretchy thing, like a pencil. After you have assembled the ingredients for this experiment, do the following. Pick up the thin rubber band, hold one end between your fingers and with the other hand give it a little tug. Mentally record how far it stretches. Next, pick up the thicker rubber band, and apply the same strength of tug as you did to the thin one. Note that it stretches less than the thin one. Finally, use the same force to tug on the pencil. It doesn't stretch at all.

I think you would agree that the word elasticity explains the results of this experiment. The first rubber band is more elastic than the second, and both are more elastic than the pencil. You can also do this experiment with underwear of different vintages if you wish.

In economics, we use the word elasticity to describe the degree of change (stretch) in one economic variable in response to some change (tug) in another. The elasticity of demand is one important application of this idea. We know from the law of demand that when a price falls, buyers want to buy more of a good, and when a price rises, buyers want to buy less. But how much more or how much less does the quantity demanded respond when the price changes? It depends on the elasticity of demand.

When the quantity demanded responds a lot to a price change, we say demand is elastic. When it responds little, we say demand is inelastic. We can be more precise by relating price and quantity change in percent terms. If the quantity changes by a greater percentage than does the price, demand is elastic. If quantity changes by a smaller percentage than price, demand is inelastic.

When a business considers a price change, it should consider the elasticity of demand for its product. One of my favorite elasticity of demand experiments from the Economics Laboratory of the Real World occurred in 1997 at the business where I worked, the University of Idaho. The Idaho State Legislature and the State Board of Education decided that we needed to raise more revenue from out-of-state students. Our out-of-state tuition was low compared to other universities in the West. We raised out-of-state tuition by about 12%.

Of course, from the law of demand, we know that fewer out-of-state students will enroll when the price goes up, but revenue might still increase if the percent decrease in quantity is less than the percent increase in price. In this case, however, the 23% reduction in quantity was greater than the 12% increase in price. Demand was elastic. Because revenue is price times quantity, revenue from out-of-state students fell. For revenue to rise with a price increase, demand must be inelastic. To raise revenue with a price increase, the percent increase in the revenue-increasing component (price increase) must be greater than the percent reduction in the revenue-decreasing component (quantity decrease). Ignorance about the elasticity of demand led to an effect exactly opposite of that intended by the Legislature and the State Board of Education.

When I related this story to my students, I always asked them to imagine sitting in the back of the room at the State Board of Education meeting where this pricing discussion took place and to recognize the opportunity for the Miller Wave. You, too, could be in this situation. You raise your hand high with just the hint of a wave. You ask politely, oh so politely, "Doesn't the success of this policy depend on the elasticity of demand?" After the blank stares, the multiple responses of "Abadaabdaabada...," the pleading glances by Board members toward their staff, who are looking at their shoes or running for cover, you sit quietly waiting for the response that never comes. As Mr. Buckley did to Mr. Strauss, you deliver a knockout punch with just a little understanding of economics. You look smart and help the University make a better decision. Let me know if this ever happens to you in a similar situation. My heart will soar like a hawk.

But Only Rich People Would Get Tickets

As I came out the door of my late afternoon class one September day, I saw the College of Business and Economics (CBE) annual picnic in full swing. Faculty grilled burgers and hotdogs. Representatives of student clubs promoted their organizations to anyone who passed in front of their booths. Captains of departmental volleyball teams scanned the top of the crowd for potential spikers. But most importantly, a long line of students and faculty members waited for free food and drink. As an economist, fresh from an introductory class on the principles of supply and demand, I didn't take a place in the food line. Instead, I walked the line looking for my current students. Finding one at last, I looked up and down the long line and asked,

"What's wrong with this picture?"

"What do you mean?" he asked.

"I mean this line. What does it tell you?"

"They need more barbecue grills," he said.

"D answer, I said, but thanks for trying."

I shook his hand and welcomed him to the picnic, choking back the urge to give a short lecture about expensive "free" food. I continued to walk the line until I spotted a young woman who had done very well on the first exam. I'd chatted with her during my office hours and knew she was smart.

"What's wrong with this picture?" I asked.

"What do you mean?" she asked, a little flustered, stalling for time. She looked like a student who had just run into a parent at a kegger.

"This line, what does it tell you?" I asked.

After a short pause, and a glance again over her shoulder in both directions, she said in her best uptalk, "The price is too low?"

"Bless you," I said. "See me after class tomorrow about becoming an economics major."

Economists hate lines. A line usually means that we are addressing the economic problem of excess demand with some method other than a price increase. At the CBE annual picnic, we decide who gets the burgers and hotdogs on a first-come, first-served method of allocation, and then by the opportunity cost of waiting. Whoever has the least valuable time is willing to wait the longest in line for food. That's not the way it works at auctions, as bidding hands remain in laps or pockets as bids rise. Every day around the world millions or more markets clear as prices rise. If they don't have to think about it, normal people are willing to tolerate markets but bring a market process into the light of day, and objections mount, and we substitute other allocation methods.

Usually, concerns about fairness defeat market processes. A zero price before the picnic may not be such a bad idea. You want lots of students to show up. But once it was clear that we had underestimated demand or overestimated faculty burger flipping ability, we could have made changes. But no one wants an economist to run the picnic. If I had been running the picnic, I would have yelled, "Hey, back there in line, anyone willing to pay $3 can come to the front of the line." Can you imagine the boos and hisses? Now, only rich students, but worse, faculty, would get food in a timely fashion if they were willing to pay. I'd have had a rebellion on my hands. I wouldn't even have had time to argue that having more money usually means people get to buy more and better goods and services. The angry crowd would have had my head if I said rich people drive more Mercedes, too, or that F. Scott Fitzgerald had said, "The rich are different from us," and Ernest Hemingway had responded, "Yes, they have more money."

Anticipating the equity objection, I could say that anyone wishing to contribute $3 to help fund poor students' hiring of tutors could move to the head of the line. This might receive more support, but probably not. If they think about it, normal people view markets as unfair, something to avoid.

We can see other, more important examples of market aversion in the Economics Laboratory of the Real World.

Tickets to the NCAA Final Four are too important to allocate by the marketplace. To get a ticket, you must be lucky enough to have your name picked in a random draw. If you're not lucky, your only hope is the black market. Normal people think that if the NCAA charged market prices, only the rich could attend the Final Four.

Tickets to many events are often priced too low, with expected results. Country singer Garth Brooks used to sell some tickets to his concerts at a low price. The result, tents in the streets. Playoff tickets for the Seattle Mariners in 2001 led to sidewalk sleeping bags in the rain. For student tickets to a football game against the traditional rival with the conference championship on the line, you'd better get there early. If we didn't do this, only rich people would get to see (fill in the blank).

At the University of Idaho, we price parking permits low. At UCLA, what we pay for the best permit wouldn't get you in eyesight of a shuttle bus stop. At Idaho, we ration parking with a special game of chicken at 9:00 on weekday mornings. She who blinks last, racing for an empty spot, gets the space. Ladies and gentlemen, rev your engines. A permit is a license to hunt, not a permit to park. But if we raised permit prices, only the rich would get to park.

Permits to float rivers managed by the U.S. government are rationed by random draw. Many want to run the Middle Fork of the Salmon River in July, but limited permits exist. If we had a river permit auction, those who valued the trip the most would be willing to pay the most and get the permit. But then only rich folks would run the Salmon.

Many well-intentioned elected officials think apartment rentals should not be left up to the marketplace. Rent control is losing its grip on many American cities, yet voters in St. Paul, Minnesota, have voted for it recently. Rent control is a legislative attempt to do what the market often cannot do, make apartments more affordable. Rent too high? Pass a law that rolls back rents and allows them to rise only when costs rise. Economists call rent control a legislated "price ceiling." A normal city council representative might think that without it, only the rich would get apartments. But attempts to legislate market outcomes have predictable effects. At the rent-controlled price, fewer apartments will be available, and more people will want to rent. At a rent-controlled price, potential landlords turn basement apartments into storage, wine cellars, and poolrooms. At rent-controlled prices, your roommate suddenly becomes more annoying. The excess demand becomes permanent, what economists call a shortage. We then use other rationing methods to address this version of the basic economic problem. Reading obituaries to scout out potential rent-controlled apartments becomes a popular pastime. Forms of discrimination other than willingness to pay come into play. All have costs.

Water and electricity appear frequently in lab reports from the Economics Laboratory of the Real World. Often when we have droughts in the West, the amount of water demanded in the summer exceeds the amount available. An economist would suggest raising the price, but normal people don't appoint economists as water managers. With higher prices, only the rich could afford water. Instead, we have odd and even watering. On odd-numbered days, those with odd-numbered addresses get to water their lawns. On even-numbered days, those across the street get their chance. We then commission a water police force to keep track of water use.

California politicians and regulators create electricity shortages when they limit electricity price increases, with predictable results, rolling blackouts. If electricity prices rise, only the rich can afford electricity!

In the late 1970s, the Organization of Petroleum Exporting Countries, OPEC, raised the world price of oil. Gasoline prices rose, at least until Congress passed a law rolling back the price of gasoline with a price ceiling. As predictable as tulips in the spring, gas lines sprouted at the pump. But without price controls on gasoline, only the rich would get to drive.

Fairness and equity are important concerns. No one, including economists, can fault another for worrying about the economic plight of those at the lower end of the distribution of income. Certainly, we economists have no special insight into fairness. But we do know that using non-price rationing to address conditions of excess demand has consequences that might be as ugly as the inequity these methods seek to address.

And we see the inconsistency in using the market to decide the prices of most everything in our market economy, when we don't have to think about it, then using non-price methods for tickets to athletic events, river trips, water, electricity, and hot dogs at the fall CBE picnic. If normal people don't have to think about it, it's OK if only rich people would get (fill in the blank).

Willie Nelson and the
Mom-and-Pop Grocery Aid Concert

I'm sure you've seen or heard of special events to aid suffering farmers. Willie Nelson's Farm Aid concerts are my favorites. A few choruses of "It's a Bloody Mary Morning" are sung in a Midwest football stadium, and millions of dollars go to help farmers. I always wait for Willie to say that all we need to do is completely legalize marijuana production and solve the farm problem, but Willie understands enough economics to know that this wouldn't work either. The increase in supply would drive prices down to near zero.

This is the problem in U.S. agriculture. We're too good at it. As supplies increase, prices fall, and with inelastic demand for food and fiber, lower prices lead to lower revenue. To stay in business, you must cut costs, and in agriculture, that usually means getting bigger. Say goodbye to the small family farm.

Unlike normal people, economists don't see a problem in agriculture, because economic losses in a market economy serve the same purpose as profits. A loss acts as a signal that you need to find another line of work. Even normal people recognize this in other industries. We don't have celebrities coming to the aid of mom-and-pop grocery stores driven out of business by the new supermarket. I've never heard of a single Grocery Store Aid concert, Barber Aid, Dry Cleaner Aid, or Restaurant Aid. We don't mourn the replacement of full-service auto mechanics by Jiffy Lube and other specialty chains.

Our romantic attachment to agriculture in America influences not only the amount of government transfers to farmers but the way we give them as well. I first learned this working summers for the Douglas County (WA) Road Department in college. Farmers in Douglas County grow a lot of wheat, but even in the late 1960s wheat ranches could not support the next generation on the farm. Some wheat growers' kids had to get other jobs. One displaced wheat grower was driving a dump truck that summer as we built roads near Mansfield. One lunch period, talk had turned to politics, what we needed to do to win the war in Vietnam, and how to solve the agriculture problem. As a "goddamned long-haired college student," I dared not touch the former subject, but I asked him how the government should solve the plight of the farmer. I didn't know that my question was an insult, that it suggested government handouts. "We need to get the government out of agriculture," he said. "We just need $3 a bushel for wheat!" $3 per bushel was a high price for wheat in the late sixties.

I resisted the urge to tell him that if a frog had longer legs, he wouldn't bump his bottom when he jumped. His statement betrayed an attitude that pervades U.S. agricultural policy. Farmers are a proud lot of independent businesspeople opposed to welfare and government handouts. But if we could just get the prices up, everything would be O.K. If prices are too low, let's pass a law that makes them higher. The result is the opposite of a price ceiling, where we force a price to remain below the market-clearing level. Here we have a price floor, with a price set above the market clearing level. Just as price ceilings lead to shortages, price floors lead to surpluses.

With a price floor, agriculture remains a popular pastime. But consumers don't see the increased price as anything about the agriculture problem at all. All they see is a higher price, and when prices are higher, consumers buy less. At higher prices, farmers want to produce more. The only way to maintain this price floor is for the government to enter the market as a buyer to prop up the price. The government now owns a lot of wheat, corn, peanuts, milk, and cheese that it must store and give away to the deserving poor.

Even this buying of agricultural products has a hint of welfare to it, so the government makes loans to farmers, for which farmers pledge the crop as collateral. Of course, there's never a plan to pay off the loan. This stealth welfare became burdensome over time, and farmers as a group, having become dependent on welfare, lowered their opposition to it. Many farm programs now make direct "deficiency payments" to farmers, the difference between a regular market price and the politically agreed on higher price. This drives economists a little crazy, leading to an explanation and criticism of U.S. agricultural policy in most economics textbooks. Of course, we don't get invited to many parties in Iowa or Mansfield, Washington.

A Sabbatical in Germany, a Depreciating Dollar, and the Price of Beer

I admit it, I love beer. My mom and dad told me once that as a toddler, I'd wait for them or one of their friends to set a finished can or bottle on the table. I'd quickly attack it like a marsh hawk on a mouse, downing the golden "squirrel pee" in a quick gulp. They asked Dr. Gordon about it. He said that if I didn't drink too much, it was OK. This was the 1950s, an easier time to raise children. Today, worrisome parents and defensive doctors would have little Jon's liver enzymes checked every six months.

With this early beer foundation, it's no surprise that when I became eligible for a sabbatical leave in the mid-1980s, I immediately thought of Germany. When I visited briefly in 1984, I was amazed at the low cost, variety, and quality of German beer. I started planning my sabbatical then.

Like most university professors, I considered sabbatical leave one of the most wonderful aspects of the job. Every seven years one had a chance to abandon what might have become everyday tedium and routine and do something to recharge, rest, and rejuvenate. What a great idea. In the mid-1980s at the University of Utah, sabbaticals were popular among faculty, and scarce in an economic sense. The quantity demanded exceeded the quantity supplied. I had to compete with other faculty to get one. I wrote a proposal about studying West German Green politics and seeing whether Green economics was emerging under the same principles. I figured that I could travel around Germany and other countries in Western Europe and talk to Greens. Of course, nothing would help a conversation with a German Green more than some good German beer.

87

Wise members of the faculty sabbatical committee liked my proposal and approved my sabbatical. We pulled our daughter out of the second half of the first grade, rented our house in Salt Lake City to a visiting English professor, arranged our finances, and flew off to Germany in January 1986.

Arranging finances took a little thought in 1986 when the ATM machine was still rare. As I was going on a two-quarter sabbatical, I would get full pay from the University of Utah. But my paycheck would be denominated in dollars and deposited in our bank in Salt Lake City. I needed to spend foreign currency for six months in Europe. After a few inquiries, we discovered that with an American Express Gold Card, we could write a personal check at any American Express office. With full university pay, our house rented out, and low prices in Europe, we expected to live well on our European journey, and, of course, drink lots of tasty German beer.

Every Tuesday in the winter and spring of 1986, I'd have Solveig help me carry a case of empty half-liter Bitburger Pilsner bottles down the stairs from our third-story walk-up apartment in Bonn. We'd place the case of empties on the seat of my bicycle, and I'd walk it carefully about a block to the nearest "drink shop," a small store that sold mostly beer and bottled water. After a few Tuesdays, the owner would greet me with a friendly *"Eine neue?"* (A new one?). *"Ja, bitte,"* I'd say. I'd give him the right amount of German currency, obtained from the American Express office, and he'd help me get the new case of pilsner on my bicycle. I'd reverse my trail to the apartment and, with Solveig's help, schlep the full case up the many stairs. I can't remember how many German marks I had to pay for a case of Bitburger Pilsner that year, but I do remember that the price, in marks, didn't change the entire six months we lived in Bonn. Unfortunately, and especially so for an economist, I'd overlooked one important factor, adverse exchange rate movements. Due to a continual change in the exchange rate between the dollar and the German mark, my beer became more expensive every Tuesday for six months, as did housing, food, transportation, clothing, and entertainment. Even though the prices in Germany did not change, in terms of German marks, I received fewer marks per dollar when I wrote my check at the American Express office every University of Utah payday.

A foreign exchange rate is simply the price of one currency in terms of another. On my previous trip in 1984, the dollar was extraordinarily strong, which meant I received near historic amounts of marks per dollar in Germany, Francs per dollar in France, and Kroner per dollar in Norway. The rate was well over three marks per dollar in 1984 and 1985 and about three marks per dollar when we got off the plane in January of 1986. But it didn't last. Every payday at the American Express office, I received fewer German marks than I had the previous payday. German prices stayed the same, but the dollar price of German beer rose every week, along with the dollar price of everything else.

Another way to appreciate this unfortunate turn of events is to realize that I was receiving a cut in salary every two weeks. Most of us are fortunate enough not to have our wages fall every payday for an extended period. It was depressing. Our time of expected prosperity and financial security on sabbatical eroded, so much so that we came back deeply in debt. At the age of thirty-eight, I had to borrow money from my parents to keep the creditors at bay until we could refinance our mortgage, take some cash from our home equity, and pay off the German beer debt.

Foreign exchange rates are important, not only for companies doing business abroad but also for university professors on sabbaticals in search of cheap German beer. I should have engaged in what economists call a forward market transaction, locking in a favorable exchange rate for our time abroad. But for once, I was a normal person, not an economist, and was carried away by the exuberance of good times that I thought would never end. It was still a great sabbatical, even at two marks to the dollar, the exchange rate when we returned to the U.S. My "wage" had fallen by one-third in six months. And worse, upon return, I didn't have any good German beer to drown my sorrows. I'll pay more attention next time.

Shameless in Seattle:

Three Economists at the Final Four

Robbie called in December 1994 and suggested that we go to the Final Four in Seattle the next April. I could think of several reasons not to go, too busy, too tired, too broke, but when he said that getting tickets would be a challenge, I couldn't resist. Like many economists, I enjoy observing markets in action. And, as a bonus, Tim would be there. I had to see if Tim had emerged from what I hoped was only a temporary bout of normalcy. I would learn in Seattle that the old Tim, the one Robbie and I loved, raged on.

In 1979, we'd had the NCAA Basketball Final Four in our Special Events Center on the Utah campus, where we then were professors. Tim was now at Syracuse, and I was at the University of Idaho. In 1979, we'd applied for tickets through the official process, a truly inefficient form of resource allocation, which required submission of money orders (not checks, credit cards, or cash) to enter a ticket lottery more than a year before the games. We didn't win the right to buy tickets in the official market and were so disgusted with the transaction costs and inefficiency that we never entered the ticket lottery again. But the unofficial market was another matter.

Tim, Robbie, and I met in Seattle for the Final Four with a personal and professional commitment to the free market in basketball tickets. In Utah, I always got my ticket outside, usually at bargain prices, and sometimes after several transactions. I knew from personal experience how it feels to hear the national anthem holding three tickets in a thin market or on the other side, not having a ticket for the biggest game of the year when the starting lineups are announced. I always got in, and rarely sat above the 17th row. Often, I sat in the pep band. I do a solid version of "Hey Baby" to this day.

Robbie had arranged for us to stay in Seattle with a former colleague and her husband. Robbie viewed staying in a hotel as a last resort, reflecting, in part, one's lack of friends and connections. In this case, the lodging issue was moot, as Seattle had been booked for months.

I arrived in Seattle about 9:30 a.m. on Saturday, the day of the Semifinals. As I drove through Bellevue, across Lake Washington, and into the Emerald City, I saw the Kingdome, the home of the Seattle Mariners, the site of the games. Without a doubt, this was an unlikely basketball arena. You could have an unbelievably bad seat in left field for these games. Information about the quality of the ticket was going to be important. Under sunny skies, I could also see a giant inflated basketball "poised on the rim" of the Space Needle. If nothing else, the weather was cooperating for a good ticket market, at least in comfort terms.

At the house, we finished greetings in a few minutes and turned to the ticket market. Robbie and Tim briefed me on our standing. Robbie had made a previous transaction with a friend of a friend, a Division III coach from back East. For $100 we would receive two tickets to the final game, but not the semifinals, often the better games. Coaches often head home Sunday after the semifinals. Coaches also avoid black market ticket sales, given the extreme enforcement procedures of the NCAA. We were directed to meet this coach at the Sheraton Hotel in downtown Seattle on Saturday before the games.

We first needed to agree on some initial parameters for our search.

"It would be good if we could all sit together," Robbie said.

"That might be tough," I said.

"What about the possibility of moving to other seats?" I asked. "Are we just trying to get in the door, or do we have to buy seats together?"

Tim answered immediately, "I bet the place is going to be jammed with little UCLA pisspots. I saw a bunch of them on the plane last night." Changing seats would be almost impossible, especially between levels.

We agreed that we wanted seats where binoculars were not necessary, at least not all the time. We guessed that the 300-level in the Kingdome was not such a place, but if worse came to worse, we'd sit there. For this, Tim and I thought that $200 would be a good deal. When Robbie found out we were talking $200 each, not in total, he became a little worried.

"I don't know if I have enough cash," Robbie said.

"Don't worry," said Tim, "Timmy's here, fanning out a fistful of $100 bills. It would not be the last such fistful we'd see that weekend.

"How long are we willing to wait before we buy tickets?" asked Robbie.

Tim said, "Prices really come down when the Fat Lady sings."

"Isn't that at the end?" I asked.

"No, when she sings the national anthem," said Tim. Robbie reminded us that it was an opera metaphor adapted to basketball by Coach Motta, or was it Yogi Berra? In any case, we agreed that we would be willing to miss the first half of the game to get a package of three tickets for Saturday and Monday.

Since I had just driven across the State of Washington, we decided, with some misgivings, that Tim would drive his rental car downtown.

"Tim's driving?!" Robbie asked painfully, recalling wild rides in Tim's infamous Volvo station wagon called "the Green Magnet."

"Don't worry," Tim said, "Parking's on me." Both Robbie and I saw images of fire hydrants and loading zones.

By 11:15 a.m., we were on our way downtown. We parked with amazing ease in a parking lot halfway between the Sheraton and the Kingdome. Because it was one of those "push your money through the slot" payment systems, it took us a little while to decide how much to pay.

"Give 'em a buck," Tim said with his knowing South Buffalo grin.

"Come on, Tim," said Robbie, "How much is it?"

"Less than our maximum willingness to pay, let's get going."

"OK, but you pay the ticket, Tim."

"No way, this is a communal deal," said Tim, knowing that in a game of relative risk preference, Robbie and I would surrender early. We pieced together the low Saturday price of $5 and headed for the Sheraton.

College basketball spilled out of the Sheraton. People were everywhere, outside and inside, bumping into each other if they tried to go anywhere. We noticed one thing immediately. Nobody was selling tickets. If you inquired of someone with the standard question, "Got any tickets?" You might find an occasional 300-level ticket offer for a single seat. Absolutely no 200-level or 100-level tickets were for sale, at least for our initial offer price of $100.

We went to the coach's room to get the tickets. After a short schmooze, we were holding two 300-level tickets for the Monday night final game. As previously agreed, we paid $100 for the two tickets. It was 11:45 a.m. The tip-off for the first semifinal game was at 2:30.

I feel uneasy in a ticket market if I'm not holding. With a ticket in hand, your options are so much greater, and options have value. You can make better trades and package deals. After milling around outside the Sheraton, Tim and Robbie sat down in the warm sun while I worked the crowd.

"Tickets," I inquired. "Got any tickets?"

Soon a guy responded to my question. "Whadaya want?" he asked.

"Whadaya got?" I responded.

"It's a 300-level ticket for today and Monday, I'm not sure where," he said. I knew it was a bad seat from the map we had studied in the car on the way down. You wouldn't even get a foul ball in this seat, let alone see a basketball game.

"Come on, make up your mind," he said, walking away, "I don't like doing this. I'm just selling this for a friend."

"Wait," I said, a little too eagerly. "What do you want for it?"

"I hear they're going for two hundred," he said.

"I'll give ya a hundred," I said as he walked away, shaking his head in disgust, yet carefully, as if not wanting to be seen.

"Okay, one-fifty," I said.

"Deal," he said.

I handed the money to him, per his instructions, and he handed the ticket to Tim. I wondered how someone who didn't like to sell tickets on the street knew of this little maneuver to avoid an illegal direct sale.

"My God, Skippy, one-fifty for this dog?" said Tim.

"Hey, how many tickets for the entire three-game package are you holding?" I said in a defensive attempt to rationalize my hasty purchase. "At least we're all three in the door Monday night."

"But we're not together," Robbie said. "And what are we going to do about the semifinals due to start in a couple of hours?"

"I think $150 for this ticket is a little high," repeated Tim. "You may have been a little hasty."

We decided that I should sell the ticket if I got a good offer. Because we had some tickets, we decided to leave the regional submarket and get to the real market, at the Kingdome. The traffic was starting to build in downtown Seattle as we walked toward the Dome. Tim challenged every intersection, almost disappointed when the light was in our direction. When Tim jaywalks, it's not enough just to get safely to the other side. You must also slow traffic with your own traffic cop hand sign, or possibly with a more widely known gesture. Tim would cross the street in this fashion, then wait for Robbie and me on the other side as we crossed, mindful of traffic even when we had the right-of-way.

Many attempts to sell our single ticket for $200 were rebuffed. I didn't enjoy the walk. I concluded that I had made a purchase significantly above the going market price. At times, even an economist has difficulty ignoring sunk cost. I had buyers remorse. Of course, I tried not to show my feelings of professional inadequacy to Robbie and Tim. Robbie would be worried, and Tim would be even more smug. I remembered the popular phrase in the College of Business and Economics back home at the University of Idaho in Moscow, "Marketing is everything." I'd have to step up the sales efforts.

I was so concerned with my overpriced ticket that I couldn't enjoy the absolute party atmosphere that permeated downtown Seattle. Loud rock music in Pioneer Square, T-shirt booths everywhere, beer, basketball fans, street people, the big city.

As we approached the Kingdome, the signs of a ticket market started to emerge, and with a ticket to sell, I liked what I saw: a sellers market. People everywhere had one to four fingers in the air. Some had signs, usually cardboard with magic marker lettering saying something like, "Need tickets," or "Need two tickets, 100-level only." One hopeful believer in the goodness of human nature had a sign, which read, "Need tickets, face value only."

"He's gonna have a long day," said Tim.

"Not a good place for an act of kindness," said Robbie.

"It's really a ploy to avoid the Law," I said. "In Seattle, ticket resale at the face value of the ticket is not illegal."

A guy who looked like he had been on the street for a while held the most interesting sign. "Beer money," said the sign, as he rattled change in his cup. He was doing well.

"That's what I like," said Tim as he threw change in the cup, "a no-bullshit approach to American entrepreneurship." Robbie and I were laughing continually. Nothing like seeing the "Old Tim" again, and he wasn't even on asthma inhalers anymore.

Immediately after I indicated that I had a ticket for sale, a forty-something everyman approached me.

"What ya got?" he asked.

"300-level, not the best seat, but not the worst either," I said, trying to be truthful, but not stupid.

"How much?"

"Two hundred."

"Hey, Dad, over here. Whadaya think, 300-level, two hundred bucks," he explained to a fatigued, elderly gentleman.

"Beats walking around," he said, wiping the sweat from his relieved brow.

I was so excited that I took the cash directly from him when I handed him the ticket. It was, of course, in the accepted medium of exchange: two crisp one-hundred-dollar bills.

"Have a good time," I said, as they left to enter the arena. Warm-ups would begin soon.

Robbie and Tim ran over immediately.

"Did ya sell it?" Robbie asked eagerly.

"You bet I did, and for two hundred. We're up fifty on the cash account," I said in a reserved, matter-of-fact tone, not wishing to show my relief too readily.

"Good going, Skippy," said Tim, "Rational arbitrage, buy high, sell higher."

We now held two tickets for the final and $50 in arbitrage earnings, which was our market position for most of the day. After I sold our ticket, we never saw another transaction. In fact, we saw no tickets for sale, just enormous numbers of people looking for tickets.

We saw half of the first game in a bar near the Kingdome. We had bad seats, even in the bar, but it was fun schmoozing with basketball fans from around the country. A guy and his wife who ran a sports bar in Tucson had a tradition of coming to the Final Four without tickets and had always gotten in, but not this year. A group of guys from Boston had come with tickets in hand but sold their semifinal tickets when they ran into a good sellers market. A high price can turn a ticket holder into a ticket seller. They, like us, had tickets to the final. We, however, were one ticket short.

After the first game we went to the front gate to check out the market. There wasn't one. Our assumption had been that losers of the first game would be selling tickets. But when we saw the sign saying, "No Pass Outs," we knew the chances of getting into the second game were zero. Since we had "saved" so much on our tickets we decided to watch the second game in a little more upscale place, one with good beer, good oysters, and a good TV. The TV was a little weak, but with the beer, oysters, and other appetizers, we didn't care.

After the game we again went down to the dome for one last chance at the market. Things were better than before; tickets were for sale. Some 200-level tickets for $300 apiece hung around for a while. I don't know what they finally sold for. We needed at least one ticket so we could all see the final. But we preferred to sit together. This would require a complex transaction. A couple of teenage guys were selling two 300-level tickets for $150 each. We then ran into another group who had three tickets together, comparable to our two, but they needed four. Their four tickets didn't have to be together. Possibilities emerged. With Robbie doing the negotiating, we struck a tentative deal. If we could get two 300-level tickets, we would trade these plus our two for three tickets together and $100. We soon found the teenage guys who, as we expected earlier, were willing to sell us their tickets for $100 each. After this transaction, we turned around to complete the second part of the deal, but our partners had vanished.

"Where did they go?" cried Robbie. "They were here just a minute ago." Robbie now felt what I had felt earlier in the day, remorse from a deal gone sour in which you were the prime negotiator. We now held four tickets, two sets of two. As we were about to call it a day, concluding that we were still in fairly good shape given another round of the market on game day, we saw our guys emerging from a nearby building.

"Where'd ya go?" asked Robbie, with a scolding tone.

"Had to pee, bad," said their leader.

We immediately forgave them, having spent a good portion of the day ourselves flushing beer through our aging plumbing.

We concluded the transaction with only one minor hitch. Cops, after a day of tolerance, were now writing tickets for something. We didn't know what the citations were for, but we were fairly sure it was for something we'd probably done several times already. And further, in a moderate crackdown, our partners in crime had a liquidity crisis.

"Hey Jimmy," the leader asked, "How much money you got?" This was not what we wanted to hear.

"I'll look," said the kid.

"OK," said the leader, "here's eighty, ninety, ninety-five, ninety-seven…Oh shoot I'm short."

Another kid handed him three bucks.

"One hundred." He said.

After a day of exchanging hundred-dollar bills, we consummated our final transaction with twenties, tens, fives, and ones. As we left, we all proudly acknowledged that we made the deal without the use of coins.

After a day in the ticket market, one involving five transactions, we now had three seats together for the final between UCLA and Arkansas Monday night. We had spent $450 on tickets and had $300 in ticket sales. We were into the final for fifty bucks apiece. Not a bad day's work, we thought, as we headed off to the car.

On Sunday we went on a hike with friends to the top of Tiger Mountain, a grueling climb to view the usual Seattle clouds covering everything. We considered it training for getting to our seats Monday night. On Monday, Tim gave a paper at the University of Washington, so he could use travel funds from one of his many grants. Robbie and I continued the bakery tour he had started Friday morning. It was a beautiful day to explore some of the lovely Seattle neighborhoods, Greenwood/Green Lake, Eastlake, Fremont, and Wallingford.

Tim arrived back at the house at about 2:30 p.m. in a moderate frenzy.

"You should see the traffic out there, let's get going," said Tim.

Robbie "the squirrel" and I had already packed our game survival cookies and other treats.

As we traveled another white-knuckle trip to the Kingdome with Tim behind the wheel, Tim persuaded us to have an open mind regarding future ticket action. We agreed. We at least had an academic interest in the market still. And who knows, we might get lucky, though Robbie and I had, in economics jargon, high reservation prices on our tickets.

We were at the Kingdome in plenty of time to enjoy the party atmosphere with leisure, having our tickets already. As we strolled around between beers, among the signs asking for tickets, and the beer money guy, we chatted with a well-dressed woman from Oklahoma. We told her of our ticket quest. She asked if we needed tickets. She informed us that she had two tickets "just a few rows behind Jack Nicholson." As she had only two tickets, Robbie and I immediately figured that was that. Not enough time, and too thin a market to do a complex transaction this close to game time.

But not Tim. He wanted those tickets. Robbie and I informed him that he was on his own, and we went off to feed the parking meter, an action that Tim thought was wasteful. We arranged a meeting place. When we returned, we saw Tim, the lady, and her husband chatting affectionately.

"Which one of you is Skippy?" she asked with a smile. What has Tim told this woman, I thought to myself. In our absence, Tim had offered her four hundred for the two tickets. She wanted five hundred and had an offer pending in the form of a guy on his way to a cash machine to get the dough. We learned later that the first machine he went to had such a long line he gave a kid twenty bucks to give him a ride on his bicycle to another one. The market works. The guy came back and bought the tickets for $250 each.

It was now time for the market to end and for the game to begin, but the final market participation had been informative. Secretly, both Robbie and I were thankful Tim didn't buy the tickets and force us to sit separately or engage in further transactions.

As we came through the entrance an hour before tip-off, I showed my ticket to a kindly-looking elderly man who was working as an usher.

"Oh, 300-level. That way." He said, "And don't worry, you have enough time to get there." Were our seats that bad?

Our seats weren't that terrible. They were the farthest from the court that any of us had sat at a basketball game, but you could follow the action on and off the court as well.

"Look at that woman with Purdue's coach Gene Kady," said Tim.

"I think it's his daughter," said Robbie, looking through another pair of binocs. "Yes, there's Mrs. Kady right there. Tim, watch the game."

"Look, there in the fourth row," said Tim. "That son-of-a-bitch runs the concessions at Syracuse. Coach Boeheim must have given him his tickets."

"These seats are fine," said Robbie, "We're all together at the Final Four."

And we were. It was a great game and a great ticket market.

Part Five

Competition, Monopoly, and Market Structure

Introduction

Much of what happens in markets depends on market structure. A normal person might guess that market structure has something to do with the physical appearance of the market. For example, the look of a Safeway store differs from an open-air farmers' market, but this is not the meaning of market structure. To an economist, market structure is a taxonomy, a classification system we use to describe different businesses and the industries they inhabit. The number of buyers and sellers in the market, the similarity of products, and the ease with which new businesses can come into a market define its structure. The economic vignettes in Part Five describe the market structures competition, monopoly, monopolistic competition, oligopoly, and a joint monopoly called a cartel.

Economics is difficult to learn, in part, because economists define common terms differently than normal people do. "A Weekend in June" shows that a normal person's definition of the term competition and that of an economist is completely opposite. No business school would encourage its students to be competitive, in the economist's sense of the term.

In the second vignette, "Uncle Emil and the Oakes Liquor Store," we find the other end of the market structure continuum, monopoly. My Uncle Emil Isakson maintained his monopoly market power in the liquor business like many businesses do today, with the help of government licensing and regulation, but an economist's partial remedy for Uncle Emil's liquor monopoly would sound strange to Uncle Emil's neighbors. No economist would be invited to a party in Oakes, N.D., for a shot of aquavit on May 17th, Norwegian Independence Day.

Monopolistic competition, as its name implies, combines monopoly and competition. "Pizza Promotion" shows that pricing power alone is not enough to strike it rich in fast food, or any other industry where businesses can easily enter the marketplace.

Most normal people would struggle to find a connection between the movie "A Beautiful Mind," the television cop drama "N.Y.P.D. Blue," and fare wars among airlines, but to an economist, each illustrates game theory in action. The fourth vignette in Part Five examines interdependent behavior in each of these examples and concludes that cooperative behavior is better for the participants than independent action. The market structure oligopoly, one with interdependence among just a few sellers, invites collusion.

"Bigness, Fairness, and the Political Economy of Antitrust," explores the ever-present temptation for sellers to increase profits through conspiratorial pricing. By examining some historical and recent cases, we see government agencies applying antitrust laws and policies to prevent this type of activity. Sellers collusion is not new. My dad wanted to eliminate cut-rate sellers from his local retail oil market in the 1960s, and Adam Smith noted business collusive behavior in 1776.

The final vignette in Part Five reveals evidence of self-interested behavior on the part of a self-avowed noble organization, the National Collegiate Athletic Association (NCAA). In "The NCAA and the Exploitation of College Athletes," we see an organization reduce the wages of college athletes, while coaches, athletic departments, and universities reap great profits from athletic events. Again, economists hold a near cynical view of a cherished American institution, a view that might keep them home on a Monday night in early April, when normal people attend NCAA basketball Final Four parties across the country.

A Weekend in June:

Economists and Competition

In any month, we can turn on our electronic devices or open newspapers and magazines to follow the enormity of professional sports. For example, in June of 2002, when I wrote the first version of this economic vignette (Yes, I'm old.), the Detroit Redwings battled the Carolina Hurricanes in the Stanley Cup Finals. Los Angeles led New Jersey 2-0 in the NBA finals. War Emblem was attempting to win the Belmont Stakes and become the first Triple Crown winner since 1978. The Williams sisters faced each other in the final of the French Open. Heavyweight boxers Lennox Lewis and the charming Mike Tyson squared off in a pay-per-view title bout. My beloved Seattle Mariners began interleague play with a series against the Chicago Cubs. This was also a World Cup year when even Americans were excited about soccer. We're crazy about sports. We love competition.

While normal people love competition in sports, only economists love competition in the marketplace, partly because we have defined competition in a way that takes all the fun out of it. In economics, we emphasize the noun competition rather than the verb compete. Competition anchors one end of the market structure continuum. Monopoly occupies the other end. Competition helps classify different markets. It's not about gamesmanship and rivalry.

Three main components define a market structure: 1) the number of buyers and sellers, 2) the degree of product homogeneity or differentiation, and 3) the ease of getting into the market. In competition, we have many sellers, a homogeneous product, and easy entry to the marketplace. No seller wants to be in a competitive market. Let's see why.

With many sellers and a homogeneous product, no seller has market power. If you raise your price above the common price in the market, buyers will go down the road and buy from another seller. Agriculture illustrates this case. If my neighbor, Gene, takes his wheat to the elevator and demands a price higher than the market price, the buyers will laugh in his face. Even though Gene is an exceptional wheat grower, his wheat is like everyone else's. Gene won't get his premium price because buyers can purchase identical wheat from other growers at a lower price.

In the market structure competition, individual sellers have no control over price. We call them "price takers." People who live on farms understand this. When farmers eat a midday meal, they listen to the radio. The Farm Report notes current prices of agricultural commodities. If prices are up, that's good; if they're down, that's bad, but the farmer can't do anything about the price. He's a price taker. He has no market power.

In a competitive market, market power is even weaker in the long run than in the short run. Suppose wheat prices rise and wheat growers make economic profits. Economic profit is transitory in a competitive market, as others will plant more of this profitable wheat in the next year, increasing the supply and driving the price back down. Easy entry plagues a competitive business.

Economists like economic competition not because of beautiful strategy and clever tactics among rivals, for there is no strategy or rivalry in this boring market structure. They like it because resources shift automatically to where consumers want resources to go. Profits attract resources, losses repel them, and resources flow toward their highest-valued uses. Few truly competitive markets exist anymore. The lure of product differentiation and limited entry is just too strong for business owners to ignore.

Uncle Emil and the Oakes Liquor Store

When I was a young boy, I met my Great Uncle, Emil Isakson, in Oakes, North Dakota. He was a farmer but also owned the local liquor store. Liquor stores needed licenses granted by the county. Uncle Emil also served on the Dickey County Commission. During his period of public service, the County Commission granted no other liquor store licenses.

My Uncle Emil had market power in Oakes. He had the only liquor store in town. He could raise the price of whiskey and people would still buy it. Of course, because of the law of demand, he sold less whiskey at a higher price, but the price increase more than compensated him for the lower amount of whiskey sold. If he raised the price too high, people would cut back their purchases too much, and Uncle Emil would make less profit. As a "price setter," he had to set just the right price.

I can imagine that Uncle Emil had to encounter many potential entrants to the Oakes liquor market over the years, and as a county commissioner, he was likely involved in discussions about this with his Norwegian-American neighbors in both official and unofficial settings. He might have said, "I'm not sure we want to open Oakes up to more liquor availability. Do we want Main Street to have more liquor store signs? Do we really want the liquor business to expand in Oakes, to have our town look more and more like downtown Fargo?" And the neighbors would frown in agreement, content to have Uncle Emil manning the last foxhole in the battle against demon rum. The normal people of Oakes hardly even thought about the extra profits, monopoly profits, which would accrue to Uncle Emil.

Economists, of course, are not normal people and would point out the implications of the liquor market structure in Oakes. We would note that the monopoly profit earned by Uncle Emil was a signal in the marketplace that the residents of Oakes wanted more liquor, not less and that a free market, one without liquor licenses controlled by Uncle Emil, would give it to them at a lower price. Uncle Emil had created a barrier to entry to the liquor market in Oakes and had reaped monopoly profit from it over time.

Economists might also point out the equity considerations involved with the local liquor monopoly and that the residents could urge the County Commission to determine the right number of liquor licenses (perhaps just one) and put them up for auction every year. This would transfer wealth from Uncle Emil to the residents of Dickey County. But the residents, as normal people, would think this was overly complicated, and mean to their neighbor and friend. And on the 17th of May, when they celebrated Norwegian Independence Day with a few shots of aquavit, they'd buy it from Uncle Emil, and would not invite any of those crazy economists over to the party.

Pizza Promotion:

The Economics of Monopolistic Competition

When I lived and worked in Moscow, Idaho, a small college town, many grown-ups would have sold their souls for another decent restaurant if they had not already sold them for better air service, an actual shoulder on U.S. Hwy. 95, or a spring that looked less like mild winter. On the other hand, we had an enormous number of fast-food establishments per capita, and this provided a good laboratory for studying a market structure called monopolistic competition.

If monopoly anchors one end of the market structure continuum and competition the other, monopolistic competition must lie somewhere in the middle. This paradoxical market structure borrows easy market entry from competition and price-setting behavior from monopoly. In developing the theory of monopolistic competition in the 1930s, Edward Chamberlin wished to inject some realism into the economic theory of markets, having found so few examples of perfect competition and monopoly.

Businesses in monopolistic competition differentiate their products. By creating differences in their products, and promoting these differences, businesses develop what my former marketing colleagues called product or brand loyalty. With product differentiation comes some pricing power in the marketplace. Unlike a wheat grower, a business with a differentiated product can raise its price and not have its sales go to zero.

Fast-food restaurants sell differentiated products. In Moscow, the pizza at Pizza Hut was different from that at Domino's, Branegan's, Pizza Perfection, Pizza Pipeline, Papa Murphy's, and Papa John's, but it was still pizza. When I once asked my students about the best pizza, they had strong preferences for a specific brand. Owners of these pizza places used valuable resources to promote the different characteristics of their brands and set prices high enough to cover these promotional costs. My farmer neighbors, by contrast, had no advertising expenditures on their income statements.

But market pricing power doesn't mean that the road to riches is paved with pizza. How many rich pizza vendors do you know? Suppose owners of pizza businesses were making a large profit. Unless pizza barons could keep it a secret, enterprising rivals would soon enter their market, increasing supply, and driving prices down toward cost. The peril of easy entry strikes again.

We have a lot of monopolistic competition in market economies. We can tell by looking at the variety of similar products. Not only pizza, but hair styling, espresso coffee drinks, and auto services, among many others. The many sellers of these differentiated products make similar ordinary incomes. To make money in this market structure you must have a NEW product difference and take the money and run before the entrants come and ruin it for you. This is an incentive to innovate, a valuable characteristic of market economies, even if the competition is not perfect.

A Beautiful Mind, NYPD Blue, and Airline Fare Wars:

Game Theory, Oligopoly, and Sellers Cartels

When Russell Crowe was nominated for an Academy Award for his portrayal of John Nash in the movie "A Beautiful Mind," normal people thought it was for his ability to convincingly capture the behavior of a paranoid schizophrenic or say anything without blabbering in the presence of the beautiful Jennifer Connelly. Economists knew it was for his mastery of game theory.

With game theory, economists explain all kinds of interdependent behavior. Often, rivals in a "game" engage in self-interested maximizing behavior that does not lead to maximum collective or joint well-being. In a scene early in the film, Nash and his graduate school colleagues are in a bar near Princeton. Soon a group of beautiful coeds enters the bar. In the estimation of Nash and his colleagues, a blonde woman in the group is exceptionally beautiful. All but Nash are thinking about how to compete with the other guys to win this beauty. One of Nash's colleagues even refers to Adam Smith, the founder of modern economics, whose famous invisible hand principle says that individual competition leads to the common good. John Nash disagrees. He notes that if they all compete for the blonde, no one will win her affection. And in the process of competing for the blonde, they will lose the other girls as well because no one wants to be the second choice. Nash suggests that if no one goes for the blonde, they won't get in each other's way and will not insult the other girls. "It's the only way we win," he says. "It's the only way we get laid."

Of course, like any genius, Nash prefers the abstract idea of a strategy to pursue the girls rather than implementing his plan, an act for mere mortals. The theory itself is more beautiful than any of the girls, even the blonde one. Nash gathers his papers and rushes back to the dorm to work on formalizing his breakthrough, his singularly new and creative idea.

Nash's (Crowe's) example in the bar illustrates one of the most common principles in game theory, the prisoners' dilemma, the idea that cooperation will lead to a better collective outcome than rivalry among participants in the game. For another example, one even involving prisoners, or at least suspects, we must turn to another popular medium, the television cop show.

I confess. I like cop shows. In the olden days, *Hill Street Blues* and *NYPD Blue* were two of my favorites. When homicide detective Andy Sipowicz (portrayed by Dennis Franz) brought in a couple of "perps" for questioning, he showed an understanding of game theory, or at least he acted as if he understood it. With two perps, the idea was to get one to rat out the other in exchange for a lighter sentence. If both thought this way, both ratted, and both were convicted. Usually, the case was weak, and "dirtbag lawyers" might get them off. Andy needed a confession.

Even though in his heart of hearts, he preferred to beat a confession out of one of the "scumbags," he knew Internal Affairs would be on him if he did. Instead, Andy and his partner separated the suspects and worked on each independently. They told each of them that if the other guy confessed first, whoever didn't confess would get the maximum sentence, and the confessor would get a light sentence. Andy didn't tell them the best strategy was to admit to nothing. No confession, no case, go free. But if each distrusted the other, a distrust fostered by the separation and the inability to collude face-to-face, the incentives to rat looked good. If no honor exists among thieves, and they don't "lawyer up," Andy's approach will work every time. It's a prisoners' dilemma. Individual, independent, self-interested action leads to ruin for the group.

Sellers in markets are often like college boys in a bar and criminal suspects facing interrogation. Consider the airline industry, an oligopoly, a market with just a few sellers. A fare reduction by one airline company will have one effect if other airlines also reduce their fares and another effect if they don't.

According to game theory, when deciding whether to lower fares, an oligopolist considers the actions of its rivals. But what will the rivals do? It's unclear. If each thinks the other will not match a fare reduction, we get a fare war. If they think a reduction will be matched, no fare war ensues.

Game theory also suggests that a joint solution will be the best for the participants in the game, in this case, a pricing game. To maximize their joint well-being, the former rivals should form a cartel and make joint decisions. The CEO of one airline company should call the others and say, "I won't lower prices if you don't," and "What would be the best price for all of us to charge?" Unfortunately for the airlines, this is illegal behavior in the U.S. You can go to jail for that. But the idea remains. Cartels emerge when oligopolists recognize the benefits of collusion and joint decision-making.

Bigness, Fairness, and the Political Economy of Antitrust

My dad drove an oil truck. He worked for the local Union Oil distributor in Wenatchee, Washington, for 33 years until he retired in the early 1980s. He was far down the organization chart for Union Oil, but he was in the oil business nonetheless. Once in the middle 1960s, shortly after I got my driver's license, we had a gasoline price war in Wenatchee. If I were willing to break with family loyalty to Union Oil and buy an off-brand, cut-rate gas, I could fill up my '51 Chevy for under five bucks. I thought this was about as good as it could get. My dad, the oil man, had a different idea. One time at the dinner table, I remember him saying, "What we need to do is clean up the oil industry, get rid of all the gyppo, cut-rate guys." Mom and I knew that this was a good time to change the dinner discussion to sports.

Dad had a sellers view of market structure. Too many sellers made business difficult. Not only were prices lower, but you had little control over price at all. If you could get rid of the cut-rate riffraff, you and the Texaco man might be able to come to a sensible agreement to stop "hitting each other over the head" on prices. Dad had good company in this view. In 1776, Adam Smith wrote in *The Wealth of Nations*, "People of the same trade seldom meet together, even for merriment and diversion, but the conversation ends in a conspiracy against the public, or in some contrivance to raise prices."

Unless you're Tony Soprano or Michael Corleone, reducing the number of sellers in the market is not easy. For one thing, the government uses antitrust laws and policies against actions by businesses that reduce the number of sellers and raise prices. Federal government regulatory agencies, such as the Federal Trade Commission, the Federal Communications Commission, and the Antitrust Division of the Department of Justice, often scrutinize mergers and collusive actions.

In 2002, both the Federal Communications Commission and the Department of Justice ruled against a merger of the nation's two largest satellite-television companies at that time, EchoStar Communications Corp. and Hughes Electronics Corp. Regulators at these agencies argued that the merger would raise prices to rural customers who, after the merger, would have one satellite-television alternative instead of two. The companies claimed this wouldn't happen and that the larger satellite company would have lower costs and provide more competition in urban cable television markets. Efficiency (lower cost) and fairness are often tradeoffs in antitrust policy.

More recently, in November of 2021, the Department of Justice filed a suit to block the world's largest consumer book publisher, Penguin Random House, from acquiring fellow publisher Simon and Schuster. Here the issue was not about market power over selling prices, monopoly power, but over the power the larger company would have over the prices it paid to authors for their work. This is what economists call monopsony power, something we'll discuss in more detail in the next piece in Part Five. Economists worry that mergers might move the economy away from a level of book publishing where marginal social benefit equals marginal social cost, the conditions for efficiency and maximum economic well-being. Non-economists, mostly normal people, would care more about whether the merger would be more unfair to authors.

Even if companies don't merge, they can increase profits by jointly restricting output and raising prices by forming a sellers cartel. The most famous sellers cartel is the Organization of Petroleum Exporting Countries (OPEC). Over the last four-plus decades, OPEC has raised oil prices by using production quotas for its members. The success of OPEC depends on the willingness of Saudi Arabia, by far the largest producer of crude oil, to control its pumping.

Even successful cartels, however, encounter innovation in and entry into the market. Recent development of "fracking" technology in oil extraction has increased supplies from shale sources and previously abandoned wells in the United States and has reduced the market power of OPEC.

OPEC has succeeded at times, but sellers cartels, including OPEC, often fail. The desire for greater profit that brings companies (and countries in this case) together is the same force that leads to cheating once production quotas are established. Every seller thinks, "If I sell just a little more at a higher price, my profit will be higher still." If they all sell more, the price falls. With OPEC, this usually happens a month or so after oil ministers have met somewhere like Vienna to hammer out an agreement.

Cartels work best with a small number of participants. Christie's International PLC and Sotheby's Holdings Inc. control over 90% of the art auction market. In 2001, both companies paid to settle a class-action suit alleging they jointly fixed fees to both buyers and sellers of art.

Adam Smith was right. Whether in the Wenatchee oil business, the world oil market, the rural market for satellite television, book publishing, or the art auction industry, sellers want to reduce the number of rivals and to raise prices if they can, and buyers want to lower the prices they pay for production resources. The antitrust laws offer some constraints on this activity. But to an economist, whether a merger or price-fixing agreement is bad and whether we need antitrust laws to prevent these actions depends to some extent on the case but also on the economic theory we use to evaluate it.

In the short run, mergers or price fixing can increase price and profit and reduce the amount sold in the marketplace to a level lower than consumers are willing to pay for. Economists would think the latter is bad and withhold judgment on the price and profit increase. But over the long run, higher market power can lead to more innovation and investment. Besides, no business can maintain a barrier to entry forever, regulators are not saints, and cartels with many participants are doomed to failure even without government involvement.

Much recent antitrust activity centers around large, high-tech businesses such as Apple, Google, and Microsoft, but not on an abuse of pricing power. Rather, recent cases focus on the alleged ability of these companies, because of their size, to limit rival companies from competing with them. For example, Apple has been accused of hindering the use of non-Apple app stores and payment mechanisms and forcing game developers to use its own lucrative (to Apple) payment system. Google has been accused of using its search engine to direct consumers to its own in-house services, and Microsoft, for decades, has had to defend itself against charges that it favors its own products, like its internet browser, in its Windows software.

Antitrust policy has a large political dimension, as well. Democrats are more ardent in their pursuit of "anticompetitive behavior." Republicans, on the other hand, tend to be more lenient toward this behavior. In 2021, the appointment of Federal Trade Commission Chair Lina Khan in the Biden administration illustrates this point. According to a report in the *Wall Street Journal*, and other news sources, Ms. Khan wants to challenge more corporate mergers and monopolistic activities and adopt regulations that reduce unfair business practices. These actions are less popular among Republican members of the commission. The political economy of antitrust is rarely dull.

The NCAA and Exploitation of College Athletes:

Anatomy of a Buyers Cartel

In November 2001, the story of DeShaun Foster graced every newspaper sports section in America. The Foster story indirectly mentioned his considerable accomplishments as a running back for the Bruins of the University of California Los Angeles (UCLA). Near the end of the 2001 season, Mr. Foster, a candidate for the Heisman Trophy, had averaged 140 yards per game rushing, the best in the (then) Pacific Ten Conference and fifth best in the country. UCLA was about to play Oregon, the eventual winner of the conference championship and contender for a national title. UCLA suspended Mr. Foster from the team and immediately performed a full investigation of his activities, an investigation that school officials hoped would keep the NCAA from penalizing the football program. Mr. Foster had committed the unpardonable sin of driving a new car loaned to him by a friend, a UCLA booster with close ties to a sports agent.

Without a doubt, this activity violated NCAA rules, and normal people recognize rule-breaking. Economists, on the other hand, see this as strong evidence of the most successful buyers cartel in history. In a cartel, market participants cooperate to increase their market power and profit. Buyer cartels can raise profit by conspiring to lower the price of goods or services members buy. Economists have a fancy term for this kind of market power: monopsony. But buyers cartel will serve us just as well, eliminating confusing jargon.

When economists call the NCAA a buyers cartel, they again limit their party invitations. Normal people cling to the noble ideal of the scholar-athlete, the Olympian merger of brains and brawn rhetorically advanced by the NCAA. However, economists dig deeper into economic incentives and behavior.

116

In this case, we find the wages of college athletes at zero, despite six- and seven-figure salaries for coaches, and millions of dollars in revenue flowing to athletic departments and their host universities.

When a worker generates profit for a business and receives compensation far below the value of this profit, we call it exploitation. College athletes receive zero wages from their schools. Recent NCAA rule changes, however, have allowed athletes to earn income from authorizing the use of their Names, Images, and Likenesses (NIL). These activities will be very lucrative for star athletes in major sports. Even athletes in sports like volleyball, soccer, and water polo can earn NIL income if they have a large enough following on social media.

The NCAA has also relaxed restrictions on transferring between schools, in effect creating an amateur form of free agency found in professional sports. Student athletes may now transfer without sitting out a year at their new school. But exploitation still exists, with coaches receiving seven-figure salaries while athletes remain unpaid by their academic institutions. We have not seen the end of efforts to increase compensation and inter-school mobility of college athletes.

Two behaviors represent a litmus test for the existence of cartel behavior. We've already seen one, the collective activity of raising the price in the sellers case and lowering it in the buyers case. Once a cartel is established, however, the other natural cartel behavior emerges: cheating. In a buyers cartel, once everyone else has agreed not to pay college athletes, and adhere to other restrictions on normal market activity, a cartel member has a tremendous incentive to cheat. In fact, this incentive is so strong that we rarely see successful cartels. The greed that creates them sows the seeds of their own destruction.

A successful cartel must control the cheating by its members. And here, the NCAA is without parallel. Loaned cars, extra recruiting trips for athletes, extravagant entertainment on recruiting visits, too-liberal shoe supplies, and trips to visit sick family members paid for by boosters can all land an athletic program on probation and limit its monetary return from the lucrative business of college athletics. Next time you see a program busted for a minor infraction, think of the cartel keeping its members in line. And be more kind to the weird economist whose favorite college basketball team was coached by Naismith Hall of Fame member Jerry Tarkanian at the University of Nevada at Las Vegas, alleged to be the best college basketball team money could buy. If true, at least "Tark" reduced player exploitation.

Part Six

Collective Goods,
Externalities, Asymmetric
Information, Market Failure,
and Government Failure

Introduction

In Part Five, we learned that monopoly, oligopoly, and cartels, can lead to market failure, where a market economy does not maximize the well-being of its people. In Part Six, we explore several other real-world market imperfections that may lead to similar failures and to an economic justification for government action to correct them. But government action can also fail to improve human well-being, something economists call government failure. This can occur from government action independent of market failure, but also from government attempts to correct market failure. No guarantee exists that the government can improve upon market failure. Its actions might make things worse, which leads to a dilemma for government policy.

In "The Lloyd Austin National Defense Telethon," a private sector company attempts to pay for a pure collective good. Like the familiar Public Broadcasting System (PBS) pledge drive or the Jerry Lewis fundraiser for Muscular Dystrophy, the company uses a national television telethon. When the company's guest host, the U.S. Secretary of Defense, appeals to Americans on Memorial Day to pledge contributions for national defense, the phones don't ring. To provide collective goods, we must avoid the "free rider problem" by using the coercive power of government taxation.

Collective goods (or bads) are often created in an economy through something economists call externalities. In "Studded Tires and Grass Burning," deep grooves in road surfaces from studded snow tires and air pollution from grass field burning are legendary North Idaho external costs. Because these external costs are collective bads, our market economy will produce too many of them. We need government action to improve air and pavement quality.

In "Helping Johnny Learn to Read," others benefit from an individual's education, an example of a positive externality, an external benefit. Because an external benefit from education has the characteristics of a collective good, too little will be provided in the market. Again, market failure justifies government action.

Negative externalities from climate change are collective bads that suggest government action to reduce their cost. In "Economics and Climate Change: Putting a Price on Carbon," we see economists' favorite type of environmental policy, economic incentives, such as carbon taxes and cap-and-trade systems. Here the important concept is efficiency, where incentive-based systems achieve environmental improvements at lower cost than command-and-control policies and production subsidies common in current U.S. climate policy.

Actions by private business do much to lessen market failures due to the lack of perfect information in the marketplace. Asymmetric information, where one party in a transaction has more information than another, can lead to moral hazard, adverse selection, and low-quality goods in a market. "Asymmetric Information: Moral Hazzard, Adverse Selection, and Signaling," shows examples of information-related market and government failure. Well-meaning government policy can create large costs from moral hazard in different policies related to deposit insurance, pension guarantees, and the Federal Reserve's "lender of last resort" actions.

Individuals, businesses, and governments often give "in-kind" gifts, those other than money. In "What are Those Free Drink Coupons Worth? The Inefficiency of In-Kind Transfers," cash is king, if we want to maximize the well-being of one who receives a gift.

The next two economic vignettes are about government failure. In "Using Taxes to Pay for Water," politics and the individual interests of water district managers align to create high-cost western water policy. No other economic rationale can explain the use of property taxes to pay for water, mostly a private good. If government produces a private good, the result is government failure. In "Protectionism: Government Failure in International Trade," political action reduces economic well-being. Due to differences in the cost of organizing groups, producers can influence democratic governments to limit imports of cheaper foreign goods, while consumers are powerless to respond with comparable action.

The case for government involvement in the provision of collective goods is not an argument for government production of them. In "Choosing a Bruise Over a Puncture Wound: Vouchers and the Collective Choice Dilemma," the existence of market failure and government failure at the same time requires creative public policy, such as education voucher systems advocated mostly by economists. This controversial type of education policy, opposed by teachers' unions and politicians they support, is beginning to win support from parents and legislators who represent them.

The Lloyd Austin National Defense Telethon:

Collective Goods in a Market Economy

I almost can't watch. Not because some great concert disappoints. No, the three tenors, Paul Simon, Joe Bonamassa, or the Highwaymen, among many others, exceed my expectations. But I know that after a great musical performance, the local Public Broadcasting System (PBS) station manager will say, "Without your help, fine programming like this won't be available." And then the pledge drive will drone on and on and on. Now, perfectly deflated, I ooze down into my Lazy Boy recliner, reach for the remote, and rue the private provision of collective goods.

Economists divide the world into two categories: private goods and collective goods. We sometimes call the latter public goods, but this introduces needless confusion. The term public good might lead a normal person to think that anything produced by the public sector or government is a public good. As the government often produces private goods as well, we will use the term collective, rather than public.

Most know the characteristics of private goods. If I consume a private good, you can't consume the same one. Suppose you are in a fast-food restaurant eating a hamburger, and I come up to you and say that I want to eat that hamburger. Of course, we both can't eat the same hamburger. If you eat it, I can't, and vice versa. If it's your hamburger, you could take pity on me and give it to me, or you could sell it to me, but the choice is yours. You could tell me to "get lost" and remind me that it's YOUR hamburger. Economists say that this private good is rival in consumption.

In addition, you can't get a hamburger in a fast-food restaurant without paying for it first, either at the cash register or, less likely but possible, from someone who already has one. Imagine what would happen in a McDonald's if you took a few explosive steps, hurdled the service counter, grabbed a Quarter Pounder and fries, and ran out the door. Most certainly, an employee would run after you in the parking lot, while a colleague called 911. While we take it for granted in everyday life, private goods require that we pay for them. Economists call this excluding people from consuming private goods if they don't pay.

Rival consumption and excludable exchange allow sellers in a market system to exist. Motivated by the incentive to earn a profit, private businesses produce and sell stuff every day. If a consumer wants a private good, she must get it for herself, and to get it, she must agree to pay before the seller will provide it to her.

But suppose that a good is nonrival in consumption and non-excludable in exchange. For example, we can listen to a broadcast radio program in my household, while not keeping you from listening to it in yours. Any other household within the broadcast area can listen, as well. In the broadcast area, the program is nonrival in consumption. And once broadcast over the airwaves, no one must pay to hear it. It's non-excludable. This presents a difficulty for producers of radio programs. If a good is provided to me, whether I pay for it or not, I might consume this good without contributing to its provision. We call this "free riding" in economics. Because of the free rider problem, an alternative funding source, advertising, interrupts many radio programs in the United States. National Public Radio (NPR) doesn't like to have this interruption, so it places ads in the form of "sponsors" at the beginning and end of programs. In addition to funding from sponsors, NPR (like its television counterpart PBS) also asks the government for money, and asks you and me, as well, through periodic fund drives. Many countries dispense with advertising and fund drives and pay for radio and TV with tax revenue.

In recent years, technological change has allowed the spread of excludable radio and television signals. Subscription services, such as Sirius-XM radio, cable television, Netflix, Hulu, and Amazon, charge for their services. The good remains nonrival but now is excludable. Subscription payments to the provider replace advertising as the funding source for these products.

While radio and TV are interesting because of their variety of funding methods, the best example of a collective good is national defense. The U.S. nuclear arsenal, deliverable from silos, submarines, and bombers, ensures the destruction of any country foolish enough to launch a first strike on the United States. This deterrent protects me and my family from, say, a Russian attack and, at the same time, protects all other U.S. families. Our nuclear deterrent is nonrival in consumption.

And once the U.S. government provides a nuclear deterrent, it can't exclude an American from consuming it. Because nuclear deterrence is a pure collective good, businesses in our market economy are not likely to provide it. Business owners recognize that selling something that no one must pay for is a losing proposition. As in all countries, we coerce people to pay for national defense through taxes. When an agent from the Internal Revenue Service asks why you paid 5% less in taxes than you should have, he won't be very receptive to the argument that you were merely free-riding on the collective good national defense.

National defense requires government coercion for funding. Few other options exist, and using them would result in too little national defense. Suppose the Biden administration wanted to reduce the burden of government taxation by substituting private funding for taxes. The President might summon the CEO of Amazon to the Oval Office. The President would point out that Amazon is one of the largest and most profitable companies in the world, and that if any company could make private provision of national defense pay, Amazon could. Not wanting to disappoint the President, the CEO might say he would give it a try. How might Amazon proceed? They would have a telethon.

Picture a warm sunny Memorial Day weekend. You come in from the yard or the golf course and turn on the TV. And who do you see on the screen? None other than Lloyd Austin, U.S. Secretary of Defense. As *The Battle Hymn of the Republic* or *America the Beautiful* plays softly in the background, Mr. Austin patriotically intones, "I'm here today on behalf of the fine people of Amazon, who have taken on the noble task of providing for the defense of our country. In keeping with the philosophy of free markets, and to lighten the tax burden of all Americans, we are asking you to help Amazon raise $750 billion for this year's national defense budget. I'm proud to have behind me on the stage, members of the Fairfax, Virginia, Daughters of the American Revolution, who are waiting to answer the phones when you send in your Pledge for a Strong America. And I must say I'm concerned that the phones aren't ringing. Without your help, there will be no ballistic missile defense, an insufficient number of U.S. ships in the South China Sea, and few ways to counter nasty rogue tyrants who threaten our democratic principles and those of our friends around the world.

"Oh, there, the phones are ringing. I thank you in advance for your pledge, and now turn the microphone over to Mary Johnson, a Social Security recipient and mother of two children in the U.S. Navy, who wants to challenge, with her pledge of $25, all Social Security recipients and mothers of military personnel to make a similar pledge. Oh yes, I hear the phones ringing. Thanks to you, it's working. God bless America!"

Economists are pessimistic about the Lloyd Austin National Defense Telethon. Thanks to free riders, the market will not work. Because national defense is a collective good, we must resort to government coercion through taxation to provide it.

Studded Tires and Grass Burning:

The Economics of North Idaho External Cost

In the summer in the Inland Northwest, if you ask an owner of lake property what they did last weekend, they will say, "We went to the lake." We have hundreds of lakes in the Inland Northwest, but after a weekend at the lake, we never feel obliged to identify which lake we went to. It's simply the lake as if there were no other. If you don't know which lake we went to, it's just as well. You are probably an evil visitor from California or Seattle looking for a place to build a mansion and docks for your impossibly large loud boat and jet skis.

On a late August day several years ago, I, too, was going to the lake. We were going to spend a week at a cabin Solveig's parents built about 50 years ago, one now surrounded by huge mansions and docks for impossibly large loud boats and jet skis. When we go to the lake for an extended period, we often take two vehicles to carry the gear, the dog, the food, and the beer. It's also nice to have two vehicles for rescue purposes. I'm an economist. I drive cars until I have squeezed every drop of physical utility from them. Breakdowns happen.

On this late-August day, I was driving our 1986 Isuzu Trooper. I loved this rig (That's what we call SUVs and pickups in North Idaho), but we only allowed it to go out of town if we were going to the lake. The Trooper, with me behind the wheel, proves correct the American aphorism, "You are what you drive." The Trooper was old, big, boxy, and slow. At 170 thousand miles, the Trooper's front end was a little loose and wobbly, so much so that ruts in the road caused sudden and significant sideways vehicle thrust. As I drove west briefly on Interstate 90 from U.S. 95 to Idaho 41, to head further north, I held firmly onto the steering wheel to negotiate the rutted road.

While big trucks might share some blame, rutted highways come mainly from studded snow tires.

In addition to the sudden sideways thrust I experienced in my Trooper, I also hydroplaned from water collected in the ruts. We no longer let Miss Budweiser or Miss Thriftway race on our Inland Northwest Lakes. We reserve hydroplaning for cars on Interstate 90. Damage from studded tires is so bad that the severe winter states of Minnesota, Michigan, and Wisconsin have banned them. In Idaho, we didn't have enough resources to do the study, but right next door the Washington State Department of Transportation estimated that studded tires did about $20-28 million of damage to state roads each year. Washington restricts studded tire use to the period November 1st to April 1st. In less regulatory Idaho, we can use studded tires from October 1st to April 15th (Hey, what if it snows on Tax Day?)

Using studded tires generates what economists call external cost. This cost is borne not by the creators of the cost, drivers with studded tires, but by the driving public and taxpayers at large. Markets don't work well in the presence of external cost. In fact, external cost is another cause of market failure and a justification for government action to reduce studded tire use.

Few economists would recommend banning studded tires because this would likely reduce the benefit of studs by more than their cost, a normative economic no-no. But a special excise tax on studded tires would make economists' hearts soar like bald eagles at Lake Coeur d'Alene, especially if the tax were set equal to the marginal damage of the studs in the tires.

Had I been driving west from Spokane on that late-August day, this vignette on external cost and market failure would now be complete. But in North Idaho, in August and September, we can incur a unique double whammy of external cost, rutted roads that are hard to see. In North Idaho, we grow a lot of grass seed. Part of the production process for grass seed is field burning, and when the wind blows the wrong way, as it was on my way to the lake, you can't see more than a few hundred feet in front of your car as it thrusts left and right from tire ruts. Mario Andretti would have had trouble negotiating these driving conditions.

After intervention by the Saint of Old Trooper Drivers, I finally made it to the Highway 41 exit and headed north. But now the traffic had virtually stopped. The smoke was so thick that police officers directed traffic at intersections. I didn't think I would ever get to the lake. Grass growers benefit from field burning and pass some of the cost on to the public at large in the form of slow and dangerous driving, smoky days at the Coeur d'Alene Resort, and respiratory illness and death. Because the costs are external, the market produces the wrong amount of field burning. Too much field burning comes from improper incentives. Economists recognize time and time again that if people don't bear all the costs of an action, they do too much of it.

Helping Johnny Learn to Read:

The Economics of External Benefit

Why is the government involved in education? Normal people, at least in the United States, consider education a right of citizenship, something we collectively do for people. It would be unfair or unjust not to provide someone with an education. Economists call this kind of good a merit good. By the merit of citizenship, a person has a right to government-provided or government-subsidized education.

Economists, on the other hand, with their predisposition toward market resource allocation, look for a different normative rationale for government provision of any good. It must have the characteristics of a collective good. If it's not a collective good, leave it up to the market, as we do with private goods such as hamburgers, pants, and shoes.

Education has much in common with hamburgers, pants, and shoes. In each case, much of the benefit accrues directly to the individual consuming the good, and this benefit is nonrival. If Johnny learns to read, he has a much higher chance of getting a job and earning a higher income throughout his lifetime. If he gets that job, someone else can't. The ability to read opens the world of literature to Johnny, as well. His life is simply easier and richer. This benefit of education goes to Johnny. No one else can consume his enjoyment from reading except him. Education is not like national defense or the preservation of an endangered species, where the benefit of consumption is entirely nonrival.

Also, we can exclude someone from educational instruction. I say educational instruction, as self-teaching and learning are much less excludable. Unlike national defense and knowledge of the existence of endangered species, schoolhouses have doors that can be closed to those who don't pay tuition. Education is excludable.

Because education has characteristics like private goods, private producers will provide it in the marketplace. Many schools are built and run by religious organizations, offering religious instruction along with reading, writing, and arithmetic. Other private schools purport to offer a higher quality education. Parents want their children to learn to read. They are willing to pay for it like they are for Johnny's Big Mac, his cargo pants, and his soccer shoes. Later, if Johnny receives training in accounting or engineering, this opens the possibility of an even more satisfying and lucrative career. Economists point out that Johnny and his parents would be willing to pay for this too.

So, if education is rival in consumption and excludable in exchange, why is the government involved? Is the justification simply for its merit good status, one related to ethics and fairness and not efficiency? Is there no economic justification for government involvement in education? Not quite, because education is something economists call a mixed good. In addition to Johnny's private benefit from education, an external benefit from his education spills over to others in the community at large. If Johnny can read, you can design an advertising campaign to sell him something. If Johnny learns about the rule of law in a civics class, he will be less likely to pursue a life of crime. If Johnny learns enough to do research in microbiology or biomedical engineering, he might discover a cure for cancer or invent an artificial kidney. Education's mixed good status stems from the mixture of private and external benefits from it.

While Johnny's private benefit from education is rival and excludable, like a hamburger, the external benefit is nonrival and nonexcludable, like national defense. Think of a local school district telethon designed to raise money to subsidize local education. It would be like the National Defense Telethon. Some would call in and make a pledge, but economists know that most people would be "free riders." We don't have to worry about the Johnnies of the world getting education to acquire their own private benefits, but too little education will be produced because of the collective nature of the external benefit. If we decide the external benefit of more education exceeds the cost of providing it, we must give Johnny and his parents an incentive to buy more of it.

131

Reasonable people, even economists, will have different estimates of the ratio of the private and external benefits from education. In the United States, we provide collectively (subsidize) a much higher proportion of primary and secondary education than we do higher education. Of course, this might reflect a decline in the merit of the good as we move beyond the basics to more specialized education. I think most economists would think that the difference in relative subsidy reflects an economically rational assessment of the ratio of external and private benefits. If college has less external and more private benefit than does elementary education, normative economics would suggest we collectively subsidize it less.

Given a justification for some government action in teaching Johnny to read, should the government build schools and hire teachers to teach him? We'll have more to say about this related question in a later vignette, where we discuss the voucher system in education. In this system, students or their parents, while still subsidized with money raised through taxation, would pay some education costs at the schoolhouse door. But more of these doors would be on private, not government schools. In any case, irrespective of the type of involvement, the economic justification of any kind of government involvement in Johnny's learning to read comes from the external benefit from that effort, an external benefit with the characteristics of a collective good.

Economics and Climate Change:

Putting a Price on Carbon

First, a question. I'm putting it on the final exam so pay attention (just kidding). What do I have in common with 28 Economics Nobel Laureates, four former chairs of the Federal Reserve System, fifteen former chairs of the President's Council of Economic Advisers, and 3,622 fellow U.S. economists? No, it's not brilliant economic research (I wish it were.). It's not that we are like Oscar Wilde's cynic, knowing the price of everything and the value of nothing. No, it's not that we make weather forecasters look good. These may be partially true, but the correct answer is that all of us signed the Economists' Statement on Carbon Dividends, the largest public statement by economists in history. You can find the details of this proposal at the website of the Climate Leadership Council, https://clcouncil.org/economists-statement. I'm not trying to signal virtuous behavior with this admission. Rather, I want to explain the overwhelming support economists have for economic incentive-based approaches in environmental policy.

The Economists' Statement on Carbon Dividends begins with the normative conclusion that climate change is a serious problem that should be addressed forcibly and immediately and that the best way to do this is with a revenue-neutral carbon tax. Revenue neutrality means that the government will refund the tax revenue to Americans through equal annual carbon dividends. Of course, the government could use carbon tax revenue to fund all kinds of activities or to reduce other taxes, but developers of the statement felt that raising revenue would also create political discussions that would jeopardize the implementation of the tax.

If an economist thinks that climate change is a problem, it's easy to take the next step and recommend an economic incentive-based approach to address it. "Greenhouse gasses" create external costs, borne not by those creating them, but by others around the world. Instituting a tax (or a fee) on carbon emissions will help to internalize the external cost. If we must pay for our climate-changing behavior, we'll change our behavior. As carbon-emitting activities become more expensive, we will find substitutes for them. And demand for these substitutes will give incentives for the market to provide them. One thing we know as economists, incentives matter.

Using an economic incentive to reduce emissions is more cost-effective than more regulatory command-and-control approaches, or government subsidies to more climate-friendly technologies. Economic evidence is overwhelming in this regard for many types of pollution control. And cost-effectiveness is important. Making our behavior more climate-friendly will require costly change. People don't like costly change. Let's make the transition to a more hospitable climate as easy as possible.

By returning carbon tax revenue to Americans with equal carbon dividends, the plan will also make climate policy fairer, because the cost of climate policy is regressive. The lower one's income, the higher the cost as a proportion of income. By returning an equal share, regardless of income, we help to redress this regressivity.

The proposal calls for a carbon tax to rise every year until we achieve carbon reduction goals. It also calls for a carbon border adjustment to guard against importing goods from other countries with less stringent climate policies. This will help preserve the competitiveness of U.S. companies and not penalize good behavior in the world marketplace.

The carbon tax is an economic incentive like an effluent charge in water pollution policy or an emissions charge in air pollution control. Ideally, the charge should be set equal to the marginal benefit of reducing greenhouse gas emissions. This would move the economy toward the point where the marginal benefit of emissions reduction equals the marginal cost, maximizing net benefit. The Climate Leadership Council's proposal is less ambitious, however, settling for cost-effectiveness, not maximization of net benefits. Whatever the tax level, theory suggests that emitters will control emissions up to the point where the marginal cost of emissions control equals the tax. As all face the same tax rate, this ensures that the marginal cost of emissions control is equal across emitters, a condition necessary to minimize the cost of emissions reduction.

With a carbon tax, we can estimate the amount of emissions reduction, but we won't know how much will occur until we see the reactions of emitters. We set a tax and see how it works. Setting a lower tax initially will ease the transition to more climate-friendly practices. The statement founders, knowing that the tax is initially low, call for raising it over time, the magnitude of the increases depending on progress toward climate goals.

An alternative form of economic incentive-based policy is a cap-and-trade system, one used successfully in the reduction of sulfur dioxide emissions in the U.S. and Canada and in the early stages of implementation of climate policy in Europe and China. With this system, we cap the quantity of emissions and allocate emission permits to emitters. The trade part of cap-and-trade comes from the establishment of a market in emission permits. Since emission permits have value in the marketplace, those who can reduce emissions cheaply have an incentive to do so and sell the permits to those with more costly emissions control. Again, the economic incentive preserves cost-effectiveness. But in this case, in contrast with the carbon tax, the quantity of emissions reduction is set, through the cap, and the market determines the price of emission permits.

Economists, in general, are much more in favor of economic incentive-based pollution control systems than are normal people. To normal people, these approaches sound too easy, and regulatory command-and-control policies sound tougher. Much research by environmental economists has demonstrated that the opposite is the case. Of course, if emissions taxes are set too low, or emissions caps made too lenient, both might fail to achieve climate goals. Here, again, the cost-effectiveness of economic incentive-based approaches is important, as lower emissions reduction cost reduces the political pressure for low tax rates and lenient caps on emissions.

Asymmetric Information:
Moral Hazard, Adverse Selection, and Signaling

In most textbooks, economists use a common method. First, we define a stylized model of a market economy and show the desirable characteristics of it. Three pillars support this stylized economy: 1) perfect competition, 2) no externalities or collective goods, and 3) perfect information. Then, we remove a pillar and examine the implications for economic well-being in the economy. Removal of a pillar exposes a type of market failure that justifies government action if the benefits of the action exceed its costs. Likewise, the exposure of government failure suggests that the government stop or modify its activity, again if the benefits exceed the costs. Economists examined the first two pillars in the late 19th and early 20th centuries. The third pillar toppled only recently.

In 2001, George Akerlof, Joseph Stiglitz, and Michael Spence received the Nobel Prize in economics for their work in the early 1970s on the economics of information, especially the implications of asymmetric information, when some parties to a transaction have more information than others. This represented official confirmation that economists had driven the final stake through the heart of the stylized model of an economy. As we will see below, both market failure and government failure result from the existence of asymmetric information. Whether we need government action, however, is much less clear than with imperfect competition and collective goods. This is due, in part, to the ability of those on the short end of information asymmetries to take actions to lessen the harm to them.

Economists worry that the existence of asymmetric information might affect the efficiency of market processes. In some instances, strong information asymmetries can cause a market not to exist. For a discipline very friendly to market processes, this is a failure, indeed. Consider the market for a bag of money in my possession. I possess almost all the information needed for this transaction. I know exactly how much money is in the bag. You don't. I'm willing to sell it to a high bidder, but I'm not obligated to sell. Would you make a bid? Probably not. I won't sell for an amount lower than the value of the money and any other sale will guarantee a loss to you, the buyer. A market won't exist.

Owners and managers of businesses are concerned about information asymmetries for reasons other than market efficiency. Failure to act when you are on the information "short side" can increase your costs and negatively affect your profit. Businesses spend to reduce information asymmetries caused by the existence of moral hazard, adverse selection, and uncertain product quality. We address these manifestations of asymmetric information in the following.

Moral Hazard

Moral hazard exists when one party to a transaction has an incentive to engage in behavior injurious to the other party AFTER the transaction. We emphasize the word after here, because another manifestation of asymmetric information, adverse selection, stems from behavior BEFORE the transaction.

The money-back breakage guarantee shows a moral hazard. This contract feature induces post-purchase behavior on the part of some buyers that is injurious to the seller of the good. Buyers have an incentive to break the item and get their money back or use the product recklessly, which increases the probability of breakage. Recognizing moral hazard, sellers of this good alter the contract, refusing to pay when they recognize reckless behavior. Or they could increase the price of the product to cover future breakage guarantee claims.

Sellers of life insurance are very aware of moral hazard in their business. If you kill yourself within a specified period, after purchase of a life insurance policy, the company won't pay. They've put an exclusionary suicide clause in the insurance policy. Likewise, if you burn your own house down, the fire insurance company won't pay. They recognize moral hazard in a fire insurance contract and protect themselves from it. Can you imagine the number of "match transformations" that would happen with the bursting of a housing bubble, a large and unsustainable increase in housing prices, without owner-arson clauses in fire insurance policies? Fires would light up the night sky. Because private actions are available to counter these examples of moral hazard, the market failure most likely doesn't require government action, based on the benefits and costs of that action.

Sometimes government actions can be the cause of moral hazard. In many of these cases, the "contract" is harder to see than in a money-back breakage guarantee or a life or fire insurance policy. Federal deposit insurance is an example. The Federal Deposit Insurance Corporation (FDIC), a government agency, sells deposit insurance to banks. The FDIC requires many banks to purchase deposit insurance, and many more choose it voluntarily. A bank with deposit insurance pays a premium and, in return, receives the guarantee that depositors won't lose their bank balances if the bank fails. Deposit insurance creates moral hazard. With deposit insurance, banks worry less about the effects of their failure on members of their community. All the grandmothers, families, small businesses, and children will get their money back if their bank fails. Released from this burden, banks accept more risk and increase the return on the assets they own. This is injurious to the other party, the FDIC, and often the general taxpayer, because of the increased probability of bank failure from riskier bank portfolios. The savings and loan crisis of the 1990s and the aftershocks of the financial crisis in 2007 and 2008 are just two examples. Critics of deposit insurance and the moral hazard it creates make a government failure argument for increased insurance premiums and other incentives to reduce behavior leading to more bank failures.

Pension insurance for corporations, provided by a government agency called the Pension Benefit Guarantee Corporation (PBGC), gives corporations an incentive to underfund their pension plans or even to declare bankruptcy. Pension insurance will pay some of the pensions that their employees would have lost from pension underfunding or bankruptcy.

Private-public corporations, such as the Federal National Mortgage Association (Fannie Mae), which provide a government-insured secondary market for home mortgages, give mortgage lenders an incentive to make mortgage loans to applicants with lower qualifications. This causes more mortgage defaults and foreclosures leading to financial instability.

Finally, the general bailout mentality underlying the Federal Reserve's lender of last resort function, gives large financial institutions an incentive to adopt more risky portfolios, knowing that the Fed will recognize in the next crisis that they are "too big to fail." Financial system stability is a good thing, as are grandmothers' protected savings with deposit insurance and insured pensions of workers. Whether the benefits exceed the costs of such government actions is a question that engenders much economic research and results in rich public policy debates.

Adverse Selection

In contrast with moral hazard, where behavior AFTER an agreement causes problems for the other party, adverse selection involves behavior BEFORE a transaction by the party with more information. The high cost of information makes it difficult for the party with less information to single out offending parties before a transaction. Insurance products commonly contain elements of adverse selection.

Consider auto insurance. Poor drivers, or those who are likely to damage vehicles for other reasons, are more likely to buy collision insurance than are better drivers or those less likely to have accidents. Insurance companies would like to have the information to distinguish between good drivers and poor drivers and to charge the latter higher premiums to cover the higher risk of loss, but this information is costly to obtain. When poor drivers buy more collision insurance than those who might have fewer claims, adverse selection occurs.

Automobile insurers use statistical discrimination to protect themselves from adverse selection. Statistical discrimination attributes to individual members of a group the average characteristics of a group. Because unmarried males under the age of twenty-five have more accidents, on average, than their female counterparts, they pay higher auto insurance premiums. Because people who have speeding tickets and reported accidents have more claims, all drivers with these characteristics pay higher premiums. Because good students, on average, have fewer accidents than poor students, all good students, even bad-driving good students, receive discounts on their policy premiums.

Insurance deductibles are another way auto insurers try to realign incentives caused by adverse selection. A deductible on a policy means the person making the claim must pay some amount, usually $100, $500, or $1,000, depending on the policy. By having "skin in the game," drivers become more cautious or less likely to submit claims, lowering the insurance company's cost.

Health insurance also suffers from adverse selection. An insurance company nightmare occurs when only people who will need or use the insurance buy it, such as those with preexisting conditions. For example, many health insurance policies have maternity coverage for women. If all purchasers of maternity insurance are pregnant, the insurance company cannot insure against the loss. They need a pool of women, some of whom will become pregnant, and some who will not. To remedy this information asymmetry, insurers outlaw preexisting conditions. If a woman has a full-term baby 5 months after purchasing a health insurance policy with maternity coverage, the company won't pay. Many illnesses are also excluded as preexisting conditions.

Preexisting condition clauses in insurance contracts are controversial, so much so that recent U.S. health care legislation, the Affordable Care Act, sometimes referred to as "Obamacare," outlawed them. For this reason, many health economists pointed out that outlawing them would increase the cost of health insurance.

Examples of adverse selection are not limited to the insurance industry. Employers are on the short side of an information asymmetry when confronted with applications from potential employees. Job applicants know their own characteristics better than potential employers do. Those who are overqualified for a position are less likely to apply for it. Adverse selection implies that many candidates for a job opening are unqualified for the position. To redress this imbalance, companies' human resource departments incur costs in the form of interviewing, testing, screening, and checking references of job candidates.

Adverse selection also enables the "lemons" problem when buyers can't determine the quality of a product prior to purchase. Consider the used car market. If higher quality cars are more costly, and buyers can't determine differences in quality, the market will not have price premiums for higher quality. High-quality sellers will face losses and choose to leave the market. This means that only low-quality cars will be sold, which, over time, could lead the market to go out of existence. Behavior by sellers prior to a transaction hurts buyers of used cars. This is adverse selection.

This problem of asymmetric information about product quality leads to another manifestation of seller behavior to deal with it. Sellers of higher quality products attempt to signal in various ways this higher quality to their customers.

Quality Signaling

If businesses with higher quality products cannot provide information about this higher quality to customers, lower quality, lower cost, and lower-priced products will drive them from the market. Warranties are one way for sellers to signal quality to buyers. If a seller stands behind the quality of a product by fixing it free of charge if something goes wrong, that can indicate quality. Advertising is another way. The amount of advertising can indicate high quality. If the advertising is not discounted as misleading, a company that touts the quality of its product might, indeed, have a quality product. I know people, however, who won't go to restaurants that advertise, thinking that advertising stems from low demand, a sign of low quality.

Product endorsements also signal quality. If LeBron James wears these shoes, they must be good. If Phil Mickelson hits this golf ball, it will be good. If John Coltrane played this brand of saxophone, it's a good one.

Signaling is not limited to product markets. College attendance comes not only from a desire for knowledge and skill but also from a credential that will signal to potential employers that a graduate has done what it takes to negotiate the terrain of one institution and, because of this, might be capable of doing the same in another. Many students offered an automatic "A" on the first day of class, would accept the deal and not attempt to learn anything in a course. They pursue a signal, not knowledge. "Dressing for success" signals. A new suit doesn't make one smarter, but it does show that a potential employee can bend to professional norms when it counts.

The Signaling Equilibrium

We can think of markets with imperfect and asymmetric information groping toward a signaling equilibrium over time. The concept is due to Michael Spence, one of the economics Nobel laureates mentioned above. Spence wrote in the context of labor markets, but the analogy to product markets applies. Following Spence, we can think of markets as characterized by repeated cycles in a loop, where buyers have beliefs about the quality of a product that are either confirmed or disconfirmed by incoming data. Based on received signals, buyers formulate their willingness to pay for a product. Based on this willingness to purchase, sellers evaluate the effectiveness of their signaling decisions and revise them accordingly. In turn, buyers observe the relationship between price and seller signals and revise their prior beliefs. Again, paraphrasing Spence, an equilibrium occurs when the components in this cycle regenerate themselves. We can think of a buyer confirming prior beliefs, his or her willingness to pay for a product of given quality remaining the same, and seller signaling behavior and pricing reproducing itself in the next round.

In a signaling equilibrium, we would expect a close relationship between price and signaled attributes used to justify that price. Furthermore, to the extent that the relationship of price to these signals is less than perfect, we would expect the relationship to improve or tighten over time, as buyers and sellers adjust their behavior to information received in the previous period. If signaling equilibria occur, private actions in the marketplace reduce market failure from asymmetric information, reducing the need for government action to correct it.

What are Those Free Drink Coupons Worth?

The Inefficiency of In-Kind Transfers and Black Markets

I'm an economist. I understand the benefit of patient accumulation. It works with money, and it used to work with airline frequent flyer miles. Save 15% of your salary every paycheck and retire a millionaire. Take a few trips a year, maybe a big one abroad, and, in a few years, you accumulate enough miles for a free ticket. But now, finding a frequent flier ticket on some airlines is like finding a political conservative on a college campus. Either no seats are available, or a seat requires twice the number of miles that the original agreement required. I've had a good experience with Alaska Airlines and their loyalty credit card and companion fare. But, once upon a time, the program I liked the most was Southwest Airlines, when they counted trips and not miles.

Back in the day, with Southwest, you didn't accumulate miles. If you flew eight roundtrips, you got a free ticket. Simple. And, as a bonus, when Southwest notified you of your free ticket, you got a booklet of free drink coupons in the mail!

The purpose here is not to extol the virtues of Southwest Airlines but to examine the economics of in-kind transfers, gifts of something other than money. Through gift-giving on Christmas, birthdays, and other holidays, normal people institutionalize in-kind transfers. Only economists recognize the superiority of cash gifts. They always fit and never have to be exchanged. Unlike in-kind gifts, cash gifts are always equivalent, in full, to their cash value.

Personal gift-giving is not the only source of in-kind transfers. An employer might give an employee a free holiday turkey. The government gives poor people free food in the form of food stamps, free medical care, or free housing. And, of course, Southwest Airlines gives frequent flyers free drinks!

What is the value of a free drink coupon? As always, in economics, "It depends." It depends on a person's preferences for alcohol. If I purchase more drinks than the coupons give, the value to me is the drink's cash-equivalent, what I would have to pay for the drink. The free drink frees up purchasing power that I can use on something else, or if I'm being picked up at the airport or using public transportation, maybe another drink.

But what if I'm a recovering alcoholic, a Muslim, a Mormon, or just a general teetotaler? In this case, the free drink coupons are worth less to me, perhaps even worthless. Here, the existence of a market would improve my benefit from an in-kind transfer. These markets are often black markets, ones frowned upon by the giver. After all, the giver must have some reason for giving an in-kind transfer and not cash. We give the poor food stamps, not cocaine or heroin stamps, beer stamps, or tobacco stamps. If one wishes to transform food stamps into contraband items, one must find a buyer in the unofficial black market who wants to buy food stamps at some fraction of the dollar. This is costly and inefficient.

I once flew from Spokane to Salt Lake City, the center of the Mormon Church. I witnessed no underground activity in Southwest drink coupons. Perhaps Mormon frequent flyers give drink coupons to their non-Mormon friends. Of course, they could receive "psychic income" from the moral superiority of throwing them in the garbage upon receipt. If they don't throw them in the trash, however, the possibility exists for mutually beneficial, interfaith exchange. If a broker could just bring Southwest Airlines' frequent-flying Mormons and Irish Catholics together in a drink coupon market, both groups would be better off.

Government in-kind transfers for food, heating, and housing are like free drink coupons. They are inefficient if we want to maximize the well-being of the receiver of the transfer. Their value to the receiver is less than it appears because some recipients of these transfers would buy less of the good if they had cash instead. As my major professor, Charlie Leven, used to say, nothing cures poverty better than money. But we must temper our economic criticism of in-kind transfers and consider the well-being of the giver, as well. Taxpayers feel better if the poor spend their transfers on food, housing, and heat and not on alcohol, tobacco, and drugs. Even economists who dislike paternalism as a matter of professional principle must agree with normal people that the well-being of the in-kind giver warrants consideration in public policy.

Paying for Water with Taxes:

Government Failure in Action

After reading a news account of James Buchanan's 1986 Nobel Prize in Economics, a biologist friend of mine considered abandoning his career with a successful biotechnology company and becoming an economist. He reckoned that only economists could win a Nobel Prize for mere common sense. The news account had said that Buchanan thought people in government organizations were rational maximizers following their own agenda, rather than passive intermediaries between the legislature and its constituents. According to Buchanan, using the government to address market failure would not necessarily lead to a net improvement in human well-being. Government could fail to act in the broad public interest and make things worse. My friend thought this was equivalent to saying that a ball tossed into the air would fall to the ground.

After a defense of the seminal nature of Buchanan's work, I noted that my own work in Western water policy also supported his views. I had been studying Western local water finance, the way we pay for water and water projects, and had found that, in the West, property taxes often accounted for a large proportion of water funding. An economic explanation of this behavior requires a Buchanan-like theory of the local water district. We pay for water with taxes because the water district, not the water user, benefits from it. Let's look at this theory more closely.

Consider a local government water district from Buchanan's perspective. What might be the goal of the district and its employees? Because the water district is not privately owned, profit maximization or shareholder wealth maximization is not the goal. Let's assume that water district managers wish to increase their income, prestige, and power. One common denominator helps the water manager achieve his or her goals, lots of water running through the pipes of the water district. I would guess that salaries of water district managers correlate directly with the amount of water running though their district's pipes. When the manager of the Metropolitan Water District of Los Angeles enters the room at the annual American Water Works Convention, heads turn. The water manager from Troy, Idaho, gets about as much attention as one of the servers at the luncheon. For managers of a local water district, the more water the better.

Unless it wants to pay for water only with taxes, the water district will have to charge its water customers. The district can influence water sales through its water pricing. With a low water price, the district keeps the quantity of water demanded high. At low water prices, people use water for the strangest things, even in the desert: green lawns, swimming pools, hosing off the sidewalk, and evaporative coolers.

The water district can lower the price of water in two ways, pursuit of low-cost supplies, an economically rational policy that develops the cheapest water projects first, or subsidizing the price of water by shifting payment away from water users to other water project beneficiaries and federal, state, and local taxpayers. Districts often choose a combination of these two options. The two options present tradeoffs, as well. For example, low-cost water development from a local project may not allow the shifting of the payment burden to others. The water district then has an incentive to pursue high-cost water subsidized by others. Such is the nature of water development in the western United States.

The water district can also increase the amount of water in the pipes by using nonprice strategies. It can avoid water conservation and substitutes for the district's water. The district can also work the political process to its benefit.

The standard economic justification for government action in a market economy comes from the theory of collective goods. For the most part, water is not a collective good. First, water is rival in consumption. If I turn on my tap for a gallon of water, that gallon is unavailable for you. Likewise, sellers can exclude people from using water if they don't pay. They can turn off their water. Water is easily excludable in exchange. Goods rival in consumption and excludable in exchange are private goods, which can be provided by businesses in the market.

Think what would happen if water users paid the total cost of their water at the tap. With higher water prices they would use less. They would pay more for water, but pay less in taxes, and would be much more careful with their water use. Less water would flow through the pipes and more would flow in streams. Water managers would have lower salaries and less power. We'd save money, have a better environment, and improve the overall efficiency of the economy. Paying for water with taxes is government failure, and Buchanan justifiably won the Nobel Prize for explaining it.

Protectionism:

Government Failure in International Trade

When I lived in Moscow, Idaho, I once visited our local plumbing and heating contractor about a bill. With a big, older house, with lots of plumbing issues, this was a common chore in our household, and it was my turn to deal with it. We always considered a bill from this contractor a suggestion, a point for further negotiation. This time they had charged for something one of their trainees had done incorrectly a year before. Of course, we got an adjustment. Most people like to pay lower prices, not just economists. We shop around, use coupons, and negotiate prices, especially for large, high-priced items. By contrast, when we act collectively through government, we seem to want to pay higher prices. We attempt to protect domestic producers from international competition, and, in the process, raise the prices of the things we buy. Economists call this protectionism. While domestic producers benefit from protectionism, consumers suffer greater losses, so, on net, economic well-being falls. This is government failure.

Like many economics teachers of my generation, I kept a file of newspaper clippings (Yes, cut out of a paper newspaper) organized according to topics I covered in class. I called this collection of files the economics laboratory of the real world. I labeled one of the fattest files "Protectionism." The file contained several articles about U.S. lumber producers complaining that the Canadian government subsidized lumber production. U.S. producers wanted to "level the playing field" by placing a tax, called a tariff, on lumber imported from Canada. Canadians are selling us cheap lumber. Shame on them. Let's pay more for a two-by-four.

Idaho, and five other western states produce all the malting barley in the U.S. We're talking beer here. In the 1990s, the

Clinton administration wanted to allow record levels of barley imports from Canada. The National Association of Barley Growers said that we must stop this. Oh dear, let's pay more for beer.

We produce a lot of wheat in the Northwest and so do our friends north of the 49th parallel. Again, in the 1990s, every year the National Association of Wheat Growers found evidence of nasty Canadians "dumping" wheat in U.S. markets, selling at an extremely low price. Oh no! Wouldn't it be neat to pay more for wheat?

I now live in Washington State, the leading producer of apples in the U.S. While much of Washington's apple crop still goes to the fresh market, we now process more and more apples into apple juice. Growers in other countries also produce apples and apple juice. In April 2000, the U.S. Department of Commerce imposed a "duty," a tax, of 52% on Chinese "dumping" of apple juice concentrate in the U.S. With Chinese exporters on the loose, let's pay more for apple juice.

Every president, Democrat and Republican, from Johnson to Trump and Biden, has placed tariffs or required some form of other restraint on steel imports. President Trump, citing national security, placed a 25% tariff on steel from anywhere other than Canada and Mexico. The Biden Administration continued this policy. Europeans retaliated with tariffs of their own. Presidents Trump and Biden argued for national security, but steel tariffs relate more to the number of electoral votes in Ohio and Pennsylvania than from strategic vulnerability. Let's get real and pay more for steel!

The foundations of protectionism go back to 16th century Europe, when monarchs shared a common economic view, that a nation's wealth stemmed from a favorable balance of trade, selling more abroad than you buy abroad. Export more than you import. This surplus of exports over imports led to the accumulation of gold and other precious metals in the country's coffers. Economists consider this one of the loose collection of beliefs called Mercantilism.

Responding to Mercantilist fervor in 19th century France, M. Frederic Bastiat wrote a satirical petition to the Chamber of Deputies on behalf of the makers of candles, lamps, and other lighting products. Bastiat asked the Chamber to pass a law shuttering all openings through which the sun's rays could penetrate France's dwellings. According to Bastiat, the sun, a foreign rival, provided intolerable competition in the form of very low-cost light. Wouldn't it be fun to block out the sun?

Adam Smith tried to jab a stake through the vampire heart of Mercantilism, in 1776, in his book, *The Wealth of Nations*, where he argued that productivity, not the trade balance, generated a nation's prosperity. Later, David Ricardo twisted that stake with his theory of comparative advantage and nearly every economist since has advocated for free international trade. But protectionism persists.

Economists have demonstrated, with both theory and evidence, that a nation gains from free trade. The costs from protectionist measures, such as tariffs and import quotas, exceed the benefits. In an economic sense, protectionism harms the public interest. Why, then, does protectionism succeed in all forms of government and across the entire political spectrum within governments? Why does it succeed in democracy? The answer lies in the economics of politics.

Suppose companies in another country produce cars that Americans like to drive. Oh, heck, let's just call this economy Japan and get on with it. When Japanese producers make better cars, for the same or lower price, Americans start buying a lot of Hondas and Toyotas. Three U.S. automakers and the United Autoworkers union have a meeting. At the meeting, they agree that Japanese automobiles are killing them, and something must be done about it. A meeting like this about domestic competition could send them to jail for violating antitrust laws. Foreign competition, however, is fair game. The auto producers and union decide to form a lobbying group to contact the president and members of congress, and ask them to restrict Japanese auto imports into the U.S. Because a small number of parties form this alliance, no one can shirk payment for the lobbying, even if they wanted to, which they don't, as they surely will benefit from the restrictions. In Washington, D.C., the president, and members of congress are only too willing to accept political contributions to hear arguments about something they think is important: American jobs, fair trade, and level playing fields.

Just representative democracy in action, you say, political sausage in the making. The other side has an opportunity to state its case. The JADA, the Japanese Automobile Drivers of America, must have lobbyists, too. But they don't, because the benefits of free trade in automobiles are diffused among millions of Americans who own Japanese cars. No JADA exists. The free rider problem makes the cost of organizing such a group prohibitive. No Honda or Toyota driver would take time out of a busy day to attend an organizational meeting. As an organizer, your only hope would be direct mail. Imagine receiving a request for a contribution to JADA. Would you rush to find your checkbook? No. It's just another worthy cause we are willing to let someone else pay for.

Opponents' organizing difficulties allow protectionism to succeed. Diffuse benefits and localized costs doom any policy proposal in representative democracy. Economists might share a normal person's view that democracy is a good political system, considering the alternatives. Economists differ from normal people, however, when they recognize that democracy is NOT a good economic system. I am more likely to go to my plumbing contractor to lower my bill than I am to contribute to an organization that would reduce my Japanese automobile prices. Because of higher organizing costs caused by the free-rider problem, a democracy will devote too many resources to limiting foreign competition through protectionism, even when the costs exceed the benefits.

Choosing a Bruise Over a Puncture Wound:

Vouchers and the Collective Choice Dilemma

A large part of economics is about choices, and how we might improve human well-being with institutions and economic systems that allow for good ones. For economists, choices are fun. If we have a choice, we have a good chance of making the right one. Normal people like to make choices among good alternatives. College professors can test this theory any nice spring day when attendance is down in their afternoon classes. But normal people don't like choosing among bad alternatives. In normal discourse, we even have a word for it, dilemma. Being on the "horns of a dilemma" means that any choice results in a bad outcome. Choosing something less bad is not much fun.

We often face a normative economic dilemma when confronted with market failure from collective goods. Consider education, for example. Much of the benefit of education accrues to the educated person, both in terms of lifetime income and better quality of life. But an individual's education also conveys benefits to others, as well. People choose their level of education to maximize their personal benefit, not the collective external benefit, leaving the latter up to others. People buy too little education. If we leave the level of education to market decisions, the market failure horn of the dilemma gores us.

But wait, what about the government? If people choose to buy too little education, we can use government taxation to coerce them to pay for more, using the standard economic justification for government action to counter the market failure from collective goods. But government legislators and bureaucrats don't all ride in to save the day wearing white hats astride white horses. I learned this first-hand in the early 1980s when consulting for the U.S. Fish and Wildlife Service, helping them estimate the nonmarket value of fishing and hunting. One day, as we were returning from lunch, I noticed some large printers stored in a corner of one of the offices. I asked a Fish and Wildlife staffer about them. He told me they were plotters that could print graphs in color, fancy equipment in the early eighties. I asked what they used them for. He said they didn't use them at all. They had some "end of year money" they needed to spend in a hurry, and this was all they could produce quickly. No rational bureaucrat returns unused budget to the legislature at the end of a year. Rather, a government agency spends the surplus funds, so the legislature won't reduce their budget in the next legislative session. Other examples of government failure include, among others, budget or staff maximization by mission-oriented agencies, overly zealous application and enforcement of regulations, government production of private (not collective) goods, and general inefficiency caused by weak incentives to control costs. Calling on the government to solve market failure risks goring by the other horn of the normative economic dilemma, government failure.

What do we do when faced with a choice between two bad outcomes, market failure or government failure? Unlike normal people, we economists enjoy a good dilemma now and then, and wouldn't avoid the responsibility of choosing the least-worst puncture wound. But we really enjoy dulling the horns of the dilemma a little bit. A bruise beats a puncture wound any day. We can dull the horns of the collective choice dilemma by using voucher systems.

With a voucher system, we attempt to utilize the best abilities of the market AND the government. We use the government to provide increased amounts of the collective good through the coercive power of taxation, but we don't allow the government to use tax revenue to produce the good. Instead, we give consumers of the collective good a voucher they can spend in the private marketplace. This increased demand calls forth more production and we solve, or at least address, the collective goods problem of too little production and consumption.

Here, we have the best of both worlds. Governments excel at using taxes to force people to pay, but governments fail as producers of goods and services. Dollar votes in the marketplace trump the ballot box and public hearings in giving people what they want for their money. For private producers to stay in business, they must satisfy consumer preferences, control costs, try new ideas, and innovate.

Let's look at a few examples of voucher systems. Knowledge of adequate housing for the poor is a collective good. We can use economic arguments to justify government involvement in housing the poor. But should we allow the government to use tax revenue to produce public housing? The history of public housing in the U.S. is not a pretty sight, literally and in a policy sense. A voucher system would take the resources raised through taxation and give vouchers to the poor to buy housing in the market.

Consider health care. Suppose we decide the external benefit of improved health in a country justifies government involvement in health care. We have two main alternatives, government production with government doctors and government hospitals, or government health insurance. The voucher alternative would use resources raised through taxation to give people vouchers to buy the health care of their choice and buy their own health insurance.

The most controversial current example of using vouchers instead of government production is in education. Government production overwhelmingly characterizes the current approach to education in the U.S. States and local school districts collect taxes, then use these resources to build and run government schools. With a voucher system, the government still forces people to pay for education whether they want to or not, but it uses the resources to give vouchers to parents of school children that they can spend in the marketplace at the school of their choice. Demand for education increases, and we address the collective goods problem. But at the same time, we harness the power of the marketplace to innovate, provide variety, and control costs.

Voucher systems become controversial when offered as alternatives to existing government production. Valid arguments exist on both sides of the issue. Voucher systems in education substitute parental choice for school board choice. Parents might not make the best decisions for their children. But do monopoly school boards make better decisions? No perfect solution to the collective goods problem exists. But economists offer voucher systems as a means of dulling the horns of this collective choice dilemma. With vouchers we'll be bumped, not gored. To an economist, a bruise beats a puncture wound any day.

Part Seven

Macroeconomics: Definitions and Issues

Introduction

In Part Seven, we step away from issues about markets and the behavior of people in them, material referred to as microeconomics. We now turn to macroeconomics, where the prefix, meaning large, applies to the entire economy. Micro, meaning small, applies to parts or pieces of the economy. For example, in microeconomics, we study prices in particular markets. In macroeconomics, we study the average of all prices in the economy. In microeconomics, we look at the output of an individual business and in macroeconomics, the output of the entire economy. Through the economic vignettes in Part Seven, we define and explain important macroeconomic concepts: Gross Domestic Product (GDP), economic growth, unemployment, employment, the labor force, inflation, deflation, recession, depression, and the miracle of productivity growth.

"Why Macroeconomics?" introduces the idea of aggregation. Economists define and measure macroeconomic aggregates because people have an interest in them. We want to know how well a city, a region, or an entire economy performs, and if these geographical aggregations perform poorly whether the government can do something to improve things.

In "Adding Apples and Oranges…," economists violate the standard norm by adding these two fruits together to create Gross Domestic Product (GDP). To do this, we use a monetary unit, like the dollar, as a common denominator. If the value of this common denominator changes over time, however, our measure of national output becomes problematic, one of many reasons GDP is a poor measure of national well-being.

In "Lawn Mowing, Burglar Alarms, Whales, Drugs, and Old Raincoats…," we see, in more detail, the shortcomings of GDP as a measure of national well-being. Even though all economists know these shortcomings, we tend to ignore them and worship at the altar of rising GDP.

The next vignette addresses the tricky definitions of employment, unemployment, and the labor force. Although I have spent much of my life not working, I've never been unemployed. My lifetime employment history and macroeconomic labor market definitions explain this paradox in "The U.S. Department of Labor and Me..."

My short and unspectacular basketball career provides the context for the next vignette in this part, "Inflation and the Shrinking Money Ruler." Just as my basketball ability would not improve if I became taller, by redefining a foot as nine inches, neither does the output of the economy increase when inflation shrinks the purchasing power of money.

Even a little knowledge of economics can help you in your everyday life. In "Inflation and the Charitable Family Pawnshop...," my brother-in-law buys a Martin D-21 guitar in 1964, sells it to me in the mid-1970s, and I sell it to his son in 1993. With the use of a price index, we were able to complete these transactions, preserve familial economic justice, and improve overall musical performance of our extended family at the same time.

"Ugly Truths About Inflation," reveals flaws in common measures of the average price level, especially the Consumer Price Index (CPI). By measuring inflation incorrectly, we enact government economic policy outside the democratic political process.

My grandfather trained as a banker, but the crisis of bank failures in the Great Depression drove him from the banking industry. In "Mr. Kinneberg, Could You Please Get Me My Money...," we examine the Great Depression and other recessions and how the use of deposit insurance, fiscal policy, and monetary policy have helped create more stable macroeconomic performance over time. If Grandpa were a young banker today, he might have retired as one.

We will explore discretionary, expansionary fiscal policy in more depth in Part Eight, but we define one of its results in this part. In "Just Charge It: The Federal Deficit and Debt," we ask whether federal debt is a burden on future generations. Of course, like so many answers in economics, "It depends."

The final vignette in this part examines the recipe for a rising material standard of living. In "Living the American Dream...," the economic lives of my parents, especially my father's, show the miracle of productivity growth. Raised on a farm in Nebraska in the Great Depression, Dad left school after the eighth grade, but luckily, as a working man in the 1950s and 1960s, the miracle of productivity growth allowed him, my mom, and me to live the American dream.

Why Macroeconomics?

Economists dichotomize their discipline into a micro (small) and a macro (large) component. I once had a libertarian colleague, let's call him Joe, who thought that the only true economics was microeconomics. And when he said microeconomics, he meant the economics of individual choice aided and coordinated by markets. He allowed into the discipline the study of voluntary associations of individuals, such as businesses, which make up the supply side of the supply and demand model. Joe thought the study of markets and market economies was more than enough to keep economists and economics students occupied. To Joe, everything else, especially macroeconomics, is a thinly veiled attempt to mess up a market economy with unnecessary tinkering and government spending and taxation. I have some sympathy for Joe's view, but I also have less libertarian fire in my belly than he does, and like most mainstream economists, believe in the legitimacy of macroeconomics as economics, not merely disguised politics.

Macroeconomics' legitimacy stems from our concern about meaningful aggregation. We identify with cities, states, regions, and national economies, not just Fred across the street and decisions made by a local auto mechanic. We want to know how well an economy performs, and whether a government can do something if it struggles.

In microeconomics, we might have questions about resources used by a business, at a specific place, producing a single product, like the number of workers in the Bennett Lumber mill in the small town of Princeton, Idaho. Why, over time, has the Bennett Mill substituted computers and other forms of capital for labor, making a sawmill a much lonelier place than it used to be? In macroeconomics, we care not for such resource minutiae. Rather, we define, measure, and track over time something called the civilian noninstitutionalized labor force, all people working or looking for work in the entire economy. We also measure the unemployment rate, the percentage of the labor force unemployed.

Likewise, in macroeconomics, we have little interest in the annual output of the Bennett Lumber mill, or even the total production of lumber in the U.S. in a year, or the total production of any single product. Rather, in macroeconomics, we define, measure, and track over time the total output of the economy. For example, we define and measure Gross Domestic Product (GDP). We'll devote more time to this later, but we can recognize now that a falling GDP for a long period would lead economists and normal people alike to wonder why GDP is falling, and whether the government can do something to arrest this decline.

In microeconomics, we might follow the price of lumber in a lumber market, say in the Pacific Northwest. What effect does Canadian lumber imports, or U.S. endangered species policy, or wilderness preservation have on the price of lumber? In macroeconomics, however, we would not study the price of lumber, but rather the average of all prices in an economy. You may have heard of the consumer price index (CPI), the average price level of consumer goods. By calculating the percent change in this and other price indexes, economists measure the rate of inflation. High inflation leads us to question its causes and whether the government might do something to lower the inflation rate.

Adding Apples and Oranges:

Keeping Score with Gross Domestic Product

At this very moment at our house, we have three apples, two oranges, four bananas, and an overripe pear in the fruit basket on our countertop. You might have something similar. Go look in your fruit basket. What's in it? Like we do, you have some of this, so many of that, and you could surely provide a list of contents like I did. But what if I say that I don't want a list of what's in your fruit basket, I want to know the total amount in the basket. Now, you might have a problem because we all know that "you cannot add apples and oranges," let alone apples, oranges, bananas, and an overripe pear.

You could address this problem by creating a more general category to which all contents of the basket belong, say fruit. In our basket, we have ten pieces of fruit. Alternatively, you could weigh the contents of the basket, and tell me how many pounds of fruit you have, a useful bit of information if you were carrying the fruit somewhere, say in a backpack.

Now, as a busybody social scientist, suppose I ask you what you have in your fruit basket, your refrigerator, and your closet. After sufficient time to check your household inventory, you could produce a list again. Suppose I again say I don't want a list. Could you summarize it for me? Can you see that the total number of items is not a very satisfactory answer? Instead of a tight and meaningful category like fruit, we have fruit, meat, cheese, vegetables, beer, butter, margarine, jam, and tonic water. Okay, because beer is food, we could summarize that we have some number, some weight, or some calories of food in the fridge. Not totally satisfactory, but it might do. But now we go to the closet. How do we combine food with shirts, shoes, pants, skirts, shorts, and blouses?

The list of things produced annually in the U.S. economy is quite a bit longer than our household inventory, but, nonetheless, we might want to know how much we produced in the U.S. economy last year, how much we're producing this year, and, perhaps, what we expect to produce in the future. People produce this stuff, and most people get their income from employment. The higher the production, the higher the employment in an economy. But the real reason we measure the amount of production is that most economists are guys, and guys like to keep score. We like to know if we are producing more from year to year and how our economy compares to others in that respect.

Fortunately, in a market economy like ours, we have prices for goods and services that make adding apples and oranges easier. We simply add the value of the goods and services together. The most added-together economic magnitude in any economy is something called gross domestic product (GDP), the market value of all final goods and services produced in an economy in a given time period, usually a year. GDP and its simple definition contain many tricky parts that highlight the perils of measuring national output.

Let's start with the first word in GDP, gross. It doesn't mean that it's big (which it is), or in the common vernacular, boorish or crude. The term gross means that some of the stuff we produce in a year replaces worn-out machines, assembly lines, buildings, and trucks. Yes, some GDP merely helps us keep up with the onslaught of mold, rust, and decay. If we subtract the value of this maintenance production, we are left with a net domestic product. I suggest you forget about this distinction and leave it to professional economists to worry about.

The next word, domestic, is a recent substitution in the U.S. Perhaps you've heard of Gross National Product, a concept we reported for years until we finally came around to what the rest of the world does. Domestic product, in contrast with national product, counts the value of goods and services produced within the borders of a country, regardless of the nationality of the producers. A country's citizens don't have to produce the goods and services or own the resources that produce them. The output of a Japanese company producing in the U.S., using Japanese workers who send their paychecks home to Tokyo, is counted as U.S. GDP. On the other hand, if I take a leave from my university and go teach in Canada for a year, the value of my teaching output would be part of Canadian GDP.

GNP counts things differently, the value of production from a country's resources wherever the production takes place. The Japanese production mentioned above contributes to Japan's GNP and our GDP, and my teaching in Canada does the same for U.S. GNP and Canadian GDP. Again, if you are confused, don't worry about it, unless you lack cocktail party material to make you look smart.

The telling third word in GDP, production, reveals that we don't count the value we get from using stuff produced in the past. This, alone, shows that GDP cannot be a measure of national well-being. Go to your closet. You probably have an old raincoat or parka hanging there. Economists have many of them. Go to your garage. Was your car produced this year? If not, it's not part of GDP. This is not a problem unless we make GDP a measure of national well-being (which we often do).

In the definition of GDP, we see the word "final." This means that we add up the value of goods and services at their final point of sale. We do this to avoid counting the production of something more than once. The value of a loaf of bread sold in the supermarket is in GDP. We don't count the value of the wheat, the value of the flour (which contains the value of the wheat), and the value of the bread (which contains the value of the wheat and the value of the flour) separately. We count these values at the point of final sale.

Because we measure the economy's production over a particular time period, GDP is a *flow* measure. It has a time dimension, like cubic feet per second and miles per hour. GDP is not a national inventory of goods we have around, only the new ones we produce in the current year.

Finally, while measuring the market value of production allows us to add apples and oranges, using monetary magnitudes introduces its own set of problems. A simple example illustrates the point. Suppose from one year to the next, we produce the same amount of stuff in the economy, but the price of everything rises ten percent. GDP rises by ten percent. Is this a good way of keeping score? Obviously not. We have not produced any more stuff, but our measure of production, GDP, has risen. We have not allowed for the shrinking of our common denominator, the dollar, the fall in its purchasing power, something we call inflation, a topic we'll discuss later in the book.

Lawn Mowing, Burglar Alarms, Whales, Drugs, and Old Raincoats:

GDP and Economic Well-Being

For twenty-four years, we lived on Paradise Ridge, southeast of Moscow, Idaho. We had a lot of lawn at our house, about an acre of irregular, hilly terrain punctuated with outbuildings, large trees, shrubs, flower beds, and other obstacles, not the lawn for a riding mower. Green and mowed, our grounds looked like a miniature Manito Park, Spokane's magnificent South Hill landmark. I ignored for years the question, why would anyone want to maintain a miniature Manito Park around his or her house.

I did all the mowing at our house, with a fleet of three self-propelled, walk-behind mowers. If all went well, I could mow all parts of the lawn in about 4 hours. In the spring and early summer, when the grass grew an inch and a half a day, I mowed almost every day.

Once, in a rare moment of standard economic rationality, Solveig and I contracted for a weekly lawn mowing service. It was her idea, nurtured by an intuitive understanding of the law of comparative advantage. If I didn't mow, I could spend 4-5 hours a week doing something more productive. I could specialize in economics or some other home improvement project and pay someone else to mow our lawn. But to apply the law of comparative advantage properly, we must consider nonmarket benefits, as well as monetary compensation.

I loved mowing. It's like vacuuming, another of my household duties. I really enjoyed doing it. There's no ambiguity in mowing, no journal editor rejecting what you thought to be your best work, no student complaining about a grade, no academic administrator failing to value your good teaching, and no consulting client wanting the moon yesterday for a limited budget. The grass was long. I mowed it. It looked great. End of story. Simplicity and bliss.

When we hired the lawn service, we paid for it by saving less. Because it involved a market transaction, the U.S. GDP went up that summer by the amount of our payments to the mowing company, even though no more lawn was mowed. When I mow my own lawn, cash registers don't ring, and the U.S. Bureau of Economic Analysis doesn't count my own lawn mowing in GDP. When we ignore the value of home production, GDP becomes a poor measure of economic well-being.

Consider a hypothetical example. Suppose, in one instance, my neighbor and I each mow our own lawns. Then, one day, we pay each other to mow each other's lawns. GDP is higher in the second case because we use market transactions. Remember that GDP is the total market value of all goods and services produced in a country in a year. When my neighbor and I hire each other for lawn mowing, we mow the same amount of grass, but GDP rises.

GDP rose in the last several decades partly because previous home production shifted to the marketplace, in the form of day-care, fast-food meals, beauty care, yard care, and house cleaning. With more and more market labor by household members, GDP rises, but we never subtract off the value of the home production that we lose when we shift lawn mowing, child-care, food preparation, and house cleaning to the marketplace. This overstates the rise in GDP. In countries with less specialization and fewer market transactions, home production remains a large part of economic activity. Ignoring it dramatically understates economic well-being.

In measuring GDP, we also ignore the composition of spending in the economy. However, all types of spending are not equal in terms of economic well-being. A peaceful, law-abiding, and harmonious economy, where we produce and consume ballet, theater, sports events, concerts, housing, food, and clothing, can have the same GDP as one where we spend on burglar alarms, handguns, divorce lawyers, air purifiers, and water filters. "Defensive expenditures" to protect us from crime, social disharmony, and air and water pollution are part of GDP, but if we spend on those things, we can't spend as much on recreation and the arts.

Likewise, we don't subtract nonmarket collective bads from GDP, nor do we add in the value of nonmarket collective goods. Suppose we hunt whales to extinction for the marketable goods we obtain from them. GDP goes up from the sale of these commodities, but the value of knowing that whales exist, a collective good, falls dramatically. We don't subtract this loss of "existence value" from GDP.

We undercount the value of leisure itself in GDP. If we work more, our income and spending will rise, and because of it so does GDP. We produce and consume more stuff, but the value of leisure activities falls. We don't subtract the value of reduced leisure activities from GDP. As more members of households enter the workforce, less household leisure exists, home production falls, but GDP rises.

We don't include the underground economy and illegal activities in GDP. As gambling, prostitution, and drugs move more to the surface of an economy, up from the underground, GDP rises. But these activities have always been with us and have provided well-being to people for millennia. But if these activities are outside the formal market, they're not part of GDP. GDP understates economic well-being because of these uncounted, underground activities.

Finally, because GDP is a flow measure, we count only the value of new goods and services produced in a year. Except for an adjustment for owner-occupied housing, GDP measurement ignores the value of service flows from previously produced assets. I have a raincoat that must be ten years old. It provides a valuable service year after year but was included in GDP ten years ago. Likewise, except for gas, oil, and maintenance, my 1997 Subaru Legacy is phantom wealth when it comes to GDP. My Subaru's transportation services, incredibly valuable to me, are not counted in GDP.

Economists are a bit inconsistent in their attitudes and behaviors about GDP as a measure of economic well-being. On the one hand, any economist recognizes the shortcomings in measurement described above and knows that total spending in an economy is a flawed measure of economic well-being. On the other hand, we wait anxiously for quarterly GDP numbers and act as if GDP growth is a good measure of economic health.

The social indicators movement, for lack of a better term, has been around intellectually for some time. In 1995, an organization called Redefining Progress started to compute a genuine progress indicator (GPI) as an alternative to GDP. They asked the question, "If the GDP is up, why is America down?"

Following the lead of Nobel Laureates James Tobin and William Nordhaus and their work on the Measure of Economic Welfare (MEW), economists were some of the main signatories in this 1995 call for better measures of economic progress. Perhaps this healthy effort will change the way the U.S. Bureau of Economic Analysis will measure economic output in the future. Perhaps they will develop additional indicators that will include our lawn mowing, knowledge of whales, less crime, cleaner air and water, illegal activities, and use of old raincoats and cars as part of the nation's output.

The U.S. Department of Labor and Me:

Employment, Unemployment, and the Labor Force

My first paid job was picking cherries for my eighth-grade basketball coach, Wes Newbill. I remember he called me Yogi, after Yogi Berra. Coach Newbill said he'd heard the real Yogi say that he was too plump to jump. After seeing me on the court, Coach applied the moniker to me, as well. However, I was lean enough to strap on a bucket, climb a 16 ft. ladder, and pick cherries in the Newbill orchard. In the 1960s, in the Wenatchee Valley, many people had small-scale orchards, what might be called today a "side hustle." Not yet sixteen, Dad had to drive me to the orchard. According to the U.S. Department of Labor, I wasn't employed. You must attain the age of sixteen to be part of the labor force, those either employed or unemployed.

I made a nickel per pound picking cherries, good money in those days, even though the work was hard. I've worked hard many times in my life, thinning and picking apples, picking peaches, and weeding around apple trees, but the hardest I've ever worked was in graduate school, studying for my Ph.D. in economics. I put in sixty or seventy hours per week. According to the U.S. Department of Labor, I wasn't working. College students are not part of the labor force unless they have another paid job while in school. My parents always discouraged me from getting a paid job during school. School WAS my job. The U.S. Labor Department didn't agree.

In the late 1960s, I played football as an undergraduate at Pacific Lutheran University (PLU) in Tacoma, Washington. This was before PLU became a national small school powerhouse under Coach Frosty Westering. They won four NAIA or NCAA Division 3 national championships under Coach Westering. We were not that good, but we tied for the conference championship my senior year. In my sophomore year, in a losing effort against California Lutheran, I intercepted a pass and ran it back sixty-seven yards for a touchdown. A few plays later, I tore a cartilage and stretched ligaments in my knee. After limping through my junior year, I had surgery and had a decent senior year. Then, after my birthday, I came up number eight in the first U.S. draft lottery; I was about to have my first full-time job, most likely in the army in Vietnam. I failed my draft physical because of my damaged knee and didn't have to work for Uncle Sam in that "conflict overseas." Even if I had gone into the army, however, the U.S. Department of Labor would not have considered me employed. According to the Labor Department, only civilians make up the labor force.

Once I became a university professor, I still worked hard, but not as hard as I did in graduate school. I had a flexible schedule and managed to include a lot of leisure in my life. I spent a lot of time not working, especially in the summer "at the lake." Even though I spent much time not working in my life, I was never unemployed. To be unemployed, you must not work AND look for a job. Many people aren't working, but only some of them are unemployed. If you are not working and not looking for work, you are not in the labor force, neither employed nor unemployed.

Macroeconomics contains many concepts related to the labor market. The labor force is comprised of the total number of people in an economy over the age of sixteen, not in the military, who are fortunate enough to be out of jail or mental institutions, and who are employed or looking for work. You don't have to work much to be employed if you receive pay. If you would like to work more, or at a higher wage, you are considered under-employed, but still employed and part of the "civilian, noninstitutionalized labor force."

We monitor the labor force in an economy because, if the labor force grows, the economy likely grows. Population growth leads to labor force growth, if a constant percentage of the population remains in the labor force. As population growth has slowed in most developed countries, because women are having fewer children in their lifetimes, growth in the labor force has declined. Recently, in the U.S., because of the aging "Baby

Boom" generation and work choices related to the Covid 19 pandemic, the percentage of the population in the labor force, the labor force participation rate, has fallen, as well. Many economists think this shrinking labor force participation will lead to lower economic growth and lower rates of return in the stock market in the future. Time will tell.

If we divide the number of unemployed people by the number in the labor force and convert it to a percentage, we get one of the most important macroeconomic numbers, the unemployment rate. This number has ranged from about 3% to 25% in the U.S. economy since 1933. Explaining this variation and figuring out what we can do to keep the unemployment rate low occupies much of economists' effort in macroeconomics.

Inflation and the Shrinking Money Ruler

My height measures a little under 6-1. I played basketball in high school way back when basketball shorts were still short. I was just okay as a high school player. I wasn't a particularly good shooter, but I shot a lot, so I averaged about 11-12 points a game in my senior year. I couldn't jump very high either, but I was stocky, so I could get a few rebounds if I got in position. For me basketball was just something to do between football and baseball.

Now suppose I had been 8-1 instead of 6-1. I would have been a much better player and potentially a professional player. How can a person 6-1 become 8-1? Simple. Just reduce the length of a foot by one-fourth, from twelve inches to nine inches. I immediately become very tall. Should I do this, contact an agent, and start practicing foul shots? Of course not. I'm not really eight feet tall with the new 9-inch ruler, because a foot is really twelve inches. And besides, if I get taller with the shorter ruler, so does everyone else, and my relative height stays the same.

When an economy experiences inflation, the money ruler shrinks. The average prices in the economy rise. We measure this average price level in several ways, but commonly with the Consumer Price Index (CPI). When the CPI rises, the value of the economy's annual output (GDP) goes up, even if we are not producing more. The "ruler" that we use to measure production has changed. I'm not taller with a shorter ruler, and an economy doesn't produce more just because prices rise on average. When the average price level rises, a dollar will buy less than it did before. The dollar's purchasing power has shrunk. We can think of inflation as a rise in the average price level or as a decline in the purchasing power of money.

A shrinking dollar is not the same as a shorter foot. In the latter, we kept the inch as the real unit of height and just made a foot nine inches. With money, this doesn't happen. Even with inflation, a dollar is still one hundred pennies, ten dimes, or four quarters. I often hear normal people who have experienced inflation say something like, "Today's dollar is only worth about 25 cents." When I hear this, I always offer to buy every dollar they have for a quarter. A dollar is still worth four quarters, but it won't buy as much as it used to.

Because we usually have inflation in the U.S. economy, the purchasing power of the dollar falls over time. To get a real picture of what is happening to GDP, we must correct for the fall in the dollar's purchasing power. In doing this, economists for once use a helpful term, Real GDP, which is GDP adjusted to take account of the shrinking money ruler.

Inflation and the Charitable Family Pawn Shop

In the mid-1970s, I bought a Martin D 21 guitar from Bob, my brother-in-law. In 1993, I sold it to his son, Scott, for the same price, adjusted for inflation. Neither of these were ordinary transactions. As participants in both transactions were members of the same extended family, justice, not efficiency, was the order of the day.

Martin guitars are like North Face tents, Selmer saxophones, and Titleist golf balls. The pros use them. They are quality products, and not cheap. Jimmy Buffett played a Martin, as did Eric Clapton, and Joan Baez. Bob bought his Martin for $256 in Seattle in 1964, on the way to his summer folk singer gig at Rosario Resort in the San Juan Islands. Bob, a fine musician, sang under Maurice Skones in the Pacific Lutheran University Choir of the West in the early sixties and did tenor solo work in Spokane for years. Once, Bob and I were with about ten others in a yurt high in the Wallowa Mountains on a guided cross-country ski trip with newlyweds in the group. Bob, as usual, was cold. As we passed around a few bottles of wine, I said, "Bob, how about a few bars of *My Romance* for the kids?" After a three-second hesitation, he cleared his throat discreetly and nailed a tight *a cappella* version of the entire song.

In the mid-1970s, Bob's musical interests had changed. He wanted a new classical guitar, which cost $342, and he didn't have the dough. He wanted to sell the Martin. I begged him not to do it. At this time, I was making a feeble attempt at guitar playing and had some extra cash. Bob sold me the Martin for $342, less than its market value at the time. In turn, I agreed to a no-sell clause. I wouldn't sell the Martin. He could borrow it at any time and buy it back whenever he wanted. I would take my interest on the loan in kind, playing better versions of *My*

Creole Belle and *On the Banks of the Ohio*. This was the first time I had served as a charitable family pawn shop. Many families have them from time to time.

As the years passed and my interests turned away from the guitar, the Martin gathered dust in my closet. Bob's son, Scott, had developed into quite a good guitar player, soon outperforming his modest beginning instrument. He wanted to buy the Martin. Bob thought it was a good idea. I did too. In 1993 I sold it to Scott for $950. Whoa! you say. Where is the justice in that? I paid $342 for the Martin and sold it for $950. Looks like pawn shop profit, not family justice. That is, until you understand inflation and the effect it has on the purchasing power of money.

Between the mid-70s and 1993 we had inflation in the U.S. Inflation is a rise in the average of all prices in the economy. During periods of inflation, a given amount of money buys fewer goods and services than it did before. The purchasing power of money falls during inflation. Whenever economists compare dollar values at different points in time, they check for any change in the average of prices between the two time periods. If so, they correct for this change in the purchasing power of the dollar.

Because of the inflation when I "owned" the Martin, the purchasing power of a dollar had fallen. It would take much more than $342 in 1993 to buy a comparable shopping cart full of hamburger, milk, beer, shirts, pants, and Swiss chard. Family justice dictated that I sell the Martin back to Scott at what I had paid originally, but $342 would understate the price of the guitar in 1993 dollars. We needed to inflate the price of the Martin to get a better estimate of its cost.

The government—specifically the Bureau of Labor Statistics—has something called the consumer price index (CPI) that we can use to measure the rise in the average price level or the decline in the purchasing power of money over time. By using these numbers, we were able to convert $342 to its equivalent purchasing power in 1993. This is where the price of $950 came from. If the government has measured inflation correctly, Scott gave up the equivalent of the same shopping basket of stuff in 1993 that I paid for the guitar many years earlier.

We preserved family contracts and justice. Bob's still playing his classical guitar. I played alto saxophone in the Hog Heaven Big Band for years, and the Martin is still in the family because of the charitable family pawn shop and knowledge of what inflation does to the purchasing power of money.

Ugly Truths About Inflation

Unless you're a self-sufficient hermit living off the grid on a secluded Inland Northwest ridgetop, you probably think about inflation these days. You've seen gas prices rise to well over $3.50 a gallon. You note that a hundred bucks doesn't put as much in a shopping cart as it used to. And if you read the newspaper or listen to the evening news, you hear that inflation affects interest rates, the stock market, and Grandma's social security check. But many myths and misunderstandings about inflation exist in the minds of normal people. I'll try to eliminate some of these in the following and deliver some ugly truths about inflation.

First, a rise in the price of one good or service is not evidence of inflation. Inflation occurs when the average of all prices in the economy rises. Deflation, rarer in modern economies, occurs when the average falls. Most of us see rising prices easier than falling ones. Gas and food prices make the news, but we take for granted the enormous decline in the price of a computer. Because some prices rise and some fall, and because they rise and fall by different amounts, we must average the price changes to determine the rate of inflation.

When economists at government agencies calculate the inflation rate, they average together the different increases and decreases in prices, but they don't perform a simple average. Rather, they give more weight to items that are more important in a consumer's budget. They give more weight to a change in the price of housing and food than they do to a change in the price of entertainment goods because most of us spend more on housing and food than we do on entertainment. But here is a fundamental problem in measuring the rate of inflation. Because every consumer has a different spending pattern, everyone experiences a different rate of inflation. We read about THE inflation rate, but there's no such thing!

The most common estimate of inflation comes from a price index created by the Bureau of Labor Statistics (BLS), a federal agency within the U.S. Department of Labor. You've probably heard of it—the Consumer Price Index, or CPI for short. But did you know that CPI inflation applies only to the average urban worker? The term average here means average spending patterns and average price changes for each of the goods and services in each expenditure category. A retired person living in a rural area has a different spending pattern and faces different price changes than the average urban worker. CPI inflation only approximates your inflation, and the more your spending differs from that of an average urban worker, the worse the approximation becomes.

And this is not the only ugly truth about CPI inflation. We also measure it incorrectly, with a systematic bias that overstates the rate of inflation. While people at the BLS work hard to correct deficiencies in inflation measurement, economists know that they overstate inflation by as much as 1% per year, maybe more. They fail to account adequately for the change in the quality of goods and services. They fail to account for consumers buying fewer of the goods and services with the steepest price increases, thereby lessening the effect of price increases. They don't incorporate new products in the index fast enough, so they miss the initial price decline as new products move through their life cycle. And finally, the BLS underestimates the American consumer's tendency to switch to discount outlets when they become available.

The overstatement of CPI inflation is such that the Federal Reserve System doesn't even use the number. They prefer something called the personal consumption expenditure (PCE) deflator calculated by the Department of Commerce. The information conveyed by different measures of inflation is no small matter. Over the four decades, from 1980 to 2020, the CPI says that the average price level rose 232%. The PCE shows a much smaller 170% increase.

If the measure of CPI inflation is so bad, why do we use it? We adjust many wage contracts with cost-of-living adjustments related to the change in the CPI. We bump up grandma and grandpa's social security checks according to CPI inflation. We adjust the standard deduction and federal tax brackets with this inaccurate measure of inflation. We don't fix it because the politics are a little nasty for incumbent members of Congress. A lower inflation rate means lower social security increases and higher taxes. Not many politicians want to hit the campaign trail with a platform of being mean to Grandma and raising their constituents' taxes. So, we study the problem and do nothing.

Let's end with a truth about inflation that might be less ugly, but no less misunderstood. This one applies to inflation no matter how it's measured. Contrary to popular belief, many are better off with inflation, especially if it rises unexpectedly. These are folks who have debt at a fixed interest rate. If you have a large mortgage at a fixed rate, or consolidated student loans at a fixed rate, and if you can count on your wage or salary keeping up with inflation, which it has historically on average, inflation is the best thing that can happen to you. Every month inflation eats away the real value of your mortgage or student loan balance by a decline in the purchasing power of money. Month after month you must work fewer hours to make a mortgage or student loan payment. Now that's a good deal. Unless, of course, you are a lender, where the reverse holds. To protect against inflation, lenders have been eager to offer variable interest rate loans. Because interest rates rise with inflation, adjustable-rate mortgages and student loan balances don't benefit from it, only those with fixed rates. Some gain, some lose from inflation. Inflation redistributes wealth and income in a sneaky way. Now that's ugly.

"Mr. Kinneberg, could you please get me my money?"

Remembering the Bad Times of Recession or Depression

When I was a kid, my Grandpa Kinneberg worked as a clerk in various departments of Sears Roebuck in Portland, Oregon. He and my grandma owned a small house in the woods on NE 127th. Every day after work, Grandpa checked the value of Sears stock in the local paper, the *Oregonian*. He received Sears stock as part of a profit-sharing retirement plan with the company. In the era before Craftsman tools became disposable and J.C. Higgins sporting goods became a joke, Sears did well. The stock went up, split, went up more, then split again. Grandpa thought American capitalism was okay. He hadn't always felt that way.

Even though my grandparents seemed financially secure, my grandpa saved on his water bill by lowering a bucket on a rope into a cistern to retrieve stored rainwater he then hand-carried to his flowers. As a Norwegian-American, he was genetically frugal, but he'd been in France in World War I and had experienced the 1930s in the United States. He'd seen hard times.

I didn't think much about it at the time, but Grandpa always seemed good with figures. He had a small bookkeeping and tax-preparing business on the side. I later learned that he'd gone to business college in Lacrosse, Wisconsin, after the Great War, yet he never had jobs that utilized his numerical talents. At least that's what I thought at the time.

Only a few years ago, in a conversation with my mother, did I find a missing piece of Grandpa's life puzzle. He had worked in a bank in Litchville, North Dakota, and had shown great promise as a young banker. Then, in 1930, the bank closed its doors. In those days, before deposit insurance, depositors lost all their money when a bank closed. My mom remembers a lady coming up to Grandpa in church one Sunday. She pleaded, "Mr. Kinneberg, could you please get me my money?" Grandpa moved the family to Ayr, North Dakota, shortly thereafter, where he drove a truck for a local oil distributor. He never worked in a bank again. I never heard him talk about it. In the early 1930s, Grandpa experienced American capitalism at its modern nadir, the Great Depression.

We usually apply the term Great Depression to the period beginning with the stock market crash in October 1929 and ending with the beginning of World War II in 1941. While the term Great Depression aptly describes those difficult, economically depressed and mentally depressing times, the term has economic meaning less precise than the term recession. A committee at the National Bureau of Economic Research (NBER), a private research organization, decides when the economy enters and exits a recession. They define a recession as a period of significant decline in total output, income, employment, and trade, usually lasting from six months to a year, and marked by widespread contractions in many sectors of the economy. Many economists define a recession as two or more consecutive quarters of declining Real GDP, which is GDP adjusted for inflation. When the contraction ends and real GDP starts growing again, the NBER marks the date as the beginning of a recovery, the early part of an expansion.

The Great Depression contained two recessions, the initial one a real whopper. The U.S. economy started into a recession in August 1929, its fourth recession of the decade. Real GDP had grown dramatically by the end of the "Roaring 20s," but like the new pleasure of driving a car on American roads, the ride had been a bumpy one. The business cycle of macroeconomic expansions and contractions had been alive and well in the 1920s. Then, on Black Thursday, in late October, the growing tree of U.S. stock market speculation snapped like a frost-laden North Idaho pine. The Dow Jones Industrial Average plunged 23% in two days, closing 40% down from its September peak. The fall would continue. No one could have imagined that times would get so bad.

In 1929, the average annual unemployment rate had been a low 3.2%. By 1933 it was nearly 25 %. Real GDP declined not for two quarters, but for 43 months in a row, falling nearly 14% in 1931 alone. In March of 1933, the U.S. economy reached the trough of the largest business cycle downturn in U.S. history. The economy started to grow again in 1933, and it grew rapidly, but the decline had been so great that the unemployment rate was still almost 10%, in 1941.

Except for a bad "double dip" recession in the early 1980s, where the unemployment rate reached double digits for the first time since the Great Depression, and in the financial crisis after 2007, post-World War II recessions in the U.S. have been mild, short, and infrequent. Long expansions have become the rule for the U.S. economy. We had uninterrupted expansions of 106, 92, and 120 months, in the 1960s, 80s, and 90s, respectively. The record expansion from mid-2009 to early 2020 lasted 128 months. The most recent recession, early in the Covid-19 pandemic, was the shortest on record, lasting only two months.

Both macroeconomic fiscal and monetary policy, topics we examine in Part 8, should receive much of the credit for trimming the depth and length of post-WWII recessions. Had President Roosevelt and members of Congress realized that they could spend on their constituents, cut their taxes, and fight a bad recession at the same time, the Great Depression might have been just another bad recession. But in 1930, politicians governed six years before John Maynard Keynes fathered the child called expansionary fiscal policy.

Little old ladies lost their money in my grandfather's bank in 1930 because deposits were not insured, which caused a bank run, and because the Federal Reserve System (Fed) did not undertake expansionary monetary policy. Had the Fed flooded the banking system with money, the Great Depression would have been much milder, and my grandpa might have retired as a banker.

Even political conservatives like President George W. Bush embraced the idea that, when facing a recession, the government should stimulate the economy through more spending and tax cuts. His father understood this political-economic axiom less well, and some say it cost him the election in 1992. No Federal

Reserve Board today would allow a contraction of the money supply in a recession. We've been leaning against the macroeconomic winds for too long now to be blown over by a downturn in economic activity.

But who knows what the future will bring? What if someday the economy doesn't respond to stimulus? What if the fiscal policy child of Keynes reaches his dotage? What if international investors usurp the Fed's control over interest rates? We might get evidence that a new paradigm is in order and change the way we approach macroeconomic policy. Until then, we'll continue to use standard tools of fiscal and monetary policy to avoid a large recession, the ones we've used with some success for sixty years. Unfortunately, for Grandpa Kinneberg, a Great Depression banker, our understanding of macroeconomic policy came too late.

"Just Charge It:"

The Federal Budget Deficit and Debt

Near the end of 2023, the U.S. government's debt held by the public totaled over $26 trillion. That's a lot of money, over 94% of U.S. GDP. Twenty years ago, the debt was about 34% of GDP. And this doesn't include debt held by government agencies, such as the Social Security Trust Fund. Should we worry about this debt, sometimes referred to as a "debt burden?" The economic answer is yes and no, which just proves the old joke that says if we laid all economists end-to-end, we'd never reach a conclusion!

It's no secret where this debt came from. Since 1962, outlays of the federal government have exceeded revenues in all but 5 years, with four of those in the period 1998-2001. The government's budget constraint is not much different from yours and mine. If our outgo exceeds our income, we have a deficit, and borrowing must finance it. As we all know, borrowing creates debt. In 2020, the federal government's deficit reached a record in absolute terms, just over $3.1 trillion. It declined to $2.6 trillion in 2021 and $1.4 trillion in 2022, with lower pandemic-induced expenditures and growing tax revenues.

Looking at the federal debt in absolute terms, however, gives a misleading impression of it. If you go to a bank to obtain a car loan or a mortgage, the loan officer wants to know your income, so the bank can assess your ability to make payments on that debt. Likewise, we need to look at the government's debt in relative terms. The federal government's debt was over five times its revenues in 2022.

Add up your mortgage, student loan, car, and credit card debt and divide it by your annual income. Your debt burden might be higher than the government's. My household's debt, from a mortgage on our principal residence and a second home "at the lake," is three times our income. By this standard, the federal government is more indebted than the Millers, but Uncle Sam is a better credit risk, as well. We Americans are often greatly concerned about our collective government debt, but much less concerned about our own private debt.

Looking at the government deficit and debt, even in relative terms, shows only part of the government's financial situation. We wouldn't examine a company's or a household's balance sheet and look only at the liability side. We need to look at assets as well. What do we get for our deficits? What do have to show for our debt? Here the analysis becomes a little more subjective and much more political.

Sometimes, deficits are justified, from a macroeconomic stabilization standpoint, to give the economy a boost in times of recession or national emergency. We needed a budget with stimulus during the Great Depression. We didn't get it. We got stimulus, by default, in World War II. We needed stimulus during the financial crisis, the "Great Recession," and the COVID-19 Pandemic and the federal government delivered it. Deficits in boom times are less warranted.

Sometimes it's a good idea to spend more than you earn and finance it by borrowing. Borrowing allows for better financial management over time. Imagine if everyone had to save the entire price of a house before they bought one. Few would own their own. Many people have huge annual deficits in the years they buy houses, but those are justified one-time expenditures on assets that they are going to enjoy for years and years. Likewise, college students today wisely borrow to finance their college costs, usually, but not always, a good investment in human capital.

All major wars require borrowing. Was government borrowing worth it to win World War II? Sure. Was it worth it to win the Cold War in the 1980s? Probably. How about the wars in Vietnam, Iraq, and Afghanistan? Many would say no. Should we borrow today to improve U.S. security at home, counter a rising Chinese military threat, build public infrastructure, and combat climate change? You must answer these questions yourself before the next election.

In our personal finances, if a deficit leading to more debt were for a better spring break party, cosmetic surgery, a new boat, or a better wine cellar, we might reconsider. A habit of saying, "Relax, put it on plastic," is not financially healthy. And if our collective deficit, leading to more debt, creates farmer, corporate, or consumer subsidies, or the equivalent of a big national party, maybe we should collectively reconsider, as well. Should we worry about the federal deficit and debt? Yes, but not in an alarmist fashion. We need to ask what we are getting for our deficits and added debt. The assets may or may not be worth the additional liabilities.

Living the American Dream:

The Miracle of Productivity Growth

In 1945, after fighting what he called the "Battle of Fort Lewis" in World War II, my father met my mother in Tacoma, Washington. They married and moved across the Cascade Mountains to Wenatchee, the "Apple Capital of the World." Later, after a frenzy of dam building in the 1950s and 60s, the publishers added "Buckle of the Power Belt of the Pacific Northwest," to the masthead of the local newspaper. A friend of my mom's had married a Wenatchee orchardist. Dad knew that he could work in the orchards if he couldn't find anything better.

In 1945, Dad didn't have many prospects better than orchard work. He'd grown up on a farm in Nebraska, the eighth of sixteen children of Silas J. Miller. My grandmother died when Dad was four years old, after giving birth to Uncle Junior, number nine in the "first family." With nine children at home, eighty acres to farm, and countless souls to bring to the Lord, the handsome Reverend Miller wasted no time finding his new wife, who was just a few years older than his oldest daughter.

Grandpa believed in three noble occupations: preaching, teaching, and farming. Unfortunately, none of these appealed to Dad in 1945. By singing gospel harmony with his sisters in tent meetings as a boy, he had acquired enough musical ability to sing for beer in Tacoma bars, but that's all the preaching he wanted. Besides, he'd married a Lutheran, and you just didn't go to the nearest street corner and start a church. You first went to college, then to seminary, then to an internship, where you waited for a call from the bishop. Dad's formal schooling had ended in the eighth grade, when he went to work on local Nebraska farms during the Great Depression. The educational requirements of preaching and teaching seemed out of reach. That left farming.

Dad's older brother, Paul, was first in line for the farm, and I have little doubt that Grandpa offered it to him. But when Uncle Paul died after the war, Grandpa offered the farm to Dad. By that time, Dad had seen "God's Country" in the Pacific Northwest and was not returning to the flat lands of Nebraska. Also, if he returned, he'd go alone. My mom was never going to be part of that life.

My mother, the daughter of second-generation Norwegian immigrants, grew up in Minnesota and North Dakota. After graduating from high school in Moorhead, she wanted to go to Concordia College, but due to the cost, she had to walk, brokenhearted, across the Concordia campus to attend what was then Moorhead State Teachers College, from which she graduated in 1942. She majored in education, one of the acceptable pursuits for women then. During her student teaching, she decided she hated it. She never saw the inside of another classroom. She worked for accountants her entire life. I have no doubt she would have been a CPA had she gone to college 30 years later.

A year or so after moving to Wenatchee, Dad got a job with the local Union Oil distributor and delivered fuel oil to appreciative Wenatchee residents for over thirty years. With the income from driving the oil truck and Mom's part-time earnings working for accountants during tax season, Mom and Dad bought a house, drove better and better cars, supported their church, Little League, Boy Scouts, and anything related to my benefit. They sent me to Pacific Lutheran University, near where they met in Tacoma. Even then, with some financial aid, it was a lot of money.

My parents and I experienced rising material living standards. As Americans, we've always wanted our children to be better off than we are. Of course, we also dream of a good social and natural environment to raise children and grow old in, about the idea of opportunity, and a belief that America stands for something good in the world.

Those in my generation were fortunate. Between the year of my birth, 1948, and the year I graduated from high school in East Wenatchee, U.S. labor productivity grew at a rate exceeding 3% per year. The amount of goods and services produced by an hour's work doubled about every twenty-four years. Even after including earlier and later eras, when productivity growth slowed, material prosperity grew and grew. From 1873 to 1973, an average thirty-five-year-old could expect to be twice as "well off" as his or her parents. After 1973, annual productivity growth has been slower on average, just .7% between 1974 and 1981. The digital revolution increased annual productivity growth to about 2% in the 1990s, but in the first two decades of this century, the growth rate averaged only 1.3% per year.

Material gains today, while still widely distributed, tend to fall more in the hands of those with more education and training. The well-being we get from the American economy grows, but some Americans have difficulty grabbing this growth. It's not like 1948 when the rising economic tide lifted even the small boat of a Nebraska farm boy with little formal education. All Dad had to do was get his family in the boat and row hard toward the dock of prosperity.

One day in the 1980s, as we were riding in a golf cart down the fairway of a golf course in Utah's Wasatch Mountains, Dad looked at the snow-capped peaks and his son, the professor sitting next to him, and marveled at the improbable life he had lived. Later, in the 1990s, not too long before he died, he said, "Just look at all we've done." He was right. We had lived the American Dream.

Part Eight

Fiscal and Monetary Policy

Introduction

In Part Eight, we examine government actions to improve an economy's performance. We start with fiscal policy in "Watching the River Flow...," a riverine analogy that shows how government can counteract a low flow in the GDP River (recession) by releasing water from behind a dam (increased spending) and reducing diversions (lowering taxes). If the GDP River floods (economic boom and inflation), economic hydrologists can reverse this process and reduce flows. Plans for government management of economic flows began with John Maynard Keynes in the 1930s, just as the federal government management of river flows began with the Flood Control Act of 1936. Natural and economic currents sometimes move together.

Keynesian fiscal policy has become attractive politics in the last fifty years on both the political left and right. In "If Nixon Said It, We're All Keynesians Now," President Nixon makes a shocking statement in January 1971 about the economics of Keynes and the policies of Keynesians.

We switch to monetary policy in the next two vignettes. "Central Banks and Worrying About Money," begins with the difference between money and income and then explains briefly how our central bank, the Federal Reserve System (Fed), changes the amount of money in the economy to affect interest rates and economic performance. In "Hello, I'm Jerome Powel..." the chair of the Fed goes door to door buying short-term government bonds in a process economists call open market operations. In this process, the money supply increases, credit eases, households and businesses borrow and spend, and GDP grows faster.

Pete Seeger's anti-war song "Where Have All the Flowers Gone?" is one of the top political songs of all time, recorded and performed by countless artists. In the title of the next vignette, Phillips Curves substitute for Flowers in the lyrics to commemorate a failure of macroeconomic theory in the 1970s. When the inverse relationship between inflation and unemployment vanished, I retreated from teaching macroeconomics until my fellow economists developed new theories which explained economic events. It was one of the finest moments in economic science.

"Supply-side Economics: A Conversation in the Oval Office," shows a politically conservative mutation of Keynesian fiscal policy. Much of this vignette is a one-act play involving a conversation newly elected President Ronald Reagan has with his advisors. Mr. Reagan needs a way to defeat the Soviets in the cold war, reduce taxes, stimulate the economy, and balance the federal budget at the same time. Supply-side economics emerges as a possible economic solution to a political problem. We still debate whether it worked, but one thing is certain. It made its originator, Arthur Laffer, famous. We named a curve after him.

Inflation is not, as popularly suggested, the "cost of living." If it were, we'd all be dead. In "Living with Inflation and Deflation Around the World," indexing protects us from inflation. Even the economic pathologies deflation and hyperinflation, while costly in a true economic sense, are not deadly. Because the politics of fighting it are so appealing, deflation rarely exists. And even hyperinflation, the result of a political problem addressed by a government creating money, can be solved if a central bank can achieve some level of political independence.

The final vignette in this part is, in a way, a capstone. From 2008 to the present, we've lived in a hyperactive macroeconomic policy environment in the U.S. "Bubbles, Busts, and Bailouts...," summarizes the macroeconomics of this era by discussing the history of and policy responses to the Financial Crisis, the Great Recession, and the Covid 19 pandemic. This has been a period of unprecedented expansionary fiscal and monetary policy, not only in magnitude, but also in innovation. Activist macroeconomic policy, especially economic stimulus, is alive and well in the United States.

Watching the River Flow:

Macroeconomic Performance in Cubic Feet Per Second

As we entered Riggins, Idaho, in late August, we read on the handcrafted sign, an Idaho "reader board," that the flow that day in the Salmon River would be 3,200 cubic feet per second (cfs). We would have to avoid many exposed rocks in the river, but with skilled boat guides, even a group of aging college professors on the Dean's retreat would have a good float and plenty of fun in the rapids. This was a low flow for the Salmon at Riggins. Some in our party noted that normally at this time of year the Salmon flowed at 8,000 cfs, and at flood stage, in the spring, often over 100,000.

Flows are important in running rivers, and in economics, especially macroeconomics. Do not confuse flows, magnitudes with time dimensions, with stocks. Here, I don't mean common stock indicating ownership in a corporation, but merely a hunk of something, a mass just sitting there. In water resources, we measure a stock of water in gallons, or cubic feet, or in acre-feet, the amount of water it takes to cover an acre to a depth of one foot. In economics, we find the stock of money in the economy, or the stock of wealth,

Monitoring macroeconomic performance is much like watching a river. Flows are often more important and interesting than stocks. The amount of water trapped behind the ice dam in the ancient Lake Missoula is not as interesting as the great Missoula flood, which scoured and drained the Inland Northwest with daily flows equal to the annual flows of all the rivers of the world today. The water behind a concrete dam is less important than the flow through its turbines generating electricity, or the flow flushing salmon smolts to the sea, or the amount used by households, measured, say, in gallons per capita per day. Gross domestic product is a flow, as is national income, the total product or income of an economy in a year.

Given the importance of flows in both water resources and economics, we use many hydrologic metaphors in macroeconomics. We illustrate a market economy with something called the circular flow model, appearing near page 50 in most encyclopedic economics texts. We talk of injections to and leakages from the circular flow of income. An overheated economy "lets off steam," a flow changing the form of matter. With an economic growth metaphor, we say, "a rising tide lifts all boats."

So, imagine an economic river. Let's call it the Real GDP River. We measure the flow rate in dollars per year, dollars with constant purchasing power. Upstream from our river flow gage, we have some tributaries and some diversions. The four main tributaries are rivers called consumption, investment, government purchases and exports. We also have two diversions from the river channel, imports, and taxes.

Suppose we have a drought in the Consumption River basin. In the real world, this metaphorical drought might occur if people become grumpy and fearful of the future and reduce their spending. The flow of the Consumption River, a tributary to the Real GDP River, now falls. Other things held constant, what happens to our river gage on the banks of the Real GDP? The arrow shows a reduction in flow. A flow reduction large enough and long enough causes a recession. Luckily, rainfall in the Consumption River drainage is very stable, but we still want to measure it. Various real-world organizations like the Conference Board, a collective of businesses, and the University of Michigan Survey Research Center monitor consumer confidence, a measure of current economic precipitation that gives some indication of future flows in the Consumption River.

The Investment River, much smaller than the Consumption River, generates more hydrologic interest. It's a very unstable river. Imagine a flash flood on the Investment River. What will happen to the flow in the Real GDP? Yes, the arrow on the gage shows a rise. In the real world, we call this an investment boom.

Use your new knowledge of economic hydrology to examine changes in flows from the Export River, one that flows into our economy from across the border, and the Import Diversion, water flowing out of the Consumption and Investment Rivers into another economy. Can you see what will happen to the gage at the river's edge?

Please note one especially important tributary, the Government Purchases River, and one important diversion, the Taxes Diversion. While much of the flow in the government purchases river relates to general government activity, the river has an interesting characteristic, dams. The federal government can keep its eye on the Real GDP River gage, and if the flow starts to fall, maybe because of a drought in the Consumption River drainage, it can let water out from behind the dams. As this water moves downstream, we will eventually see the Real GDP River start to rise again. If a prolonged boom threatens a flood, the government can close spillways on the dams and reduce the flow of the Real GDP River.

Likewise, the government can control the gate of the Taxes Diversion. If flow in the Real GDP River starts to fall, the government could close the gate on the Taxes Diversion a little, leaving more water in the Consumption River. This would feed the Real GDP River and make its flow rise. In the real world, we call adjusting flows at these dams and diversions discretionary or compensatory fiscal policy. The government watches the Real GDP River gage and adjusts flows from the dams on the Government Purchases River and the flows out through the gate of the Taxes Diversion to compensate for changes in flows in the Consumption and Investment Rivers.

And finally, a note on the history of hydrological economic thought. All the dams on the Government River were built after 1936, as were the discretionary gates on the Taxes Diversion. The engineer responsible for the design of this system was a British economist by the name of John Maynard Keynes. His blueprints appeared in a book entitled *The General Theory of Employment, Interest, and Money*. Before Keynes, if the flow of the Real GDP River fell, the government, upon advice from their economic engineers, would say, "Flows in the river are going down. Don't worry. It will rain soon." The early years of the Great Depression were very dry. The rains came gradually in the 1930s, and the flow in the Real GDP River rose again, but the largest jump in flow came from a persistent thunderstorm called World War II.

If Nixon Said It, "We're All Keynesians Now!"

Richard M. Nixon was full of surprises. As a sitting vice president, he lost the 1960 presidential election to a young and inexperienced politician, John F. Kennedy, only to drop down a political notch and lose the gubernatorial election in his home state of California two years later. After most counted him out of any political future, he came back and won the presidency in 1968. A hawk on the Vietnam War, he fought the communist movement under Ho Chi Minh in Indochina, yet he later withdrew U.S. forces from Vietnam. An ardent anticommunist, he opened diplomatic relations with communist China. And most surprising of all, he taped conversations in the Oval Office that led to his resignation. Nixon was never dull.

In January 1971, midway through his first term in office, Mr. Nixon also surprised anyone who knew anything about macroeconomic policy. On January 4th, he'd done a live television interview with reporters from the three major networks and one from the Public Broadcasting System (PBS). In a February 9th commentary in the *National Review*, William F. Buckley, Jr. reported that Howard K. Smith from the American Broadcasting Company (ABC), one of the interviewers on January 4th, noted that Mr. Nixon had said, "I am now a Keynesian in economics." According to Mr. Smith, Mr. Nixon made his remark in an informal conversation after the formal interview. Mr. Smith considered the President's statement akin to a Christian in the Crusades, saying that, all things considered, Mohammed was right. Mr. Smith thought he had caught Mr. Nixon committing an act of political economic heresy, and to Mr. Smith, it couldn't get much better than that. He'd been one of the most strident at writing off Mr. Nixon's future political career in 1962.

Over time Mr. Nixon's statement has appeared in different versions. Later in January, *The Nation* reported something shorter, "I am now a Keynesian," with no economics qualifier. When I asked my colleagues about Nixon's statement about Keynes, they concurred that he said, "We're all Keynesians now." Several textbooks use this statement as a lead-in to a discussion of Keynesian economics. I've used it in class. The story even got a chuckle or two once in a great while, usually from a history or political science major, or a baby boomer of any stripe. But if Mr. Nixon said anything about Keynes in 1971, he appears to have implicated no one else in his conversion. His statement was a singular, personal one.

What was so surprising about aligning himself with the followers of economist John Maynard Keynes, the greatest economist of the 20th century? How could one word, Keynesian, illicit such a reaction? Why would conservative commentator William F. Buckley, Jr. say that a lot of people were snickering about the remark? Some of it has to do with Mr. Nixon and his tenuous relationship with both the Left and the Right in U.S. politics. But much of the snickering and surprise stemmed from the political philosophy of macroeconomic policy. And to understand this, we need to start with the ideas of Keynes.

British economist John Maynard Keynes was the most influential economist of the 20th century. He died in 1946, almost 23 years before the first Nobel Prize in Economics. Had he survived in age to his middle eighties, he would have been the first recipient of it. He was that good. If there were an Economics Hall of Fame, he'd be in it. Books by Keynes fill a good portion of the history of economic thought shelf in my humble library, and books about his colorful life, his economic theories, and his public service and public policy prescriptions could fill many more.

To understand the essence of Keynesian economics and Mr. Nixon's alleged allegiance to it, we must revisit the U.S. economy in the middle of the Great Depression, in 1936. Economic conditions in 1936 had improved from the depths of the Great Depression, in 1933. The economy had been growing for four years, but the deep decline in real GDP from 1929 to 1933 still left the unemployment rate at nearly 17%. Economists had no idea how to get out of this economic mess. In fact, the reigning classical orthodoxy in economics stated that markets, given time, would adjust to and eliminate high unemployment. The economy would correct itself. In 1936, we just needed to wait.

In 1936, Keynes published his most important book, *The General Theory of Employment, Interest, and Money* (usually referred to as *The General Theory*). This book is not an easy read. Most economists have not read all of it. Nobel Laureate Paul Samuelson, whose textbook taught Keynesian economics to generations of college students, described *The General Theory* as follows: "It is a badly written book, poorly organized; any layman who, beguiled by the author's previous reputation, bought the book was cheated out of his five shillings... It is arrogant, bad-tempered, and not overly generous in its acknowledgments. It abounds in mares' nests and confusions... In short, it is a work of genius." The opacity of *The General Theory* would later lead to much interpretation by economists, and to the inevitable question about the relationship of Keynesian economics to the economics of Keynes himself.

Keynes theorized that fluctuations in spending in the economy, what he called effective demand, caused macroeconomic fluctuations in output, employment, and the price level. For example, when businesses saw a decline in spending and a decline in effective demand, they cut back production and fired workers. A recession ensued. Real GDP fell, and unemployment rose. A decline in spending could come from consumers, foreigners, the government, or businesses themselves if they thought the future looked bleak. Why buy new plants and equipment, for example, when they have so much idle capacity already?

Keynes saw market capitalism as inherently unstable, and the internal self-correcting mechanisms too weak or too slow to rely on. Keynes used his scientific theory of the business cycle, the ups and downs in economic activity, to advocate a normative economic policy. The government should increase its spending to compensate for declines in private spending and decrease its spending when irrational speculation causes an inflationary boom. Of course, writing in 1936, Keynes concentrated more on the recession side of the business cycle.

Keynes also emphasized government spending rather than tax reductions as a means of stimulating the economy. He preferred public expenditures on railways and housing, but he praised even pyramid building in ancient Egypt and cathedrals in the Middle Ages as macroeconomic wealth builders. Keynes thought stimulating the economy by wars and earthquakes would be preferable to doing nothing, the prescription of the classical orthodoxy. Consider the following government policy suggested, perhaps tongue in cheek, by Keynes:

"If the Treasury were to fill old bottles with banknotes, bury them at suitable depths in disused coal mines which are then filled up to the surface with town rubbish, and leave it to private enterprise on well-tried principles of laissez-faire to dig the notes up again... there need be no more unemployment and, with the help of the repercussions, the real income of the community, and its capital wealth also, would probably become a good deal greater than it actually is. It would, indeed, be more sensible to build houses and the like; but if there are practical difficulties in the way of this, the above would be better than nothing."

Keynesian policy to fight a recession creates an increase in the federal government budget deficit. If the government leaves tax revenue initially unchanged and increases government spending, it encounters the same situation you do when you spend more than you earn. You and the government have a deficit, one that must be financed by borrowing. Unlike the last five-plus decades in the United States, with deficits in all but four years, in the early 1930s deficits were bad politics. In 1932, even presidential candidate Franklin D. Roosevelt, later author of the activist New Deal program, ran on a balanced budget.

American conservatives abhor Keynes' ideas and the implications of his policies. I often suggested to my Idaho students that they could do an experiment over summer break. Merely walk through a town in conservative southern Idaho, shout out the name John Maynard Keynes, and see how long it takes before someone throws a rotten potato at you.

In 1971, a Republican president like Richard Nixon might have been reluctant to advocate Keynesian policies. One does not criticize market capitalism, encourage government activism, and advocate (even wasteful) public works and budget deficits to charm the right-leaning wing of the Republican party. Keynesian policies fit much more snugly with the political Left, American Progressives, and Democrats, not with Republicans. Howard K Smith had some basis for his surprise upon discovering Nixonian Keynesianism.

Keynes, an ardent socialist in 1936, worried deeply about inequality in the distribution of wealth and income, and especially with what he called the rentier aspect of capitalism, where the rich received unearned income merely from having their wealth invested at interest. Tucked near the end of *The General Theory*, in a chapter entitled "Concluding Notes on the Social Philosophy Towards Which the General Theory Might Lead," Keynes placed what a political conservative would consider his most damning ideas. According to Keynes, we need a socialization of investment, an increase in government spending on capital goods so large as to make capital not scarce. Drive the interest rate to zero. Fortunately for Mr. Nixon in January 1971, even few economists had read Chapter 24 of *The General Theory*.

Mr. Nixon adopted a moderate form of Keynesianism in 1971. He was not advocating the more radical leftist ideas of Keynes, but 35 years after *The General Theory*, most economists believed that the government and the central bank had a role to play in macroeconomic stabilization. And when unemployment is too high, and an election looms, which is always the case, few presidents can resist the urge to stimulate the economy.

In the 1971 television interview, in a response to a question about the high rate of unemployment in the economy from PBS correspondent Nancy H. Dickerson, Mr. Nixon said, "What we are going to do first is to have an expansionary budget. It will be a budget in deficit, as will be the budget in 1971. It will not be an inflationary budget because it will not exceed the full employment revenues. We also, according to Arthur Burns, will have an expansionary monetary policy, and that will, of course, be a monetary policy adequate to meet the needs of an expanding economy."

This seems like a reasonable version of Keynesian economics. The reference to full employment revenues means that the budget would be in balance if the economy were at full employment. An ardent Keynesian might suggest a larger deficit, but at least Mr. Nixon was not advocating a balanced actual budget for 1971. Expansionary monetary policy, while viewed by Keynes as largely ineffective in the Great Depression, certainly would be an element of Keynesian policy in milder recessionary times.

Mr. Nixon solidified his Keynesian macroeconomic policy credentials later in the same response. After predicting a good economic year for 1971, and a "very good year" in 1972 (the election year) Mr. Nixon said, "Now having made that prediction, I will say that the purpose of this Administration will be to have an activist economic policy designed to control inflation but at the same time to expand the economy so that we can reduce unemployment, and to have what this country has not had for 20 years, and that is a situation where we have full employment in peacetime without the cost of war and without the cost of excessive inflation."

With his pledge of government activism to reduce unemployment and control inflation, Mr. Nixon buried again the ghost of Herbert Hoover and what we now know to be the flawed macroeconomic policy of the early 1930s. He also buried the ghost of the restrained macroeconomic policies of the Eisenhower/Nixon administration, policies that, in part, led to the Kennedy victory in 1960. Yes, he was a Keynesian in economics, but more important to Mr. Nixon, he knew that being a Keynesian in economics was good politics the year before an election. The electorate wanted the government to expand the economy, to do something about unemployment. If they were all Keynesians now, so was he!

"Hello, I'm Jerome Powell. I'd Like to Buy Your Government Bond."

A woman hears a knock at her door in the middle of the afternoon. Someone must be selling something, probably vacuum-cleaners or religion. She opens the door and sees a man standing on the porch. He's nice looking, with well-trimmed gray hair and friendly eyes. He looks good, with a nice dark blue suit, a laundered white shirt with French cuffs, and a silk tie with a tasteful, conservative pattern. His black shoes shine like he just left the stand at the airport.

"Hello," he says, "I'm Jerome Powell. I'd like to buy one of your government bonds."

"My what?" she asks.

"One of your government bonds," says Mr. Powell.

"Say, haven't I seen you somewhere before? Yeah, on TV, or in the newspaper."

"Perhaps you have," he says, "I'm Chair of the Board of Governors of the Federal Reserve System. Most people call us the Fed."

"That's it." she says. "You're the guys who change the interest rate."

"That's right." says Mr. Powell.

"So, why aren't you out changing interest rates?" the woman asks, "Instead of coming around here trying to buy, to buy…."

"Government bonds." he says.

"Yes, government bonds. Why are you buying government bonds?"

"Because that's the way we change the interest rate," Mr. Powell says. "When we buy government bonds, we write checks to people who sell them to us. These people deposit these checks in their banks. Because bank deposits are money, we now have more money in banks, and bankers are willing to lend this money at lower interest rates. It's sort of supply and demand.

The supply of money goes up in the banking system, so there's a greater supply of loans by bankers who have the money. This lowers the price of a loan, the interest rate. Are you familiar with supply and demand analysis?"

"Oh yes. I was a finance major in college."

"Good for you." says Mr. Powell. "Well, what about it?"

"What about what?" she asks.

"Do you want to sell one of your government bonds?"

"I'm not sure. I don't think so. My portfolio is pretty much balanced." she says.

"What did you pay for your government bonds?" asks Mr. Powell.

"I can't remember exactly, but it was near the initial time the bonds were issued. It was probably about their face value, $1,000."

"I'll give you $1,250."

"No kidding?" she asks.

"No kidding." he says.

"Make it $1,300 and you have a deal." she says.

"Done." says Mr. Powell.

As he wrote the check, Jerome Powell knew the money supply was increasing, and interest rates on bank loans would decline when this and many more checks he would write that day found their way into checking accounts. He also knew that rates had already fallen. At the new higher price of $1,300, the yield on the bond had fallen, and the yield is an interest rate. We calculate the yield by dividing the fixed amount of cash received per year from the bond by its price. As the price had gone up, the yield (interest rate) had gone down.

"By the way," the woman says, "what do you do with those bonds, anyway?"

"Oh, I slip them in the bottom right drawer of my desk." Mr. Powell says.

I suspect that you doubt whether Jerome Powell, Chair of the Fed, would go door to door conducting monetary policy. You're right, he doesn't. But he and his colleagues at the Fed direct the New York Federal Reserve Bank to enter the general market for existing government bonds. To increase the money supply and lower interest rates, they buy bonds. To decrease the money supply and increase interest rates, they sell bonds. It's much easier than going door to door but has the same effect. Bond sellers get checks from the Fed, which they deposit, increasing the amount of money in the banking system. When the Fed sells bonds, bond buyers write checks to the Fed. Their bank account balances fall. With less money in their banks, bankers are stingier with loans, and interest rates rise.

"Being the Fed sounds like a pretty good business." the woman says.

"We do earn quite a bit of interest on those bonds we own." says Mr. Powell. "But we have to give most of it back to the U.S. Treasury."

"That doesn't seem fair." she says.

"It's not so bad. We pay our employees very well, and have the best cafeteria in Washington, and tennis courts right outside."

"Oh, I get it." she says.

Central Banks and Worrying About Money

Have you ever worried about money? Before you answer, I must warn you that this is a trick question. Your answer doesn't depend on whether you're religious and believe that "God will provide." It doesn't depend on your wealth or general anxiety level. The answer does, however, depend on whether you know a little economics.

Most, if they worry about financial matters at all, worry about income, not money. The two are not the same. Despite the common vernacular, you don't "make money," unless you have a counterfeiting operation in the basement. Rather, you earn income by dragging yourself out of bed on cold, dark winter mornings and showing up for your job. Money is not income. Money is a special type of asset, a liquid form of wealth, one that you can spend. You must choose the kinds of assets you want to own, but this asset allocation, while important, should not cause worrisome sleepless nights.

Money in an economy is the sum of currency, traveler's checks, and balances in accounts you can spend. It's something our central bank, the Federal Reserve System (Fed), worries about a lot. Through its monetary policy, the Fed can change the amount of money in the economy, and when it does, it affects interest rates. Interest rates affect spending, and spending affects the general level of economic activity in the economy. If the Fed creates too much money, we get inflation, or, in extreme cases, hyperinflation. Too little money can lead to a recession. If the Fed totally screws up, like it did in the early 1930s, we can have a Great Depression and deflation. Now that's something to worry about!

After the Financial Crisis in 2008 and recently during the Covid 19 pandemic, the Fed went on a money creation binge. Consequently, interest rates rested at historic lows for years. The

Fed also added a new characteristic to its monetary policy, something called "quantitative easing (QE)." In the past, the Fed operated mostly in the market for short-term government bonds, those with maturities of less than a year. This affected an interest rate called the Federal Funds Rate, the rate banks pay each other for short-term, often overnight, loans. This then reverberated through the financial system, affecting other interest rates, as well. With QE, the Fed acted in the longer-term government bond market, buying long-term bonds and assets called mortgage-backed securities. The latter are collections of mortgages from the U.S. mortgage market. QE lowered long-term interest rates, especially mortgage rates, and stimulated the U.S. housing market.

When my parents bought my boyhood home, in the early 1960s, their mortgage rate was 5%. Due to inflation's effect on rates, when Solveig and I bought our first home, in 1977, our rate was 10 ½ %. Our later mortgage rates landed in the 4-8% range. A few years ago, we refinanced our mortgage for 2.75%. Some of this reflects the low-inflation, pre-pandemic economic environment, but rates have been affected, as well, by the Fed's strong, expansionary monetary policy, QE.

In 2023, following an era of "easy money," the Fed reversed course to control post-pandemic inflation. Interest rates rose rapidly, creating stress in financial markets. Uncertainty about the path of monetary policy had everyone worrying about money, and worrying, too, if tightening by the Fed would cause a recession. As I write this in early 2024, no recession has occurred, and the Fed is signaling that it will lower interest rates this year. Some worry that this might reignite inflation. Others worry that the Fed's recent tightening may still cause a recession. With money, there is always something to worry about.

Where Have All the Phillips Curves Gone?

Science, Macroeconomics, and the Anomalous 1970s

I'd been teaching since 1974, first on the frozen plains of the St. Lawrence at Clarkson College of Technology in upstate New York, and then at the University of Utah in Salt Lake City. I enjoyed teaching, especially the introductory course. No matter where you teach, you always have students who like a good economics story, one about how the world works. But in the late 1970s, teaching the principles of macroeconomics became downright unpleasant. We didn't have a very good story about how the macroeconomic world worked anymore. I'm not sure whether economics was suffering what Thomas Kuhn called a paradigm shift, but some of our theories didn't predict or explain economic events very well, especially our theory of the relationship between inflation and unemployment.

I was no more than four or five years out of graduate school. At normal rates of decay, my intellectual economic capital should not have depreciated so rapidly. As in all disciplines, economics graduate training teaches the new generation the standard theory, the received doctrine. There's an old saying, if you want to know something about standard theory, ask a graduate student studying for Ph.D. qualifying exams. I'd been trained well, but certain macroeconomic anomalies perplexed me. In the U.S. economy, we were having high and increasing inflation and high and increasing unemployment, at the same time. In the late 1960s, Arthur Okun, Chair of President Lyndon Johnson's Council of Economic Advisers, had developed what he called the Misery Index, the sum of the inflation rate and the unemployment rate. In the late 1970s, this index read about 18-20%.

This wasn't supposed to happen. In 1958, British economist A.W. Phillips examined inflation and unemployment data from the first half of the 20th century and concluded that when the unemployment rate rose, the rate of inflation fell. U.S. economists Paul Samuelson and Robert Solow, both later Nobel laureates, showed the same thing with U.S. data two years later. This statistical relationship called the Phillips Curve, confirmed the reigning theory of inflation and unemployment at the time. Before the 1970s, all had been well in macroeconomic science, as the facts of the world confirmed economic theory.

We had learned from Keynes that higher demand in the economy eventually caused inflation. Absent a recession, more spending would force the economy's teapot to let off steam from overheating. Macroeconomic policy was merely an exercise in choosing the desired combination of inflation and unemployment and using government fiscal policy to maintain the right level of spending in the economy. Too little total spending? Increase the budget deficit. Too much spending? Reduce the budget deficit, or run the opposite of a deficit, a budget surplus.

The policy had worked in the 1960s. Following the Kennedy/Johnson tax cut in the early 1960s, increased government spending on the Vietnam War, and the war against poverty at home, the 1960s economy expanded for the rest of the decade. All the while, however, inflation remained with us, and it crept up ever so gently over the decade. We came to expect inflation, the cost of having unemployment low. Phillips, Samuelson, and Solow had shown us this years ago.

Then came the 1970s. Two things had changed. First, after a decade and a half of rising prices every year, people now expected inflation all the time and they wanted to protect themselves from its erosive effect on their purchasing power. We protected social security recipients every year by increasing their monthly checks according to changes in the consumer price index. Unions bargained for cost-of-living adjustments in their wage contracts. Even nonunion workers demanded cost-of-living increases in wages and salaries during their bargaining with employers. I can remember helping my non-economist university colleagues who made presentations to the legislature in Utah about cost-of-living adjustments in faculty salaries.

Employers obliged. If inflation rose, we expected wages next year to be higher as well. Employers passed on the wage increases in the form of higher prices. The average price level rose, a self-fulfilling prophecy. We call this type of inflation cost-push inflation to contrast it with the demand-pull, Keynesian variety. Economists talked about a wage and price spiral.

Then we had the Yom Kippur War in the Middle East, a disruption of oil supplies, and the consequent increase in oil prices. The Organization of Petroleum Exporting Countries (OPEC), previously ineffective as a sellers cartel in oil, raised prices even more. These "supply shocks" raised production costs and companies passed these costs along in the form of higher prices. Inflation was now even higher, and when the economy went into a recession, inflation remained high. We had inflation and recession at the same time. Some called this stagflation.

The macroeconomic models of the 1970s could not explain stagflation. The Phillips Curve was no longer a stable relationship between inflation and unemployment. Like the 1960s antiwar song, "Where Have All the Flowers Gone?" economists wondered where all the Phillips Curves had gone. Our favorite story told to college freshmen and sophomores was no longer true. I opted out of teaching macroeconomic principles for a few years. As an untenured assistant professor trying to publish and not perish, and with what I considered to be more fruitful research outlets, I decided to wait for others to develop new theories to explain the new macroeconomic facts, and then for those who write textbooks to distill this down to something I could understand, and then relate it to my students.

I remember at the time that I was confident, as were most economists, that this theoretical realignment would occur. We had faith in the discipline. In fact, economists were well on their way to producing a theory to explain the new facts. In graduate school in 1973, I had taken a special summer seminar in which we studied the work of Edmund Phelps, Milton Friedman and others, whose work in the late 1960s on the effect of inflation expectations in labor markets suggested why the Phillips Curve might not work as we had thought. This was part of something called the expectations revolution in macroeconomics, for which Robert Lucas of the University of Chicago won the Nobel Prize a few years later. Friedman and Phelps also won Nobel Prizes.

By the time I came to the University of Idaho in 1989, the scientific process had worked itself out. Facts had challenged standard theory. Economists had checked the facts, and they seemed correct. The problem had been with the theory. Economists produced a new theory about inflation and unemployment that explained the facts, and talented textbook writers found ways to cut through the thickets of algebra and substitute graphical models approachable by college students. I consider it one of the finest moments in economics. Of course, the moment lasted a decade or two, and had me sitting on the sideline of macroeconomics education longer than I wanted to, but we did it. We have a good macroeconomic story once again.

Supply-side Economics:

An Oval Office Conversation in Early 1981

Ronald Reagan defeated President Jimmy Carter in the 1980 presidential election, winning 44 states, nearly 51% of the popular vote, and over 90% of the electoral vote. While many would attribute some of this landslide to the unfortunate Iran hostage crisis befalling Mr. Carter, much of the victory stemmed from voters' dissatisfaction with the performance of the U.S. economy. In 1980, we had stagflation in the United States, high inflation, and a recession at the same time. The unemployment rate was 10%. Middle-income families had difficulty qualifying for home mortgages as interest rates rose to double digits. We had a deficit in the federal budget, and we'd had one for a decade. The stock market had gone nowhere in the seventies.

In 1980, people could still remember the sad story of an impeached president forced to resign and high gasoline prices caused by foreign oil-producing nations, many of them small Arab sheikdoms with cultures light years from ours. America's military superiority in the world was in question. The U.S. defense budget, as a proportion of the total federal budget, had fallen for years. Spending on social programs was rising rapidly. The American people worried about their economy and their place in the world.

Ronald Reagan offered himself to the American people as an agent of politically conservative change. In September 1980, in a campaign speech to the International Business Council in Chicago, Mr. Reagan said that the United States must reduce tax rates, balance the budget, and strengthen its national defense, an ambitious political and macroeconomic policy agenda.

After the election, Mr. Reagan and his team had to craft legislative proposals and policies to carry out their mandate. The following contains stylized dialog, a one-act play centered on a fictional conversation in the Oval Office in early 1981 about the vexing question of how to balance the budget and meet the rest of the President's agenda.

(As the curtain rises, most of the players sit in the Oval Office waiting for the president's arrival with his chief of staff, James Baker. Seated at a small table are budget director David Stockman and Murray Weidenbaum, chair of the Council of Economic Advisers. Ed Meese, a political strategist, will arrive later. The president and Mr. Baker enter.)

MR. WEIDENBAUM
&
MR. STOCKMAN: Good morning, Mr. President.

THE PRESIDENT: Good morning, gentlemen; please sit down.

(The four spend a short amount of time exchanging pleasantries before the President begins the meeting.)

THE PRESIDENT: Even though I am the president, and you have no choice, I'd like to thank you both for coming over this morning.

(Laughter)

THE PRESIDENT: And thank you for how hard you've been working. I know these are busy times, but our work is very important. The future of this great country and the entire world is in our hands. I know Jim has briefed you on our topic this morning, but I'd just like to offer a personal note. In meetings with members of Congress, and especially the press, I keep getting questions about how we are going to reduce taxes, increase defense spending, and balance the budget at the same time. I keep telling them what you all told me to say, that we hope to control overall spending with cuts in social spending, but I'm seeing a lot of skepticism. I need to know what to say. I know we can do it, but what do I say to the American people? Jim, maybe you can take it from here.

MR. BAKER: Thank you, Mr. President. Well, I think you all see the problem. We've inherited a terrible mess from the Democrats. We've got to increase defense spending to make America strong again. We'll do what we can to hold the line on social spending, but cutting social programs is going to meet opposition on the hill, on both sides of the aisle. And we have to reduce the burden on the American taxpayer. It's been a while since I took economics in college, but if taxes go down and spending goes up, it's logical that the deficit is going to rise. The President has been pretty vocal throughout the campaign, and through his whole political career for that matter, on the need to balance the budget. I don't know if two out of three is going to fly politically. Opponents are going to throw the deficit in our face and

	jeopardize the tax cut package and defense buildup. Murray, do you have any ideas?
MR. WEIDENBAUM:	Well, maybe a few, but it's possible we're just going to have to live with a bigger deficit for a while. It looks like we're going into a recession. Few economists would argue against increasing the deficit to combat a recession. It's sort of standard fiscal policy, one legacy of Keynes that has withstood the test of time.

(Startled as if awakened from the beginning of a daydream)

THE PRESIDENT:	Oh my God, Murray, you're not suggesting that we practice Keynesian economics. I've always thought that's something we have to fight, not practice.
MR. WEIDENBAUM:	Well, that depends. In the past, Keynesian economics has been associated with fine-tuning the economy. I'm not advocating that. Our philosophy must be that the U.S. economy can, for the most part, stabilize itself, and we don't want to be fine-tuning it. But because we want to reduce taxes for other reasons, all I'm saying is that when an economy is going into a recession, you won't get much flak from the economics community. We point out that we hope to have a balanced budget when we are out of the recession.

And while we might take some political heat on the deficit issue, members of Congress like to stimulate the economy. Even Nixon said, "We're all Keynesians now."

THE PRESIDENT: Surely, that was in a moment of weakness or desperation. Anyway, I'd sure not look to Nixon for economic policy guidance. His strength was foreign policy. For heaven's sake, he instituted wage and price controls.

MR. BAKER: I think you are right on target there, Mr. President, but history aside, let's get back to the issue at hand. Murray, anything else?

MR. WEIDENBAUM: I'm not offering political advice here, just observations of an economist. But we can note that we are doing something different than the fiscal policy Democrats would do. They'd be more likely to increase spending than cut taxes.

MR. BAKER: I like that, Murray. We have a conservative fiscal policy: fighting a recession and reducing the tax burden of government at the same time.

THE PRESIDENT: Ooh, that's good, Jim. That's what I like about you, Jimmy; you can take something an economist says, something that usually sounds like gibberish to me—no disrespect to you, Murray, it's an occupational hazard—and turn it into something we can use in a speech.

MR. BAKER: Thank you, Mr. President. David, you haven't said much. What do you think?

MR. STOCKMAN: Sitting where I am, I'm very concerned about the budget deficit. If the economy declines in the next several months, tax revenues are going to fall, even before we cut tax rates. We need to be aggressive in cutting social spending. If we can't do that, I'm really worried. Our economists have done some preliminary calculations, and some of the scenarios for the budget deficits are pretty frightening.

MR. WEIDENBAUM: I'd like to support attempts to hold the line on spending. Our preliminary projections at the Council are similar, if not more alarming, than David's. One thing no one has mentioned is financing the deficit. The Treasury is going to have to borrow a lot of money in financial markets, and this might push up interest rates and compete with businesses for a limited amount of capital.

MR. BAKER: I've made a note to talk with
                                    Don Regen about financing
                                    issues. He's giving a presentation
                                    to the American Bankers
                                    Association this morning. I know
                                    he'd like to be here, but we
                                    thought we needed to get out
                                    front on some of the economic
                                    agenda with his speech.

(Mr. Meese enters, and all exchange greetings.)

MR. BAKER: Ed, I'm glad you're here now.
                                    We've made some progress on
                                    clarifying the problem we face
                                    but haven't figured out what to
                                    do about it. I'm afraid this deficit
                                    thing could hurt us.

MR. MEESE: I think I might have an idea.
                                    When I was reading Jim's memo
                                    about this meeting, I
                                    remembered a conversation I had
                                    with one of our staff who had
                                    been poking around at the
                                    American Economic Association
                                    meetings a week or so ago in
                                    New York. We were looking for
                                    some material, something new
                                    that we could use to support our
                                    mission. I don't really care if
                                    economists endorse our program
                                    or not, but it never hurts to have
                                    some economic theory in
                                    reserve. It's like a clinch in
                                    boxing, you use it to buy a little
                                    time while people look at you
                                    dumbfounded.

(laughter)

MR. WEIDENBAUM: Now, Ed, we're really not that bad.

THE PRESIDENT: Not you, Murray, I've always understood the things you say.

MR. WEIDENBAUM: Thank you, Mr. President.

MR. BAKER: I'd love to continue this discussion about the ability of economists to communicate with non-economists, but the President has a busy schedule today. Ed, what's your idea?

MR. MEESE: Well, my staffer got a little tired of listening to technical papers, so she went into the hotel bar for a break. She ran into an economist who had been helping us out in the campaign and he introduced her to a young economist by the name of Arthur Laffer from USC.

THE PRESIDENT: Well, that's encouraging, everything good starts in California.

(laughter)

MR. MEESE: Apparently, this guy, Laffer, was pretty entertaining. He had a bunch of professors and graduate students engaged in a rather lively debate around the table. They were all writing equations and drawing graphs on cocktail napkins, and Laffer seemed to be holding his own. Laffer had drawn this one picture the others jokingly called the "Laffer Curve." My staffer didn't understand the graph, but the main idea was that a cut in tax rates could lead to such an increase in economic activity that tax revenues would go up, not down.

THE PRESIDENT: Boy, that makes sense to me. I've always thought the answer to all our economic problems is to get the government out of the way of the American people.

MR. BAKER: Let me see if I understand. Can we cut tax rates, increase defense spending, and lower the deficit at the same time?

MR. MEESE: That's right. Laffer's calling it supply-side economics. It's different from what the Democrats would do. They'd just throw more money at social problems, increasing demand in the economy. Nothing is produced but bureaucracy. By cutting tax rates, people get to keep more of what they earn. They have an incentive to work more. Businesses have an incentive to invest more. According to Laffer, with lower tax rates, we even get less cheating on income taxes.

THE PRESIDENT:	I've always been in favor of honesty.
MR. BAKER:	And the economists in the bar were buying it?
MR. MEESE:	Well, not entirely, but they didn't dismiss it out of hand, either.
MR. BAKER:	That's interesting. Murray, David, have you heard of this supply-side economics?
MR. WEIDENBAUM:	I've heard of it, sure, but the term supply-side economics— that's new to me.
MR. BAKER:	But will it work, Murray?
MR. WEIDENBAUM:	That depends on many things, including the magnitude of the rate cuts and the response to them, and, of course, what happens on the spending side. One thing we do know is that if we cut tax rates, there is a supply response, so even if tax revenues fall, they won't fall as much as they would if you just sent people tax rebate checks in the mail.
MR. BAKER:	That's exactly what the Democrats are proposing in Congress right now. They're worrying that the rich are getting a tax cut.

THE PRESIDENT: I never could figure out what those Democrats have against rich people.

MR. WEIDENBAUM: The empirical evidence is a little sketchy on how long it would take for tax revenues to increase after a cut in rates. Actually, it worked for Kennedy. I bet Walter Heller, who had my job under Kennedy, wished he had thought of the term supply-side economics.

THE PRESIDENT: Kennedy did this supply-side economics? I always thought he was one of the best Republican presidents.

(laughter)

MR. WEIDENBAUM: Yes, Kennedy started the process, and Johnson carried it out. They cut taxes, fought a war, and balanced the budget.

MR. BAKER: I love it. If the Democrats criticize us, we just throw Kennedy in their face, give them Laffer's theory, walk out of the room, and get on with the business of making America great. David, what do you think?

MR. STOCKMAN: We really need to cut social spending.

MR. BAKER: Well, that's all the time we have today. Let's start fleshing out this supply-side economics thing. Let's get the speechwriters coming up with something the President is comfortable with.

THE PRESIDENT: I'm comfortable with it already. I'm going to tell the people that we'll cut their taxes, defeat the Soviets, and balance the budget. And, the whole thing is backed up by economics and has a history of success, even under the Democrats. Thank you all very much.

(As they leave the Oval Office, Ed Meese smiles broadly. Murray Weidenbaum looks at David Stockman. David Stockman looks at Murray Weidenbaum. Each has a slight hint of a frown.)

MR. WEIDENBAUM: Well, David, I guess we are political appointees!

MR. STOCKMAN: At least I don't have to go back to a university when this is done.

MR. WEIDENBAUM: I hear you. Take care. Let's keep in touch on this.

Living with Inflation and Deflation Around the World

In the two decades before the COVID-19 pandemic and the unprecedented macroeconomic stimulus in response to it, inflation had fallen so low in the U.S. that the Fed worried about deflation, a decline in the average price level. Japan had experienced persistent deflation episodes for two decades. In my lifetime, we have never had to deal with prolonged deflation in the U.S. We have not had high and persistent deflation since the Great Depression. From 1929 to 1933, the U.S. price level fell nearly 25%. Good, you say? Wouldn't it be nice to have prices falling for a change? But wages are prices too, and if our wages fall more than prices, our purchasing power falls. If we have debt, and who doesn't in the modern U.S. economy, the real (adjusted for inflation) value of that debt rises with deflation. We must work more to make our monthly mortgage payments. Just as an indebted farmer "lost the farm" in the 1930s, an indebted suburbanite might lose the house if persistent deflation returned.

Inflation has been the economic norm in the U.S. for over eighty years. After World War II and the elimination of price controls, the U.S. price level rose like steam from a boiling pot. Then, in the 1950s, we had creeping inflation ranging from about 1% to 3%. Though low, many worried about this rate of inflation. With 2% inflation per year, a dollar would lose half its purchasing power in 36 years. In the 1960s, tax cuts, government spending for the Vietnam War, and more domestic spending on "Great Society" social programs at home boosted demand in the economy. By December 1969, the CPI was 6.2% higher than a year earlier. In the 1970s and early 1980s, the rapidly expanding money supply, together with supply shocks (oil price increases), drove the inflation rate to double digits. In the last 30 years, the average inflation rate has trended downward. Between 2014 and 2020, U.S. inflation averaged about 1.5%.

Because we've long experienced inflation, we've adapted to it rationally. We no longer expect zero inflation. In the late 1970s, Solveig and I obtained a home mortgage with a 10.5% interest rate. Some paid much higher rates then. The high inflation of the period led to expectations of high future inflation, and lenders protected themselves with an inflation premium. The 10-year yield on U.S. treasury bonds peaked at just under 16% in 1981.

In addition to the inflation premium on interest rates, we also live with inflation through explicit and implicit cost-of-living adjustments in wage contracts. We index for inflation income tax brackets and the standard deduction on U.S. tax forms. When inflation occurs, the standard deduction and tax brackets increase. Banks offer variable interest rate loans with rates lower than those on fixed-rate loans. The flames of unexpected inflation burned banks in the 1980s. Banks, especially savings and loan institutions, were locked into assets with low, fixed rates, while rising inflation drove their cost of attracting deposits higher and higher. We often call inflation a rise in the cost of living, but closer inspection reveals this is not the case. If inflation raised the cost of living, we'd all be dead, especially in times of rapid inflation.

When inflation rates get very high, economists call it hyperinflation. How high is high? From August 1922 to November 1923, in the Weimar Republic of Germany, the average monthly inflation rate was 322%. In October 1922, the monthly inflation rate was 25,500%. Prices doubled every 3.7 days. But the well-known German hyperinflation is not the record. That honor goes to Hungary, when, for a year after World War II, inflation rates averaged 19,800 % per month. The price level, at times, doubled every 15.6 hours. And hyperinflation is not confined to distant history. In January 1994, in the former Yugoslavia, the price level doubled in 1.4 days. Likewise, in Zimbabwe, in November 1998, the price level doubled in 24.7 hours. In 2018, in Venezuela, the average price level rose 65,000% in a year.

This list of countries gives us a hint about the causes of hyperinflation. None are examples of political and social stability. And that's where hyperinflation starts, with a government in trouble and its hand on the money printing press. Hyperinflation results from an attempted monetary solution to political problems faced by a shaky government. Most political problems suggest to politicians that some form of government spending is the answer. But tenuous political tenure doesn't lead to increased taxes to finance this spending. Hyperinflation starts with an increase in the federal government budget deficit. Massive deficit increases can be financed only one way, by the creation of money. In some countries, the government that makes budget policy also controls the central bank. In this case, the government simply writes checks. If the central bank is separate from the government, hyperinflation can result if the central bank accommodates government spending by buying all the bonds the government issues to finance its deficit, which economists call monetizing the debt.

The distortions of price signals, the unwanted wealth redistribution, and the enormous "shoe leather" costs associated with keeping up with hyperinflation eventually bring it to an end. Stopping hyperinflation requires stopping the causes we noted above. The government must get the budget deficit under control. The central bank must make a credible commitment to a more modest rate of increase in the money supply. The medicine tastes terrible, but it works.

In the latter part of the 20th century, we didn't have hyperinflation in the United States, but we struggled with persistent inflation. President Richard Nixon imposed wage and price controls in 1971, attempting to reduce inflation. A few years later, inflation rose again. His successor, Gerald Ford, handed out WIN (Whip Inflation Now) buttons in the White House. Inflation continued. President Jimmy Carter had the energy crisis and hostages in Iran to worry about, not economic policy. Inflation rose. Ronald Reagan capitalized on the bad economy of the Carter years, and after the 1980 election turned the cold war and tax cuts into some of the largest budget deficits in history.

The budget deficits of the early 1980s could have bred increased inflation had the Fed accommodated. Yet inflation declined in the 1980s in the United States, largely because a Fed chair named Paul Volker slammed on the U.S. monetary brakes, and real interest rates (interest rate minus inflation rate) rose. The inflation rate fell to under 2% in 1986. Monetary policy can control inflation, but it can be economically painful.

Volker passed the monetary baton to Alan Greenspan shortly thereafter, and inflation has trended downward and stayed low for years. It was about 5.5% in 1990, but only 1.2% in 2020. In the years after the Financial Crisis of 2007- 2009, and the economic strains of the Covid-19 Pandemic, the federal government ran record budget deficits. The Fed, through accommodative "quantitative easing," has bordered on debt monetization. In April 2022, the annual inflation rate was 8.5%. It averaged in the 6-7% range in 2022, and the Fed has raised interest rates to combat it. In early 2023, high inflation persisted, but it moderated throughout the year. In early 2024, when I write this, lower inflation has caused the Fed to pause its interest rate increases and to signal future rate reductions. Time will tell if we can control inflation without causing a recession, but in the meantime, we're living with inflation again.

Bubbles, Busts, and Bailouts:

The Financial Crisis, Great Recession, Covid-19 Pandemic and Unprecedented Macroeconomic Stimulus

Tumult describes the U.S. economy in the first decades of this century. A housing market and related financial assets bubble started things off. In a bubble, an asset's price rises to a level much higher than that justified by underlying fundamentals. Of course, as bubbles usually relate to something new, it's hard to identify these new underlying fundamentals during a bubble. We identify a bubble only with hindsight after the bubble bursts.

Economists and historians have identified many past bubbles: the tulip mania of the 17th century (the Tulip Mania), the international trading companies of the 18th century (the South Sea Bubble), stock funds in the 1920s, internet stocks in the late 1990s, and the housing market and new housing-related financial assets in the early and mid-2000s.

A good bubble usually requires debt to make it happen and then burst. Economists and other financial professionals call debt-financed investments "leverage." Just as levers help lift things up, financial leverage can elevate rates of return when asset prices are rising. However, leverage amplifies negative returns as well. Leverage, after a bubble bursts, can turn a decline or downturn into a crash, as attempts to refinance debt meet a lack of liquidity.

Mortgage debt grew rapidly in the early 2000s. People with positive equity used their houses as collateral for home equity lines of credit. The Miller family bought two cars and a sailboat financed with tax-deductible home equity borrowing. Fortunately, the family's economist didn't think of the home equity loan as a cash machine, just loans that we paid back over time at favorable terms. Others were not so disciplined.

Many forces combined to create a runup in housing debt leading to the housing bubble. We obsess about home ownership in the United States, one component of the American Dream. This dream, combined with well-intentioned egalitarian urges in the U.S. populace and its elected representatives, has led over time to incentives for home ownership, such as the home mortgage interest tax deduction. Also, the federal government created organizations such as the Federal National Mortgage Association (Fannie Mae), a private, quasi-government corporation that provides a secondary market in home mortgages. With explicit and implicit backing from the government, this business borrows in financial markets and then uses the funds to buy mortgages from banks and other institutions who issue them. When these institutions don't have to "hold the paper," and sell their mortgages to Fannie Mae, they are less diligent in screening borrowers. Economists and real estate experts suggest that the popular thirty-year mortgage, which makes homeownership more affordable, would not exist without the actions of Fannie Mae and its counterparts in the real estate market.

The U.S. government, through laws such as the Community Reinvestment Act, urged U.S. financial regulators, such as the Federal Reserve, the Federal Deposit Insurance Corporation, and the Office of the Comptroller of the Currency in the Treasury Department, to encourage regulated financial institutions to lend to low and moderate-income households. To an economist, lower-income lending usually means riskier lending. A frenzy of low-income mortgages proliferated in the housing bubble, most with adjustable interest rates and some using interest-only payments with a future "balloon payment." Borrow now, pay only interest, and later, after your house price has continued to grow, refinance, and make the balloon payment. This is good advice if your house price continues to rise and rates stay low, but it turns into a prescription for foreclosure if these conditions change. Some in the press called these mortgages NINJA loans, an acronym for borrowers with no income and no job—a risky loan, indeed.

Financial institutions packaged these sub-prime mortgages into collateralized debt obligations (CDOs) and sold them to a public of eager buyers little concerned about the details of the financial instruments they were buying. A CDO is a bundle of assets turned into its own asset (a derivative) and traded in the market. In the early and mid-2000s, the most important CDOs were mortgage-backed securities (MBS), bundles of mortgages, especially risky, sub-prime mortgages.

In booms, manias, and bubbles, speculators want to buy now because the price will only go up. Of course, prices go down, as well, after the bust. In 2008, the boom in U.S. financial markets started to unravel. It's hard to pinpoint a specific beginning to what came to be called the Financial Crisis, as the issuance and leveraged trading of sub-prime MBS had been going on for years. The stock market, a leading economic indicator, had begun to decline in October 2007, somewhat caused by worries about the sub-prime mortgage market and the value, or lack thereof, of portfolios containing large amounts of these assets. Investors also worried about declining home sales and rising mortgage foreclosures, and the questionable financial footing of unregulated investment businesses called hedge funds. In fact, the U.S. Treasury, responding to these worries, convinced large U.S. banks to create a "superfund" with which to purchase "toxic assets" owned by distressed banks and hedge funds. These efforts at the Treasury Department were spearheaded by the Secretary of the Treasury, Henry Paulson, former Chairman of the Board and CEO of Goldman Sachs, Inc., a Wall Street titan.

Secretary Paulson, a financial market veteran, knew that financial institutions hoard cash when they become worried about the health of their portfolios. They stop lending to each other, and when this happens, liquidity dries up in financial markets. Debt comes due and must be refinanced, and with a lack of liquidity, the risk of default looms. To stem a downward spiral of defaults, the Treasury and Fed often function as sources of liquidity, either through direct loans or through the arrangement of loans to, or direct acquisition of, troubled firms by other healthier ones. This willingness to provide liquidity and prevent financial crises gives rise to something called the "too big to fail doctrine," which leads to "bailouts" in the financial system.

In March of 2008, the Treasury and Fed applied the too big to fail doctrine in the case of Bear Sterns, an 85-year-old investment firm, by arranging a merger with JPMorgan Chase and Company, now the largest bank in the U.S. The union was an arranged marriage, a "shotgun wedding," with a bride pregnant with debt and hemorrhaging cash. JPMorgan Chase would later, in September, acquire Washington Mutual, another arranged marriage. My family's home equity loans, though not sub-prime, had been with Washington Mutual.

The financial branches of the federal government, along with the Fed, had a busy 2008 and 2009. The venerable Wall Street institution, Lehman Brothers, failed in September 2008, with the Fed and the Treasury watching the demise, unable, yet, to make direct loans to a company in such a crisis, or to get anyone else to acquire it. That same day, Bank of America acquired the Wall Street household name, Merrill Lynch. The Treasury also put Fannie Mae and other secondary mortgage market institutions in conservatorship, essentially nationalizing them. Throughout 2008, Ben Bernanke, Chair of the Fed and Henry Paulson, Secretary of the Treasury, sought and received from Congress and the President new authority to create an alphabet soup of new lending and other bailout authority. Meanwhile, real GDP declined, and the unemployment rate rose to over 10%. The U.S. stock market continued the biggest bear market since the Great Crash of the 1930s, declining over 50% by March 2009. Beginning in December 2007, we experienced our deepest and longest recession since the Great Depression, a period now called The Great Recession. The economy didn't return to growth until June of 2009. It was a good time to teach macroeconomics, but that's about all that was good then. To someone hoping to retire in fewer than ten years, especially an economist, these were unsettling times.

I worried about retirement savings in 2008 and 2009. In another decade, I'd hoped to retire; hopes dashed almost daily as potential stock market rallies fizzled at the market close. Would I have to work forever? Would I have to memorize the question, "Could you please wheel me to my classroom?" This time, unlike my behavior after the 1987 stock market crash, I stayed the course, putting money every two weeks into a declining stock market. It wasn't much fun, but there were few better alternatives.

While the Fed pumped money into the economy, buying all kinds of financial assets, and kept interest rates historically low year after year, government fiscal policy quickly turned expansionary in the Great Recession and beyond. As we've noted in previous vignettes, it's not hard, politically, to be a Keynesian.

Nearing the end of the Bush Administration in 2007, after a long economic expansion, at the beginning of the financial crisis and just before the recession, the federal budget deficit was $161 billion, 1.1% of GDP. As Barack Obama took office, the estimated deficit for 2009 was $1.186 trillion. No doubt, Mr. Obama inherited red ink from his predecessor. With the automatic stabilizers of declining tax revenues and increased spending, like more unemployment compensation and supplemental nutrition payments (food stamps), the deficit ballooned to over $1.412 trillion in 2009, nearly 10% of GDP, the highest level since World War II.

In 2009 the government enacted discretionary, expansionary fiscal policy, as well. The American Recovery and Reinvestment Act (ARRA) of 2009 authorized increased spending on infrastructure, healthcare, and education, along with some tax cuts. While this type of policy always affects the economy with a lag, the Congressional Budget Office later estimated that by 2011 the decline in real GDP was between .4% and 2.3% less than it would have been without the stimulus. Deficits remained high in the years following the recession, partly due to slower than anticipated economic growth, but they declined as a percent of GDP until reaching 2.4% in 2015, before rising to 3.2% in 2016, Mr. Obama's last year in office.

The financial crisis and Great Recession certainly demonstrated that the federal government, under both Democrat and Republican leadership, had become increasingly willing to undertake strong, active measures to counteract downturns in the economy and threats to financial and economic stability. Nothing compares, however, to the extraordinary measures

235

taken to combat the economic devastation pursuant to the first wave of the Covid 19 pandemic. Both voluntary and government-mandated lockdowns threw the economy into a rapid downturn in the winter and spring of 2020. The federal government responded with extraordinary fiscal measures, expanding unemployment compensation, and undertaking three waves of direct payments to low, middle, and upper-middle-income households. Solveig and I received each round of stimulus checks, even though we were far from destitute. This fiscal stimulus, the continued easy money policies by the Fed, and the development of Covid 19 virus vaccines led to a V-shaped recovery in the U.S. economy in 2021. Then, a combination of supply chain disruptions and constraints, combined with policy-induced demand stimulus, renewed inflation in the economy.

In the spring of 2023, the Fed pressed on the monetary brakes. Rising interest rates and reckless risk-taking in the previous era of low rates led to the failure of Silicon Valley Bank, the second largest, after Washington Mutual, ever to fail. Bailouts were in full swing again. With lending and deposit guarantees beyond previous limits, the Treasury, FDIC, and the Fed moved to provide financial stability once again. Despite recent Fed tightening, booms, busts, bailouts, and extraordinary fiscal stimulus are still alive and well in the U.S. economy.

Part Nine

Economics and Personal Finance

Introduction

While a general knowledge of economics will make you smarter, a better citizen, and a more interesting party guest (if you don't overdo it), understanding the economics of personal finance will make you richer. Every normal person does personal finance. Here, we see it done in an economist's style. And because personal finance is, well, personal, we'll see a bit of my personal finance in Part Nine. These personal snapshots are aids to understanding issues such as saving for retirement, asset allocation, risk and return, diversification, and the time value of money, among others.

We begin with a story about liquidity preference, which is the economic jargon for how much of your wealth you wish to hold in the form of money. In "Uncle Scrooge and Liquidity Preference…," a six-year-old economist learns that liquidity has many benefits but a substantial cost: foregone compound interest.

In "It Pays to Wait…," the perspicacious observations of the toddler Keynes, an ancient Persian story, a 1960s junior high school riddle, and environmental alarmism illustrate the power of compound interest and exponential growth. In personal finance, time is on our side, but we must be patient.

I show my age when I use the archaic vinyl music metaphor flip side to describe the relationship between compound interest and discounted present value. As compounding leads to a higher future value, discounting leads to a lower present value. This tricky economics principle complicates a common real-world problem, the first D in "The Four Ds: Divorce, Division, Death, and Discounting." Discounted present value analysis also applies to deferred compensation in professional baseball contracts, lottery winnings, real estate investment, education investment, and energy-efficient appliances.

Financially desperate people frequenting payday loan offices are much more likely than the federal government to default on their loans. In "Payday Loans and U.S. Government Bonds...," lenders add a risk premium to annual interest rates on loans to riskier borrowers, sometimes as much as 500 %. Here, the economist again turns down the music at a rollicking party by cautioning that high returns in financial markets are mostly because of risk. Free lunches don't exist, and if you ignore risk in financial planning, you may have to get a payday loan to buy yours.

Once we know about the relationship between risk and return, our next personal finance task is to make risk as low as possible for any rate of return we wish to receive on our portfolio of assets. This requires diversification. We begin with the geographical diversification by a 1970s graduate student in "Always Keep a Copy of Your Dissertation in the Trunk of Your Car." We can diversify financial portfolios by including a variety of asset types and concentrating on the direction and magnitude of the variability of the returns on these assets.

Hall of Fame economists David Ricardo and John Maynard Keynes made fortunes speculating in financial markets, but most economists are much more boring in their approach to accumulating wealth and riches. In "Get Rich Slowly with Seven Rules for Riches," we apply the principles previously learned in Part Nine: compound interest and doubling time, risk and return, asset allocation, diversification, and patience. I also confess, in this vignette, that I have not always walked the walk as I've talked the talk, but I hope you can learn from some of my mistakes.

Uncle Scrooge and Liquidity Preference

In my childhood neighborhood on the Old Rock Island Road in East Wenatchee, Washington, most kids liked comic books. *Batman, Spiderman, Flash Gordon*, and, of course, *Superman* were always popular. I didn't care much for the action heroes. I can only remember two comic book characters I liked. One was a fat little kid named Tubby in the comic *Lu Lu*. Tubby, Lu Lu, and their friends had a great clubhouse. As a chunky little kid, myself, I liked Tubby a lot. But my all-time favorite comic book character was Donald Duck's uncle, Uncle Scrooge McDuck. I never liked Donald himself, a holdover from the cartoons at the Saturday matinee. I found his voice so irritating. Uncle Scrooge, however, to a budding six-year-old economist, was sublime.

Maybe you remember Uncle Scrooge and his castle with the money bin, where he kept his billions of dollars of cash, mostly coin, that he pushed around with what we called, in those days, a bulldozer. I imitated my comic book hero by converting my weekly allowance and cash gifts into coins. I often dumped my total financial wealth onto my bed and pushed it around with cupped dozer hands, *a la* Uncle Scrooge.

Like Scrooge McDuck, I, too, was a harmless miser, not a malicious one like Dickens' Scrooge. From an early age, I didn't like to spend. It had something to do with my first purchase. I had saved several months to buy a pair of underwater goggles. They cost $1.25 at the Southend Variety Store. I can remember counting out the money on the counter as my mom and dad looked on proudly. The next weekend at Lake Chelan I discovered that they leaked uncontrollably. I've been a reluctant spender ever since. To this day, I live in a modern baseball household, where my wife, Solveig, is the Designated Spender. Without her, I'd be living in a one-room hovel and have a huge Scrooge-like bank account. It's a little sick, I know.

It wasn't long before my miserly ways began to differ from those of my hero, Uncle Scrooge. Scrooge held his wealth in one form only. Financial professionals use a portfolio metaphor to describe someone's collection of wealth. A portfolio is something you keep your wealth in. Assets make up wealth. If you have a diversity of assets, you have a diversified portfolio. How about that! Sometimes finance and economics terms have meaning. Scrooge's portfolio consisted almost entirely of the cash in his money bin. He had few other assets. His portfolio was not very diversified. Yes, he owned some real property, his castle, and some big cars and bulldozers, but mostly he had cash. He had no savings account, stocks, or bonds. Any economist would tell Scrooge that his portfolio was too liquid, a term we use to describe some assets.

Liquidity is the ease with which we can turn an asset into something we can spend, money, a medium of exchange. Scrooge held nearly all his wealth in the form of money. He had an extreme preference for liquidity. This is costly to anyone, but especially to a miser, who doesn't spend much anyway.

My first lesson in liquidity preference came from my mom. One day, when I was playing Uncle Scrooge on my bed, Mom came into the room and said, "You ought to open a savings account and earn interest."

"What's that?" I asked.

"It's something you do at the bank. You know what a bank is, don't you?"

"Not really," I said. "I usually stay in the car when you or Dad go inside."

"A bank is a place where you can put your money and earn more money."

I was immediately leery of banks. If my money was at the bank, I couldn't push it around my bed with dozer hands.

"I kind of like having my money here with me," I said. "You know, like Uncle Scrooge."

"I know you do," she said, in that sympathetic tone all good moms use when they are about to try to get you to change your mind.

"But let me tell you about the other part, interest. At a bank, you earn money with your money. If you leave a dollar in the bank for a year, at the end of that year you will have $1.02. In another year, you'll have 1.04. After a while, you even earn interest on your interest."

Mom paused as she looked at my knitted brow. I was thinking as hard as a six-year-old could think.

"What do I have to do to get that extra money?" I asked.

"Nothing," she said, "You just have to wait."

"Nothing?"

"That's right," she said. "Of course, you can't spend any of it for a year."

"That's okay," I said, the young miser.

"Could I keep a little at home?" I asked, "So I can play a little Uncle Scrooge."

"Actually, that's a good idea," she said. "Everyone needs to have some cash around, but not so much that you lose that interest."

"Okay," I said. "But now that I'm going to put money in the bank and earn, int, ah int…"

"Interest," she said.

"Yeah, interest. If I'm going to have a bunch of my money at the bank, maybe I could have an increase in my allowance."

"We'll see," she said.

It Pays to Wait:

Compound Interest, Doubling, and the Time Value of Money

At the age of four and a half, someone asked British economist John Maynard Keynes the meaning of interest. Young Maynard replied, "If I let you have a halfpenny and you kept it for a very long time, you would have to give me back that halfpenny, and another too." The precocious youngster had captured the essence of the time value of money in one crisp sentence. First, he had to lend someone a halfpenny. He could not buy anything with that halfpenny now, but in time, if he could wait, he could spend much more than his original halfpenny. Money saved at interest grows over time.

Young Maynard had also explained interest in terms of its doubling time. A fascination with doubling time is not limited to precocious toddler economists. In an old Persian story, a clever member of a King's court offers to give a beautiful chessboard to the King, if the King would give him, in return, one grain of rice for the first square on the board, two grains for the second, four for the third square, eight grains for the fourth, and so on. For each additional square on the board, the courtier would receive double the amount of rice. The King was feeling rather good about his bargain when the storehouse workers delivered a little over one thousand grains of rice for the 11th square on the board. The King started to take notice when the 20th square yielded over half a million grains of rice. For the 30th square, the King had to deliver well over five hundred million grains of rice. Far before the game reached the 64th square, the King's grain reserves were exhausted. Such is the power of doubling.

I remember a riddle I learned in junior high school. Which would you rather have, one million dollars or the sum from a penny doubling every day for a month? You get the value of the doubling penny on the 30th day. If you take the initial million, your sucker bet proves P.T. Barnum right. Choosing the doubling penny requires patience in the early days of the month. In the first few days, the doubling doesn't generate much growth. On the first day, you have two cents, four cents on the second day, and eight cents on the third. At the end of the first week, you are only up to $1.28. Even at the end of the second week, after fourteen doublings, you're still at only $163.84. On the 21st day, your gamble would yield just over $21,000, far short of a million dollars. But look what happens in the last days of the month. On the 27th day, you jump for joy as the value goes over $1.3 million. And then the real fun begins. $2.68 million on the 28th day, almost $5.4 million on the 29th day, and on the glorious 30th day your wealth doubles again to over $10.7 million. Too bad it's not March, you say, or any other month with 31 days. Don't get greedy!

Economists and other scientists call this exponential growth. Each application of the growth rate applies to the accumulated previous amount. Outside of economics, the principle of doubling and exponential growth has negative, if not frightening, connotations. In 1972, with environmental alarmism in the U.S. and around the world, a group called the Club of Rome published a book entitled *The Limits to Growth*. The authors of the book argued that exponential growth of economic output and population went hand in hand with exponential growth of pollution and depletion of resources and that we had better start limiting growth now before compounding problems surprise us later. A fundamental story in this book made use of yet another children's riddle, this time one from France. It's the metaphor of the lily pond, or as others later called it, the principle of the 29th day.

In this story, the lily pond symbolizes the earth's fixed resources, and the exponential growth of water lilies is economic output. The riddle then goes as follows. Suppose we know that the area covered by water lilies in the pond doubles every day, and further, if allowed to double daily, lily growth will choke off all other life in the pond in 30 days. As you watch the mass of water lilies growing slowly in the beginning days, you become complacent, and make a mental note that you will start beating back the lilies when they cover half the pond. When do you rise to action? On the 29th day! You have one day to stop the water lilies from choking off life as we know it.

The growth rate in all the stories above is a hearty 100%. But the principles of doubling time and exponential growth apply with lower growth rates, as well. A particularly useful rule of thumb is the rule of 72. If we take the percent growth rate and divide it into 72, we obtain an estimate of the number of periods it takes for a sum to double. If a bank account is earning compound interest at the rate of 10%, the account will double in a little over seven years (72 /10 = 7.2). If the interest rate is 7.2%, the account will double in 10 years (72/7.2 = 10). If the rate is 3.5%, the account will double only after 20 years. In the late 1990s and mid-2000s, it was common to see someone's asset portfolio grow in value at 35% a year. I, along with my baby-boomer colleagues, was thinking about early retirement, if our net worth could double twice in four or five years. Everyone should experience irrational exuberance at least once or twice in a lifetime.

With this in mind, we can only speculate why the young John Maynard Keynes thought it would take a long time for his halfpenny to double. Perhaps he thought the interest rate he could receive from the borrower was low. At 1% interest per year, he'd only have 1.01 halfpennies at the end of the first year. At that rate, it would take seventy-two years (72/1 = 72) to earn enough interest to double his halfpenny. On the other hand, at the age of four and a half, even a year is a long time. The young Keynes might have had what economists call a high rate of time preference. He might have been impatient. He didn't like waiting to spend. Or, on the other hand, young Keynes might have had a much lower rate of time preference, but the borrower could have had a poor credit history. The borrower might take the halfpenny and move to India, never to be seen again. Each of these facts would increase the minimum acceptable interest rate to young Keynes, the compensation he required to save, to forego spending now. At a 100% rate of interest, the halfpenny would double in less than a year.

Unlike exponential growth of cancer cells, pollution, or resource depletion, the time value of money, compound interest, and exponential growth all have good connotations in finance and economics. If one starts at a young age, saves a modest amount of one's income annually, and receives compound interest, one can retire at a reasonable age and live comfortably on accumulated wealth. If a country's output per capita grows at just 3% per year, each generation is twice as prosperous as the previous one. Exponential growth and its near relative, compound interest, are good for those who can forego spending now. John Maynard Keynes knew this at the age of four and a half. It pays to wait. Most members of my generation, and perhaps yours, are far less knowledgeable.

The Time Value of Money and the 4Ds:

Divorce, Division, Death, and Discounting

Frank and Jill are getting a divorce. At least all signs point that way. After 36 years of marriage, Frank is still trying to find himself. Jill is not willing to let him search anymore, at least not with the woman he's been seeing for the past two years. She asked him to give her up. He wouldn't do it. Jill now thinks that even if he did, it wouldn't matter. Before Frank and Jill can achieve the first of our 4Ds, divorce, they must confront the remaining three, division, death, and discounting. And when they do, time becomes an important economic consideration.

Because more than half of U.S. marriages end in divorce, many Americans know about division, "splitting the sheets," deciding who gets the lawnmower, who gets the couch, and who gets which half of the financial assets and liabilities. After 36 years of marriage, Frank and Jill have some financial net worth, the value of their assets minus the value of their liabilities. Assets come in many forms. Money in the bank, a portfolio of stocks or mutual funds, and equity in a house are just three examples. Liabilities are usually various forms of debt, such as the mortgage loan on the house, credit card balances, or outstanding student loans. We can determine the value of these assets and liabilities easily because each is a money lump sum now. With a few phone calls, we could get all the values, add them up, subtract the negative from the positive, and determine Frank and Jill's net worth. Then we just divide by two. Simple.

But complications exist. Frank is 60 years old and had planned to retire in six years. He will receive an annual pension from his employer based on some fraction of the average of his three highest years of salary. This is an asset, a good thing financially, but it doesn't come in the form of a money lump sum today. Jill thinks she is entitled to half this retirement income, or equivalent compensation in lieu of it.

The next D now comes into play, death. If Frank dies, his pension stops. Jill has no survivor benefit. Economists help lawyers out here by creating a statistical life, noting Frank's mortality. The expected pension from Frank's 95th year is much less than from his 70th year because the probability that Frank survives to the age of ninety-five is much lower than it is to age 70. Fortunately for the forensic economist (Yes, that's what they are called.), the U.S. Census Bureau has estimates of the probability that people of Frank's age will live to each higher age. We can find the expected amount of Frank's retirement income in any year by multiplying Frank's survival probability by the pension amount. If the payment in the future year is $40,000, but Frank only has a .75 probability of making it to that age, his expected payment in that year is $30,000 (.75 X $40,000).

Once we have the expected retirement payments in all future years, we're not yet ready to divide them up. We need to convert this flow of expected retirement payments over time into a lump sum so we can compare it with and add it to Frank and Jill's other assets. Without a lump sum value for Frank's retirement income, Jill would have to wait until Frank retired to get half his pension, and then receive checks every year. But once we convert the future flow of expected payments to a lump sum, both Frank and Jill can "cash out of" their marriage and avoid messy contact in the future.

When converting this flow of retirement payments over time into a lump sum today we confront the final D, discounting. Discounting is an abbreviation for discounted present value analysis. It's a special way we add up the expected annual retirement payments in Frank and Jill's divorce settlement. Each of these payments is a different financial event in time. And if financial events happen at different times, they have different values today, in the present. They have what economists call different present values.

Suppose I ask you to give me $1,000 now, a financial event, and tell you that I will give it back to you in five years, another financial event. Even with zero risk that I won't pay you back, and even if you expect zero inflation in the next five years, you will not lend me the $1,000 on these terms. Because interest rates are positive, if you have $1,000 today, you could put it in the bank and earn interest. The future value of the $1,000 would be $1,000 plus the interest earned. Letting me use the money for five years means you would forego that interest. $1,000 in hand today is worth more than $1,000 five years from now. The present value (today) of $1,000 in the future is less than $1,000, because of the foregone interest. Because of the possibility of earning interest, money has a time value.

The farther a financial event lies in the future, the lower its present value today. Waiting longer for something like a retirement payment means you have more foregone interest than having the payment today. Waiting creates an opportunity cost. When converting a flow of financial events over time to a lump sum, economists multiply each future event by a discount factor with a value of less than one. The farther forward in time, the higher the discount factor, the more we discount the event. The present value of Frank's expected retirement, a lump sum today, is less than the undiscounted sum of the future expected payments. If Frank or his lawyer overlooked this fact, Frank would be over-compensating Jill in the divorce settlement.

While discounting is important for divorce and division, the practice has many other useful applications. Many businesses pay key employees deferred compensation. It's especially prevalent in sports businesses. Before the Texas Rangers traded Alex Rodriguez to the New York Yankees, he was the $250 million shortstop, $25 million a year for ten years. That's a lot of money, but the discounted present value is not $250 million. If someone wins a million dollars in a lottery, they might receive the winnings in ten annual installments of $100,000. The present value of ten annual payments of $100,000 is less than one million dollars.

We use discounted present value analysis when we are considering paying a lump sum today for some expected annual flow of financial returns in the future. How much are you willing to pay for an apartment building? It shouldn't be more than the discounted present value of your net returns in the future.

How much are you willing to pay for an energy-efficient refrigerator? It will cost more than the cheaper watt-guzzler now. But unless you worship at the shrine of the sustainable society, the extra cost should be less than the discounted present value of the future savings on your electric bill.

How much income are you willing to forego now from quitting you job and going back to school, with hopes of a higher income in the future? You ought to look at the present value of the increase in your expected annual earnings before you submit you resignation.

Divorce, baseball salaries, lottery winnings, real estate investment, purchasing energy-efficient appliances, and investing in education, are only a few of the decisions we can improve by understanding the time value of money and discounted present value analysis. Sometimes being an economist is not that abnormal!

Payday Loans and U.S. Government Bonds:

The Economics of Risk and Return

At Mary's job, she's paid at the end of the month. Halfway through the month, her car dies. She shops around, and the cheapest repair is $400. Mary needs a car to get to work, get to class at the university, and take her kids to school. Before she divorced, she declared bankruptcy with her former husband. He's still a loser. She has little hope for child support payments. Her credit report reads like a horror novel. She has maxed out her credit cards and can't get new ones. Loan officers at banks and credit unions look the other way when she comes in the door. But she needs a short-term loan to fix her car. Mary needs to borrow enough to get to her next payday. She can pay off the loan then. It's time for a "payday loan."

If Mary's car were in working order, she could get a title loan. She would surrender the title of her car to the lender as collateral, along with a set of keys for the "Repo Man," if needed. But loan companies have another option for the financially desperate whose cars won't run, a check advance loan. The loan company would accept a check from Mary in the amount of $480 and would agree not to cash it until Mary's payday at the end of the month. By then, Mary's paycheck would have been deposited in her account and the check would be good. The loan company would call first to make sure that the account balance was high enough. Mary would receive $400 in cash. Whoa, you say, what happened to the other $80? That's the interest payment. The check advance fee is $10 per $100 borrowed per week. $400 for two weeks is $80. The annual interest rate is 520%.

In the aftermath of the financial crisis of 2007 - 2009 and the economic shock of the COVID-19 pandemic, the federal government ran large budget deficits. Like Mary with a dead car, Uncle Sam had to borrow to finance the deficit. When Uncle Sam borrows, he has more and better choices than Mary. He can borrow with 30-year bonds, or for shorter terms, say five or ten years, with debt called notes. Uncle Sam also borrows a lot with debt called U.S. Treasury bills. These are not crisp tens and twenties, currency, but rather short-term debt, usually paid back within three months. In November 2021, the interest rate on U.S. Treasury bills was near zero, .04%.

That's quite a difference; .04% for Uncle Sam and 520% for Mary. It doesn't seem fair to normal people that Mary, down on her luck, gets gouged with a payday loan when the government can borrow at near-zero interest. Unlike normal people, economists would point out that this difference is a response in a market economy to the relationship between risk and return.

Many kinds of risk inhabit loan markets. The most important is the risk of default, where a borrower does not pay back the loan. Given Mary's credit history, she has a high default risk. Uncle Sam has never defaulted on a loan. If he faces financial strains, he can always borrow more, or, conspiring with the Fed, create money. To protect themselves from the risk of loaning to Mary, lenders tack a risk premium onto her interest rate. But isn't this risk premium excessive? The financial market has something to say about this. After adjusting for risk, all interest rates in the market are the same. If they weren't the same, participants in financial markets would make adjustments until they were.

If there are no barriers to entering the market and Mary's high interest rate really is excessive, lenders will enter the payday loan market. This increase in the supply of payday loans will drive down the interest rate on these loans until it doesn't pay to enter the industry. In a broader, social sense, we might be concerned about the level of financial desperation that drives people like Mary to the payday loan market, but the high interest rate would be economically justified.

The relationship between risk and return applies in all financial markets. Another form of risk is associated with the variability of the rate of return. Take shares of corporate stock, for example. Stocks might pay something like an interest rate on a loan or bond, a payment called a dividend—a distribution to the stockholder of some of the company's profits. You can also earn income in the stock market by buying shares at one price and selling them at a higher price; a fortunate circumstance called a capital gain. But if stock prices fall and you sell, you earn a capital loss.

The variability of stock prices makes them riskier than, say, U.S. Treasury bills. Over the long term, the average return on stocks is higher than that on treasury bills, to compensate investors for this higher risk. Among individual stocks, the variability of the stock's price is inversely related to the rate of return on the stock. The more variable the price, the higher the risk, and the higher the return must be to compensate for that risk. There are no "free lunches" in financial markets.

Remember this principle; except for differences in risk, all rates of return are the same. Very smart people all around the world keep their eyes and their programmed computers focused on risk-adjusted rates of return. If rates of return move outside a range justified by differences in risk, these smart people sell the losers and buy the winners, driving up rates of return of the former and driving down rates of return of the latter. It's like opening another payday loan store when the difference in rates of return between payday loans and U.S. Treasury bills is no longer justified by the difference in risk.

This relationship between risk and return is important knowledge not just for economists and financial planners. It is one of the most important practical principles of personal finance. When someone attempts to sell you a high-return asset at an investment seminar, in your living room, or in an advertisement in the newspaper, your first question should be, "What is the risk?" Because, if you always pursue high rates of return without considering the high risk causing these returns, it won't be long until you are standing next to Mary at the payday loan store borrowing at 520% a year to get your car repaired.

Always Keep a Draft of Your Dissertation in the Trunk of Your Car:

The Principle of Diversification

When I was writing my Ph.D. dissertation, dinosaurs inhabited the Midwest. Sometimes I feel old enough to have seen Theropods roaming the banks of the Mississippi near Washington University in St. Louis, but I'm referring here to another large, extinct species, the IBM 360 computer. Before desktop computing or even remote terminals, we had to submit statistical programs in person to the elite "keepers of the code" at the computer center. We often ran these "jobs" after midnight to reduce computing costs. When we retrieved our computer printouts in the morning, we were often chagrined to see only a thin stack of paper. Another misplaced comma had caused another day's delay.

Because we submitted the jobs as stacks of IBM computer cards, and card readers often turned into card eaters, smart graduate students in the Nixon era learned about backup procedures. These were not in the "cloud," on portable hard discs, or thumb drives, but rather duplicate stacks of cards.

Production of printed documents in the early 1970s was equally Cretaceous, involving longhand or typed drafts and then the services of a typist. After I had accumulated about one-half inch of printed pages, I began to move beyond the fear of hungry card readers and to worry about the possibility of different kinds of disasters. What if our apartment burned, or if the Weather Underground bombed our graduate student offices on campus? What if someone stole my daypack with the only draft of my first three chapters? In these times, smart graduate students distributed their literary eggs among many physical baskets. As economics graduates, we thought of this in terms of something called diversification, in this case, geographical diversification in the storage of a physical asset, our life's work to date. I kept one copy of my budding dissertation at my office, one at our apartment, and one in the trunk of our new 1973 Plymouth Duster. (I had a working wife!) I wasn't great at statistics, but I knew that the probability of disaster destroying my dissertation at all these places was exceedingly small.

Financial diversification is not much different from a graduate student keeping a copy of his dissertation in the trunk of his car. The assets are different, but the principle is the same. You need to own more than one type of asset, and these assets should have different chances of bad things happening to them at the same time. You don't want your eggs of wealth in one financial basket.

The main risk for financial assets like stocks and bonds is not fire, theft, or political maliciousness, but simply a decline in value. Sometimes asset values grow, making the return on owning them high. Sometimes values decline and returns can be negative, even highly negative. The variability of the return on an asset is a measure of the riskiness of the asset. Because assets have different amounts of variability, they have different levels of risk.

The ideal asset has a high rate of return and a low level of risk. Unfortunately, as we learned in the previous vignette, higher rates of returns are associated with higher risk, not lower risk. Investors require higher returns to compensate for higher risk. The goal of diversification is to hold a portfolio of assets that gives you the highest return for the level of risk that you are willing to accept. How do you do this?

Let's look at stock ownership. Companies in different sectors of the economy have different patterns in the variability of their returns. For example, the returns of companies in the lodging sector have different variability than those of companies in the home entertainment sector. If a pandemic cuts down on travel, hotels, and motels, take a beating, but sellers of home entertainment equipment and video streaming subscriptions prosper. Owning shares of stock of companies in each of these sectors, in the right proportion, could cushion your portfolio in downturns. Of course, owning the right proportion of stocks is the key. If stock returns are perfectly negatively correlated, for example, you get diversification but no return. If one goes up, the other goes down by the same amount. Again, the goal is to get the same return for lower risk, or vice versa.

Financial professionals can help investors diversify their portfolios not only among sectors of one economy but also geographically across different economies of the world. The rates of return of companies with different sizes are not perfectly correlated either, offering opportunities for diversification. You can diversify beyond stocks into corporate and government bonds, real estate, precious metals, cryptocurrencies, art, and baseball cards. While the future often does not replicate the past, financial professionals can use research and simulation based on historical data to improve a portfolio's performance for a given level of risk. At least, with this goal in mind, you can ask the right questions and move in the right direction. No investment portfolio is perfect, but some are less imperfect than others.

Get Rich Slowly:

Seven Rules for Riches

Chance creates some wealth. You might get lucky and win the lottery, but do you want to count on luck to fund your retirement? If you don't, the following seven rules might help you create riches. They're not sexy. You won't get rich quickly. They're neither new nor original. They might work for you if you are willing to get rich slowly.

The first rule is: START EARLY. If you start accumulating wealth when young, time is on your side. Time allows compound interest to strut its stuff. The more time you can accumulate wealth, the more doublings you get. Remember the Persian courtier and the chessboard we noted in an earlier vignette, or the penny doubling every day for a month, or the doubling water lilies about to cover the pond on the 29th day. You need to harness the power of compounding to get rich slowly.

To accumulate wealth, you must save. Saving means spending less than you earn, NOW. This is painful for normal people, especially those in their 20s and 30s, whose unwillingness to defer gratification is a prime reason for violating rule number one. The philosophy "Eat, drink, and be merry today, for tomorrow we're old" increases the chance of little merriment in old age. It's hard to save, easy to defer the tough decision. That's why it's important to follow the second rule for riches: SAVE REGULARLY, preferably on some form of financial autopilot. How much you need to save regularly depends, in part, on how well you did with rule number one, when you started saving.

The third rule is a corollary of the second: SAVE OFF THE TOP. When you get your paycheck, save before you spend. Financial planners and personal finance columnists often call this "paying yourself first." If you only save what's left after the spending is done, you won't save much and will have a greater chance of violating rule number 2. Payroll deductions work great. It's much easier not to spend what you don't see in your take-home pay.

Once you've decided to regularly save a percentage of your paycheck, "off the top," you must decide which assets to buy. What are the best financial investments for you? This is where risk comes in. The safest investment you could make is in U.S. government bonds, but the rate of return on these is low. To get a higher return, a higher compounding interest rate, and a shorter doubling time, you must follow rule number four: ACCEPT SOME RISK. This is another reason to follow rule number one. The longer you have until you need to draw on your accumulated wealth, the more risk you can accept and receive compensation of a higher rate of return. If you have thirty or forty years until you need retirement income, you could wait out several downturns in the stock market and ride the ensuing recoveries to riches. If you are going to retire in a few years, your exposure to risk should be lower.

Once you decide to accept some risk, don't accept more risk than is necessary to achieve some targeted rate of return. You should follow rule number five: DIVERSIFY YOUR PORTFOLIO. Purchasing shares of corporate stock in mutual funds provides a good opportunity for diversification, across sectors of the economy, business sizes, and geography. Among mutual funds, I like index funds. These are collections of corporate shares of stock designed and managed to match the performance of some stock index. For example, an S&P 500 index fund would try to match the performance of companies tracked in the S&P 500 index, the largest five hundred corporations in the United States. You could invest in a total stock market fund, where you own a piece of U.S. capitalism, diversified across all sectors of the U.S. economy. You could add an international index fund for more geographical diversification, or funds made up of smaller companies to diversify across business size.

Buying mutual funds yields benefits beyond those from diversification. If you buy funds with low annual fees, you can also satisfy rule number six: MINIMIZE TRANSACTION COSTS. These include charges such as broker commissions and portfolio management fees. The more you pay in transaction costs, the less your savings can compound and double over time. You also don't have to spend a lot of time and money trying to pick good individual stocks and bonds.

Finally, the seventh rule: BE PATIENT. It takes a while. The Persian Courtier didn't receive much grain on the first few squares of the board. Returns from the doubling penny are puny the first couple of weeks of the month of daily doubling. But in time, watch out. That last doubling period is the best. Your wealth won't grow every month. Sometimes, even a well-diversified portfolio loses value, but, if history is a guide, it will turn around. World capitalism, in the long run, is a good bet. And, in a downturn, because you are following rule number two and saving regularly, you will be buying pieces of world capitalism at bargain prices.

Okay, you say. Laying down rules is easy. I've talked the talk, but did I walk the walk? Well, therein lies a short tale. I'm retired now, after 43 years as a college professor, and, so far, Solveig and I live a financially comfortable life—not lavish, but comfortable. I followed most of the seven rules for riches but also had some plain good luck.

I did well on rule number one, largely because I was lucky. I had great parents who devoted their lives to me and emphasized education in my life. I always liked school and performed well in it. Once I started school, I did it for twenty straight years, leaving with my Ph.D. at the age of twenty-six. It took a couple of years and two jobs before I was able to contribute to a retirement plan, a good one, TIAA-CREF. I made the decision to save regularly, off the top, satisfying rules two and three. I contributed the minimum to this retirement plan, a mistake, but I was lucky again. The universities I worked at more than matched my contributions for forty years. Free money always helps.

I satisfied rule number four by placing some of our savings in the stock market, but, in hindsight, my asset allocation (50% stocks, 50% bonds) was too conservative, when I was young. I corrected this in the 1990s and 2000s. My first extreme violation of rule number four came after the stock market crash of 1987. The S&P 500 stock index fell over 33% in just a little over three months. I retreated in fear from the stock market for two years and missed the rapid recovery it made after the crash. Learning my lesson, I was never completely out of the stock market again. I rode the bear market of the "Dot-Com Bust" down almost 37% in 2000-2001, putting 100% of my (matched) savings in the stock market every two weeks. Likewise, after the financial crisis of 2007 – 2008, I did the same thing, riding it down 52%, buying stock index funds every paycheck.

After these two successful financial roller coaster rides, the 2009 bear market and the Covid-19 pandemic bear market of early 2020 were easy. Without my automatic bi-weekly retirement fund contributions, however, and the lack of discipline to buy regularly in the downturns, I benefited less from the ensuing bull markets. Fear is not good for wealth accumulation. It gets into the brain of even this economist. I do much better, in general, on some form of financial "auto-pilot."

I've done well on rule number six. I've been lucky that innovation in financial markets has continued to reduce annual fees for stock index and other funds. One fund I own has an annual fee of .04%. Low transaction costs can help make up even for some bad investment choices.

As for rule number seven, I was as patient as some health problems allowed me to be. I was lucky to have a job that I could do until I was 69, when I retired. I experienced little heavy physical lifting in my profession, although I found the mental heavy lifting of faculty meetings to be extremely taxing in later years. Working to almost sixty-nine also allowed my social security benefits to increase.

Our greatest luck, however, was related to timing. I retired into one of the strongest bull markets in history. A common portfolio killer is a bear market in the early stages of a drawdown, where one must sell stocks in a down market to live. Fortunately, Solveig and I did not have to test our resolve, and perhaps our marriage, by greatly reducing spending in an early retirement downturn. My lovely tolerant wife has been my final piece of good luck. She's a very normal person, married to an economist for over 53 years. We've been through a lot but stayed together, avoiding the costly Ds, Divorce, and Division. As one of my best friends says, after four divorces, "There are only so many times I can split my company." A long marriage, an eighth rule for riches? I think so.

Acknowledgments

I wrote this book over more than two decades. I apologize to anyone whom I've forgotten to mention here who has helped me along the way. I do remember, fondly, the following. A few thousand students at the University of Idaho read many of these economic vignettes and have responded positively to them. I thank you all.

Thanks to my friends Lee Huskey and Robert Mayer, who have encouraged my writing for decades, and to my dissertation advisor, mentor, and friend, Charlie Leven, who taught me the power of storytelling in economics. Members of my writing group, Jack and Jan Praxel and Mike and Paula Durgan, very normal people, have listened patiently as I've read to them some of the pieces here and other writing.

Thanks to Susan Becker, at the Department of Business at the University of Idaho, who provided valuable clerical assistance; and to Sue Eller and Russel Davis, who helped me navigate the publishing process. I enjoyed a sabbatical leave from the University of Idaho in 2003, where many of the ideas for this book took form.

And finally, thanks to Solveig, my love and life partner these fifty some years, for never giving up on me. I have been, like this book, a continuing work in progress benefiting from her loving guidance.

About the Author

Jon R. Miller is Professor Emeritus of Economics in the College of Business and Economics at the University of Idaho, where he taught for the last 28 years of his career. He also taught at the University of Utah in Salt Lake City and at Clarkson College in Potsdam, New York. He received a B.A. from Pacific Lutheran University and A.M. and Ph.D. degrees from Washington University in St. Louis, all in economics.

While Professor Miller was an active and widely published researcher in his career, in the fields of regional economics, environmental economics, and the economics of wine, his true love was teaching, especially the introductory course. It is from this course that the "economic vignettes" of this book emerged. He received the First Interstate Bank Student Excellence Award for teaching in the College of Business and Economics and was a University of Idaho Alumni Award for Excellence recipient three times. Born in Wenatchee, Washington, Professor Miller has spent most of his life as a resident in and champion of the Intermountain West, especially the Inland Northwest. This sense of place greatly influences his writing. He currently resides in Spokane, Washington, with the Spokane native, Solveig, his wife of 54 years, whom you will meet frequently in this book.

Notes

Most normal people dislike footnotes. Some hate them. I see their point. Footnotes distract a reader from the flow of a piece of writing. They often cause needless interruptions. I'm a little normal, in this respect, but I'm also an academic and feel obligated, at times, to provide citations and other information that might amplify a point and provide additional information for those with a deeper interest in a topic. For this reason, I've pursued a middle way here. I've placed chapter notes at the end of the book, not at the bottom of the page. Because my "chapters" are short, I've not even included numbered notes on pages.

I've highlighted actual references in bold print for easy identification and kept their number to a bare minimum. I provide web addresses for online sources. Because websites arise and then vanish, I note the day I accessed the information. Sometimes, if the source material is voluminous, I simply suggest keywords for an online search.

Finally, because some of this material has appeared elsewhere, in a previous version, I cite these sources, mainly for academic attribution reasons. You really don't need to seek them out in most cases, as my later revisions tell the same story as well or better. Likewise, if you are satisfied with the exposition in the text itself, please feel free to ignore these notes entirely.

Economists Say the Darndest Things:
Reflections on Economists and Normal People

Certain writers generate an enormous amount of commentary on their work. Adam Smith is one of those writers. If you wish to read the source of Smith's invisible hand principle, see:

Adam Smith. 1976. *An Inquiry into the Nature and Causes of the Wealth of Nations*. The University of Chicago Press. p. 477. Many editions of this work have been published over the last two-plus centuries. This edition was published in the work's bicentennial year.

Lest you think I made up the statement about an economic theory of marriage, you could look up a journal article by Nobel Prize winner Gary Becker. **Gary S. Becker. 1973. "A Theory of Marriage: Part I."** *Journal of Political Economy* **81 (July-August): 813-846**. I don't recommend that you try to read this article unless you know a fair amount of calculus. A quick peek at it, however, reveals many characteristics of the method of modern economics.

Maps, Model Airplanes, Barbie, and Ken:
Using Models to Understand Reality
I wish I could tell you that I extracted Whitehead's "fallacy of misplaced concreteness" from reading him in the original, but, alas, reading Whitehead, and philosophy in general, gives me a headache. A very readable explanation of the concept, where I discovered it, appears in **Herman E. Daly. 1977.** *Steady State Economics.* **San Francisco: W. H. Freeman and Company. pp. 46-47, and 105**.

Science, Advocacy, and the Miller Wave:
Positive and Normative Economics
Like Whitehead's idea, the "fallacy of misplaced concreteness," I found the Joan Robinson statement in **Herman Daly's** *Steady State Economics* **(1977, p.4)**. While I find Robinson much more approachable than Whitehead, I have yet to find the exact quote in her original 1962 radical economics classic. However, something similar appears there. See **Joan Robinson. 1962.** *Economic Philosophy.* **Chicago: Aldine Publishing Company. p. 119**.

We will examine rent control and other "price ceilings" in Part Four of this book, in "But Only Rich People Would Get Tickets."

An Economist's Christmas
I'm certainly not the first to note economists' funny ideas about Christmas giving. For an amusing treatment of the topic, see a video from the **Marginal Revolution University:**
https://www.youtube.com/watch?v=UH28iJ7lVfg.

Accessed November 15, 2023. Alternatively, you might just search the internet on the topic "economists and Christmas giving."

Economists have funny ideas about other aspects of Christmas, as well. Some would argue that decorating one's own tree and wrapping presents is inefficient. Better to hire someone to do it and specialize in what you do best. This is an idea about "comparative advantage" that we will examine in Part Two, in "Associate Deans, Babe Ruth, and Hawaiian Pineapples…"

For a fun discussion of this and other "cheapskate" behaviors of economists see **Justin Lahart. 2010. "Secrets of the Economists Trade: First Buy a Piggy Bank." *Wall Street Journal*. January 2:**

https://www.wsj.com/articles/SB126238854939012923. Accessed January 13, 2024.

Also, see **Justin Wolfers. 2010. "Are Economists Cheap? Or Do We Just Believe in Comparative Advantage?" Freakonomics: The Hidden Side of Everything. January 5. https://freakonomics.com/2010/01/are-economists-cheap-or-do-we-just-believe-in-comparative-advantage/** Accessed November 15, 1923.

Humans, Econs, and Normal People

More complete references for Thaler's books are as follows: **Richard H. Thaler. 2015. *Misbehaving: The Making of Behavioral Economics*. New York and London: W. W. Norton & Company**, and **Richard H. Thaler and Cass R. Sunstein. 2009. *Nudge: Improving Decisions About Health, Wealth, and Happiness*. Revised and Expanded Edition. New York: Penguin Books.**

Thaler's Markowitz story appears on page 208 of *Misbehaving*.

In Part Three, in "Giving up Hope of a Brighter Past," we'll explore sunk costs and rational economic decision-making.

Backpacking with the 948 Boys:
The Basic Economic Problem

Many guides for hiking on the Colorado Plateau exist today, but in our early backpacking years, we mostly relied on Bruce's edition of **Michael R. Kelsy. 1999. *Canyon Hiking Guide to the Colorado Plateau.* Kelsey Publishing**, and my copy of **Rudi Lambrechtse. 1985. *Hiking the Escalante.* Salt Lake City: Wasatch Publishers, Inc.**

There is no better place to read Edward Abbey than in a canyon of Southern Utah, although today I can't believe I carried books (even paperback) this heavy in my pack. If you hike in Southern Utah, maybe you want to leave an orange at home and take along **Edward Abbey. 1968. *Desert Solitaire: A Season in the Wilderness.* New York: Ballantine Books**, or **Abbey. 2000. *The Monkey Wrench Gang.* New York: HARPERPERENNIAL-MODERNCLASSICS**. For something lighter and more compact, you might choose **John Muir. 1980. *Wilderness Essays.* Salt Lake City: Peregrine Smith, Inc.** When we hiked the Rainbow Trail near Navajo Mountain, I carried along the small yet heavy hardback version of **Terry Tempest Williams. 1984. *Pieces of White Shell: A Journey to Navajoland.* New York: Charles Scribner's Sons**.

How Big is the Pizza?

While the diameter of the 24-inch pizza is only 60% larger than the 15-inch pizza, the area you can eat of the giant one is almost 2.6 times larger, 452.39 square inches, compared to 176.71 square inches for the smaller one. I'm sorry, but the teacher in me can't resist reminding you that the area of a circle is found by squaring its radius (1/2 the diameter) and multiplying by *pi* (3.1416).

Dealing with Drought:
Command, Market, and Green Economic Systems

To draw out the differences in economic systems, I have understated the use of pricing mechanisms to encourage water conservation. For example, the city of Tucson was an early innovator in using pricing methods, especially summer "peak-load" pricing, to curtail water use. For an excellent and readable account of this and other innovations in Tucson, see **William E. Martin, Helen M. Ingram, Nancy K. Laney, and Adrian H. Griffin. 1984.** *Saving Water in a Desert City.* **Washington, D.C.: Resources for the Future, Inc**.

Economists, faced with persistent resistance to water pricing for conservation, continue to advocate for it. For a recent discussion of the potential for water pricing and drought in the arid West, see **Matthew E. Kahn and Bhaskar Krishnamachari. 2023. "A New Strategy for Western States to Adapt to Long-Term Drought: Customized Water Pricing."** *The Conversation* **(February 13)**. **https://theconversation.com/a-new-strategy-for-western-states-to-adapt-to-long-term-drought-customized-water-pricing-197382**. Accessed November 21, 2023.

Associate Deans, Babe Ruth, and Hawaiian Pineapples: Stories of Comparative Advantage

Economists love comparative advantage examples. While the associate dean story is mine, and I think the brain surgeon one, as well, the others here are part of the textbook and oral tradition in economics. Sometimes, these stories diverge from actuality. I learned the Billy Rose story from Charlie Leven, my dissertation advisor, as Billy Rose, the world's fastest typist. If you search the internet for Billy Rose, you find that he was not a fast typist, but, rather, a fast stenographer.

Evidence of Lanai's comparative advantage in tourism comes from numerous news accounts of billionaire Larry Ellison's purchase of the island and his efforts to turn it into a tourist destination for the wealthy. I bet this doesn't involve growing pineapples. See, among many other accounts, **Ariel Zilber. 2022. "Life on Larry Ellison's Hawaiian Island Is So Expensive Only the Super-Rich Could Afford It."** *New York Post.* **(June 9)**.

https://nypost.com/2022/06/09/life-on-larry-ellisons-hawaiian-island-is-only-for-the-super-rich/.
Accessed November 22, 2023.

The Babe Ruth story has a solid foundation in the literature of economics, something studied and published in a peer-reviewed professional journal. See **Edward M. Seahill. 1990. "Did Babe Ruth Have a Comparative Advantage as a Pitcher?"** *Journal of Economic Education* **21 (Autumn):402-410**. Seahill notes that part of the reason for Ruth's comparative advantage in playing the outfield for the Yankees was that the Yankees' pitching staff was so good that the opportunity cost of Ruth playing the outfield was low.

Marginal Tax Rates and the Three-Martini Lunch

For an amusing synopsis of the Baucus-Reid tax proposal and the Jimmy Carter and Gerald Ford quotes, see **Newsweek Staff. 2001. "American Beat: Martinis for Victory!" Newsweek.com. (October 21): https://www.newsweek.com/american-beat-martinis-victory-154047.**
Accessed November 26. 2023.

References for the Jim Wright quote are harder to track down. See **William E. Farrell and Warren Weaver, Jr. 1984. "BRIEFING;** *New York Times.* **Martinis and the Man." December 5. Section A, page 26**
https://www.nytimes.com/1984/12/05/us/briefing-martinis-and-the-man.html. Accessed November 26, 2023.

A brief digitized summary of Wright's comments on the three-martini lunch to a dinner audience appears online at **https://www.nytimes.com/1984/12/05/us/briefing-martinis-and-the-man.html**.
Accessed November 26, 2023.

Auctions and the Clearance Sale:
An Introduction to Supply and Demand Analysis

As with many sayings, sources for the quote about parrots and supply and demand are hard to track down. For years, I thought the quote was from Oscar Wilde. It sounds like something he would have said. Thomas Carlyle, who called economics the "Dismal Science," is a good choice, as well. If

you like tracking down quotations, check out **Quote Investigator. July 19, 2013.**
>**https://quoteinvestigator.com/2013/07/19/parrot-econ/**
> Accessed November 27, 2023.

Racehorse Venereal Disease, Freshwater Rough Fish and Convention Prostitutes

No one could make up this story about VD among horses. I wish I had. Luckily, all editions of the University of Utah student newspaper have been digitized. If you wish, check it out at **T.G. Moore. March 30, 1978. "VD affects racehorses." Associated Press article in *The Daily Utah Chronicle*. p. 11. https://newspapers.lib.utah.edu/ark:/87278/s6q285j0/23315 145**
> Accessed November 28, 2023.

Unfortunately, in an uncharacteristic act of decluttering, when I retired and moved from Moscow, Idaho, to Spokane, Washington, I disposed of several boxes of class materials I'd used for decades. In a file in one of those boxes resided the freshwater rough fish article. Online searches with Google and the *Wall Street Journal,* using specific keywords, yielded no results. Phone conversations with *WSJ* customer service staff revealed that digital archives only went back to 1996. I choose not to delay the publication of this book, awaiting a (planned) deeper search of physical sources. This must await (He says optimistically.) a second edition.

Please know that I have no political motivation for using this article about the actions of members of the Democratic Party. In fact, given the makeup of our two main parties in the U.S., the article's laugh-generating ability in my classes would have been enhanced had the convention been one for Republicans. See **Associated Press (New York). May 28, 1980. "Prostitutes' convention rates to rise: 'More risk, more cost.'"**
The Daily Utah Chronicle. **p. 1.**
> https://newspapers.lib.utah.edu/ark:/87278/s60g7rgc/23 320251
> Accessed November 28, 2023.

270

"But Only the Rich Would Get Tickets."

As is often the case, the origin of quotes is not as straightforward as the evolution of them appears. For one view of the protracted exchange between Fitzgerald and Hemingway, see **Quote/Counterquote. July 12, 2020. "The rich are different"... The real story behind the famed "exchange" between F. Scott Fitzgerald and Ernest Hemingway.**

http://www.quotecounterquote.com/2009/11/rich-are-different-famous-quote.html.

Accessed November 29, 2023.

For another take on the exchange, see **Erik Sherman. March 12, 2015. "The Rich are Different: They Can Walk Away."** *Forbes.*
https://www.forbes.com/sites/eriksherman/2015/03/12/the-rich-are-different-they-can-walk-away/?sh=74d933013a3d

A Weekend in June: Economists and Competition

Like the term "competition," the term "economic profit" has a special meaning in economics. This profit is not what normal people think of as profit, accounting profit, revenue minus cost, or sales minus expenses. Because economists define costs as opportunities foregone, and these include items such as the salary of a business's owner-operator in her next-best alternative, and an alternative return on capital invested in the business, economic profit is less than accounting profit. Zero economic profit does not drive a business from the industry as it is earning a normal rate of return on owner-labor and capital investment.

Pizza Promotion:
The Economics of Monopolistic Competition

American economist Edward H. Chamberlin's work emphasizing the implications of product differentiation in markets first appeared in 1933 and was revised and republished into the 1960s. See, for example, **Edward H. Chamberlin. 1962.** *The Economics of Monopolistic Competition: A Re-*

orientation of the Theory of Value, 8th ed. Cambridge, MA, and London: Harvard University Press.

Bigness, Fairness, and the Political Economy of Antitrust

As an economist with a weakness for real books, I have several editions of Adam Smith's classic work in my library. For the source of Smith's quote about businesses contriving to raise prices, here is another standard reference, available in used bookstores, thrift shops, and yard sales. **Adam Smith. 1937.** *An Inquiry into the Nature and Causes of the Wealth of Nations.* **New York: The Modern Library. Random House, Inc. p. 128**.

One popular target of the Biden Administration's FTC is the vertical merger, where companies acquire key suppliers and integrate them into their company. For just one example of a discussion of the pros, cons, and politics of this approach, see **Sarah E. Needleman and Dave Michaels. 2022. "FTC Sues to Block Activision Deal: Agency takes aim at Microsoft's biggest purchase ever on competition grounds."** *The Wall Street Journal.* **December 9. P. A1**.

The NCAA and the Exploitation of College Athletes: Anatomy of a Buyers Cartel

The power of the NCAA to limit compensation paid to college athletes is declining rapidly as I write this note near the end of 2023. Nevertheless, this historical power still provides one of the best examples of a buyer cartel. For a synopsis of the Deshaun Foster case, see **Steve Henson and Mike Bresnahan. 2001. "Foster's Season is Suspended."** *Los Angeles Times.* **November 8. https://www.latimes.com/archives/la-xpm-2001-nov-08-sp-1744-story.html**.
Accessed December 14, 2023.

The Lloyd Austin National Defense Telethon: Collective Goods in a Market Economy

As I put the finishing touches on this piece in the Holiday Season of 2023, I think of chestnuts roasting on an open fire.

While I don't have any roasted chestnuts, I do have this economic vignette about collective goods, an "old chestnut" in my traditional teaching archive. When I wrote the first version of this piece, Caspar Weinberger was U.S. Secretary of Defense. Oh My!

Studded Tires and Grass Burning:
The Economics of North Idaho External Cost

A previous version of this piece was published as a guest column in the main daily newspaper in the Inland Northwest, *The Spokesman-Review*. See **Jon Miller. 2005. "Driving U.S. 95 and Studying Econ 101." Special to *The Spokesman-Review*. Sunday, August 28. Guest Column. Roundtable section. p. B7**.

Like most economists, I try to take care of my cars so they can last a long time. To me, if a car starts, goes, and stops, it's probably OK for a little longer. But no one can avoid "acts of God." In 2017, in a big windstorm where we lived, on Paradise Ridge in Moscow, Idaho, a 130 ft. Douglas fir fell on and destroyed the Trooper. It may have been one of the longest-running Troopers, at 188 thousand miles. Sadly, I'd just bought a new set of (non-studded) tires.

For information on damage from studded tires in Washington State, see **Washington State Transportation Commission. 2019. "Studded Tire Fact Sheet." https://wstc.wa.gov/wp-content/uploads/2019/07/Studded-Tire-Fact-Sheet.pdf**.
Accessed December 15, 2023.

Economics and Climate Change:
Putting a Price on Carbon

For an insightful, respectful, yet mildly critical analysis of the "Economists' Statement," see **Michael L. Davis. 2019. "Five Questions for 3,508 Economists." *Regulation*. Cato Institute.**
https://www.cato.org/regulation/summer-2019/five-questions-3508-economists. Accessed December 18, 2023.

Asymmetric Information:
Moral Hazard, Adverse Selection, and Signaling

The Nobel Prize in Economics is a little different from the other Nobel Prizes. It was established in 1968 and first awarded in 1969. The prize is funded by the Swedish Central Bank. For a summary of the work of Akerlof, Stiglitz, and Spence, from the organization awarding the prize, see **The Royal Swedish Academy of Sciences. 2001. The Sveriges Riksbank Prize in Economic Sciences in Memory of Alfred Nobel, 2001: Press Release. October 10.** **https://www.nobelprize.org/prizes/economic-sciences/2001/press-release.** Accessed December 18, 2023.

Paying for Water with Taxes:
Government Failure in Action

This piece is based, in part, on some research I did in the early 1990s that was published in an academic journal, *Land Economics*. I was never quite sure why it appeared in a special section of the journal called "Speculations." I hope it was because the editor thought the piece was too interesting and well-written for academic work. For more depth and documentation on this issue, see **Jon R. Miller. 1993. "On the Economics of Local Water Finance: The Central Utah Experience."** *Land Economics* **69 (August): 299-303.**

For a discussion of the work of and biographical information on James M. Buchanan, Jr. and information on other economics Nobel laureates, see **The Sveriges Riksbank Prize in Economic Sciences in Memory of Alfred Nobel 1986. "James M. Buchanan, Jr.: Facts."** **https://www.nobelprize.org/prizes/economic-sciences/1986/buchanan/facts/.** Accessed December 29, 2023.

Protectionism: Government Failure in International Trade

As I noted in the preface to this Notes section, I don't wish to be overly academic here. However, Bastiat's protectionist satire is very funny and warrants a reading in the original. It can also serve as a useful piece for any argument you might wish to make against protectionist measures that raise the cost of things you wish to buy. See **M. Frederic Bastiat. 1870. "Petition from the Manufacturers of Candles. Wax-lights, Lamps, Chandeliers, Reflectors. Snuffers, Extinguishers; and from the Producers of Tallow, Oil, Resin, Alcohol, and Generally Every Thing Used for Lights." Chapter V11.** *Sophisms of the Protectionists*. **New York: American Free Trade League. pp. 73-80.**

Adding Apples and Oranges:
Keeping Score with Gross Domestic Product

I reveal my age, when I say that the U.S. "recently" changed from GNP to GDP reporting. It happened in 1991. Only "yesterday" to me. For more on this, and a link to the original Bureau of Economic Analysis article on the conversion, see **Kelly Ramey. March 2021. "The Changeover from GNP to GDP: A Milestone in BEA History."** *Survey of Current Business* **101:3. U.S. Department of Commerce. Bureau of Economic Analysis. https://apps.bea.gov/scb/issues/2021/03-march/pdf/0321-reprint-gnp.pdf**. Accessed January 2, 2024.

Lawn Mowing, Burglar Alarms, Whales, Drugs, and Old Raincoats: GDP and Economic Well-Being

The questioning of GDP as a measure of economic well-being got a good start from two economics Nobel laureates in the early 1970s. See **William D. Nordhaus and James Tobin. 1972. "Is Growth Obsolete?" in National Bureau of Economic Research.** *Economic Growth, Fiftieth Anniversary Colloquium, Volume 5*. **pp. 4-17.** A version of this paper also appears in **Robert Dorfman and Nancy S. Dorfman. Eds. 1977. "Measures of Economic Welfare."** *Economics of the Environment: Selected Readings. 2nd ed.* **New York: W. W. Norton & Company, Inc.**

The movement to provide an alternative measure to GDP has fallen on hard times recently in mainstream economics. Efforts on my part to find a continuation of a GPI series have proved futile, indicating that my hope for progress in this area will not be fulfilled soon.

The U.S. Department of Labor and Me: Employment, Unemployment, and the Labor Force

Information on current and historical magnitudes of the economic concepts mentioned here can be found at the very user-friendly website for the **U. S. Bureau of Labor Statistics. https://www.bls.gov.**

Inflation and the Shrinking Money Ruler

The federal government has no Bureau of Inflation Statistics, but the Bureau of Labor Statistics, the same outfit that keeps track of all the labor force data, has much information on the average price level, as well. The CPI, computed for different components of the U.S. population, can be found online at the **U.S. Bureau of Labor Statistics. https://www.bls.gov/cpi/.**

Inflation and the Charitable Family Pawn Shop

On the home page of the U.S. Bureau of Labor Statistics website, **http://www.bls.gov**, (when I accessed it in early January 2024), you can find a nifty inflation calculator. Just type in a dollar magnitude at some date in the past, click on calculate, and you can find the higher dollar amount you would need today, to purchase the same market basket of goods.

Ugly Truths About Inflation

A previous version of this piece was published as a guest column in *The Spokesman-Review*. See **Jon R. Miller. 2005. "Inflation isn't what you think it is." Special to the Spokesman-Review. Sunday, April 24. "Your Money" column in the Business section. pp. D3, D4.**

On the Bureau of Labor Statistics website, you can find many different consumer price indices calculated for different population groupings using the same method and for the same population groups using different methods. One alternative, the "chained" CPI, is worthy of more in-depth study should inflation (mis)measurement pique your interest.

"Mr. Kinneberg, could you please get me my money?"
Remembering the Bad Times of Recession or Depression

For the NBER definition of recession, along with charts and tables showing the history of the U.S. business cycle, see the NBER website at:

https://www.nber.org/research/business-cycle-dating. Accessed January 8, 2024.

For a formal reference to Keynes' influential work, see the note accompanying "Watching the River Flow...," in Part Eight.

"Just Charge It:" The Federal Budget Deficit and Debt

You can find federal budget and debt information by searching and clicking around at the website for the Congressional Budget Office: **http://cbo.gov**. I find the site for the Federal Reserve Bank of St. Louis to be more user-friendly and exhaustively complete for macroeconomic data. These data go by the name "FRED," an acronym for Federal Reserve Economic Data. The homepage can be found at **http://fred.stlouisfed.org**. For federal debt held by the public and debt as a percentage of GDP, respectively, see

https://fred.stlouisfed.org/series/FYGFDPUN
https://fred.stlouisfed.org/series/FYGFGDQ188S

Accessed January 8, 2024.

Watching the River Flow:
Macroeconomic Performance in Cubic Feet per Second

I don't recommend that you sit on the beach or by the fire and read Keynes' influential classic, but if you can find a copy in a used bookstore, bits and pieces of it are worth a look. It first appeared in 1936, but it was republished in several later editions. This is the latest edition in my library. **John Maynard Keynes. 1964.** *The General Theory of Employment, Interest, and Money.* **London: Macmillan & Co. Ltd.**

If Nixon Said It, "We're All Keynesians Now."

Many years ago, I tracked down the transcript of the Nixon interview through a conversation with staff at the Nixon Foundation, **https://www.nixonfoundation.org**. They must

have sent me the document or directed me to its source in a collection of President Nixon's papers. Fortunately, since then, the interview has become more readily available online at the American Presidency Project. **Richard M. Nixon. 1971. "A Conversation With the President," Interview With Four Representatives of the Television Networks." January 4. American Presidency Project: Documents. UC Santa Barbara.**
https://www.presidency.ucsb.edu/documents/conversation-with-the-president-interview-with-four-representatives-the-television. Accessed January 9, 2024.

The comments here of American Broadcasting Company news correspondent Howard K. Smith are those attributed to him by William F. Buckley, Jr. in **WM. F. Buckley Jr. 1971. "On the Right, The Right – Radicals, Are You a Keynesian?" editorial column.** *National Review* **23 (February 9): 162-163**.

For the report of President Nixon's statement in *The Nation*, see **Editors. 1971. "I am Now a Keynesian."** *The Nation* **212 (4) (January 25): 99-100.**

Later in his editorial, Mr. Buckley also refers to an earlier symposium in *Encounter* magazine with the theme "we are all Keynesians now." This could be the source of my colleagues' assessment of Nixon's statement and that of many others. For one early contribution in *Encounter*, with a negative answer, by a giant in the history of economic thought, see **Roy Harrod. 1964. "Are We Really All Keynesians Now?"** *Encounter* **(January): 46-50. https://www.unz.com/print/Encounter-1964jan-00046/**. Accessed January 9, 2023.

Samuelson's amusing views on The General Theory appeared in **Paul Samuelson. 1946. "Lord Keynes and the General Theory."** *Econometrica* **14 (3): 187-200.**

Keynes' statement about stimulating the economy by burying banknotes in abandoned coal mines and landfills appears on page 129 of *The General Theory*. See citation in notes for "Watching the River Flow…"

All the Nixon quotes come from the transcript of the interview provided by The American Presidency Project, cited above.

Central Banks and Worrying About Money
Parts of this piece appeared in a guest column in *The Spokesman-Review*. See **Jon R. Miller. 2005. "What does new monetary policy mean? It depends." Special to *The Spokesman-Review*. "Your Money" column in Business section. Sunday, January 30, 2005. pp. D3, D4**.

Where Have All the Phillips Curves Gone?
For information on Economics Nobel laureates Phelps, Friedman, and Lucas, as well as other recipients, see **https://www.nobelprize.org/prizes/lists/all-prizes-in-economic-sciences/**. Accessed January 10, 2024.

Supply-Side Economics:
An Oval Office Conversation in Early 1981
For the complete text of Candidate Reagan's speech to the International Business Council in Chicago, see **Ronald Reagan. 1980. "Remarks at the International Business Council in Chicago." September 9. The American Presidency Project. Documents. UC Santa Barbara.**
   https://www.presidency.ucsb.edu/documents/remarks-the-international-business-council-chicago.
Accessed January 10, 2024.

Living with Inflation and Deflation Around the World
Rather than burden you with endless citations for historical high inflation numbers, I urge you to type hyperinflation into your favorite search engine. However, as the experience is extreme AND recent, for information on Venezuelan hyperinflation, see **Statista. 2024. "Average inflation rate in Venezuela from 2002 – 2024. Economics and Politics:**
   https://www.statista.com/statistics/1392610/average-inflation-rate-venezuela/. Accessed January 10, 2024.

Uncle Scrooge and Liquidity Preference

Unfortunately, future six-year-old misers might have to be "trust fund babies" or offspring of rich parents to read some of the Uncle Scrooge comics. Uncle Scrooge has become a victim of the culture wars in the United States. In February 2023, the Walt Disney Company decided against future publishing of parts of *The Life and Times of Scrooge McDuck*. As economists would expect, prices of existing copies are rising rapidly. Some of these developments can be found online by using a search engine with a topic like "Uncle Scrooge banned." For examples of Uncle Scrooge prices, see prices on eBay: **https://www.ebay.com/itm/295965295704**.
Accessed January 13, 2023.

Bubbles, Busts, and Bailouts:
The Financial Crisis, Great Recession, Covid-19 Pandemic, and Unprecedented Macroeconomic Stimulus

For a brief introduction to the history of bubbles, see **Jon Hilsenrath. 2021. "How to Spot a Bubble: A Field Guide."** *The Wall Street Journal.* **Saturday/Sunday, May 8-9, p. B7**. For more depth, see the classic by the late Charles Kindleberger, first published in 1978, but revised to keep up with recurring financial crises. **Charles P. Kindleberger. 2000.** *Manias, Panics and Crashes: A History of Financial Crises, 4th ed.* **Palgrave (Macmillan)**.

Much of my understanding of the history of the financial crisis has been gleaned from countless news accounts over the years, but the most important source for an understanding of U.S. financial markets in the mid-2000s comes from **Michael Lewis. 2011.** *The Big Short.* **New York and London: W. W. Norton & Company.**

It Pays to Wait: Compound Interest, Doubling, and the Time Value of Money

According to Sir Roy Harrod, the Keynes quote about the halfpenny was an answer to a question from his father about the meaning of interest. It is quoted widely, but the original is from

Roy Harrod. 1951. *The Life of John Maynard Keynes*. New York and London: W. W. Norton & Company.
Both the Persian chessboard and the lily pond stories appear widely in the literature of personal finance and environmental alarmism. I first found both in **Donella H. Meadows, Dennis L. Meadows, Joergen Randers, and William W. Behrens III. 1972. *The Limits to Growth: A Report for the Club of Rome's Project on the Predicament of Mankind*. New York: Universe Books. p. 29**.

The Time Value of Money and the 4Ds: Divorce, Division, Death, and Discounting

A more recent example of the time value of money applied to athletes' salaries is the recent $700 million, 10-year contract of baseball player Shohei Ohtani. The Los Angeles Dodgers will pay Ohtani $2 million a year for ten years, deferring $680 million for that time. See **Mike Axisa and Dayn Perry. 2023. "Shohei Ohtani contract: Explaining $680 million deferral in Dodgers deal with unique Andrew Friedman clause." December 13. cbssports.com.**
https://www.cbssports.com/mlb/news/shohei-ohtani-contract-explaining-680-million-deferral-in-dodgers-deal-with-unique-andrew-friedman-clause/.
Accessed January 13, 2024.

My economist's heart soared like an osprey when I read in the first sentence of another news account that Ohtani's contract "… offers a wonderful lesson in the time value of money." See **Neil Irwin and Courtenay Brown. 2023. "Ohtani's big bet on inflation and the U.S. dollar." Axios.com. December 13.**
https://www.axios.com/2023/12/12/shohei-otani-dodgers-contract. Accessed January 13, 2024.

Payday Loans and U.S. Government Bonds: The Economics of Risk and Return

A previous version of this economic vignette appeared in *The Spokesman-Review*. See **Jon R. Miller. 2005. "Interest rates are all about risk level." Special to *The Spokesman-***

Review. "Your Money" column in Business section. Sunday, September 11. pp. G3, G4.

Get Rich Slowly: Seven Rules for Riches

A previous version of this piece appeared in *The Spokesman-Review* around college graduation weekend in 2004. See **Jon R. Miller. 2004. "Time is on your side: Young investors' discipline will be repaid with interest."** *The Spokesman-Review.* "Your Money" column in Business section. Monday, May 9. p. A9.

Index

284